1900
(JP HB 16.99)

DREAM BIG

THE HENRIETTA MEARS STORY

"How much we loved and admired her as a Christian and as a friend. For a wonderful lady who never married, we think hers is the richest life possible, filled to overflowing, with many and varied blessings. We know of no other woman who could boast of so many children in the Lord, and we are sure they have risen up to call her blessed."

—Dale, Roy and the Rogers Family

"For many years I marveled at Dr. Henrietta Mears' remarkable God-given gifts and her dynamic qualities which enabled her to reach unknown numbers of young people for Christ. Hers was a heavenly vision, and it never dimmed. She was our friend and memories are precious."

—Dr. Charles E. Fuller (1887-1968)
Founder, Old Fashioned Revival Hour

"In my mind, Henrietta Mears was the giant of Christian education—not only in her generation, but in this century. She was an extraordinary combination of intellect, devotion, and spirituality; an administrative genius, a motivator, an encourager and a leader.

"I thought of Henrietta Mears as a female Apostle Paul; in fact, I often referred to her as the 'Epistle Paul.' There is simply no way to exaggerate her effectiveness as a teacher, communicator and inspirer.

"In a very real sense Miss Mears is responsible for my family. Not only had she been counselor to Doris and me through the years, but she introduced us in her office. I understand that she predicted the introduction would turn out the way it did. There is not an area of my life that her influence has not touched with great significance. Philippians 1:3 expresses my sentiments perfectly concerning her."

—Dr. Richard C. Halverson
Chaplain, United States Senate

"Those influences which have meant most to us have been those times of prayer where we have both heard and felt her grasp the throne of God and give it a good shake!"

—Colleen and Louis H. Evans, Jr.
National Presbyterian Church
Washington, D.C.

"Dr. Henrietta Mears was truly one of the great women of the twentieth century and one of the greatest influences of my life. It is impossible to express adequately the deep gratitude which my wife, Vonette, and I feel toward this special servant of God with whom we shared the same home for 10 years and with whom we had the privilege of serving our dear Savior.

"She directly discipled hundreds of young men and women whom God led into full-time Christian ministry. Today, no doubt, thousands of additional disciples whom they influenced are, in turn, introducing millions of other people to Christ.

"Her life was a life of spiritual multiplication and the world is a better place in which to live because she surrendered her life to the Lord Jesus Christ to serve Him with all her heart. Vonette and I are privileged to be among the many whose lives she touched."

—Dr. William R. Bright
President,
Campus Crusade for Christ

"She was my teacher long before she ever heard of me. When I began my work among young people in 1933 I read everything she wrote and listened to everyone who could tell me about her. I tried my best to do things the way she would want them done. Then came the happy years when we worked together at Forest Home."

—Dr. Jim Rayburn
Founder, Young Life Campaign

"I think Miss Mears had the greatest capacity for loving people of almost anyone I know....Some of us talk about love. Miss Mears loved. No wonder God used her!"

—Ruth Bell Graham
Author, *Legacy of a Pack Rat, It's My Turn* and others

"The best thing I ever did for Hollywood Presbyterian Church was to get Miss Mears as Director of Christian Education."

—Dr. Stewart P. MacLennan
Pastor, 1921-1941
First Presbyterian Church
Hollywood, California

"My memories of Henrietta Mears can prompt a tear or spark a smile. The tears come when I think of the magnificent impact she had on so many lives, including my own. I have never known anyone who called young people to Christian commitment with more integrity and effectiveness. Her ability to spot people with spiritual gifts and groom them for Christian service was utterly uncanny.

"The chuckle comes when I think of her powers as an enthusiastic conversationalist. Her sense of humor, her welcome stories, her vast experience, her driving intensity all warmed my heart and challenged me in Christian service. God blessed her with a gift of friendship which thousands of people sensed in the years of her ministry and were blessed by—I among them."

> —Dr. David Allan Hubbard
> President, Fuller Theological Seminary
> Pasadena, California

"The times of prayer with her through the years, in many places and for many purposes, are among the fondest memories because they brought me so close to our Lord."

> —Dr. Robert Boyd Munger
> Professor Emeritus
> Fuller Theological Seminary

"I caught from Henrietta Mears, as from no other woman, the Christian life, not only from her teaching, but also from her living. Daily I drew from her personal, vibrant, positive, practical, persuasive words and life-style, which God allowed to penetrate my life. To me she was one of the greatest Christians of all time. She generously shared her life with Bill and me and that caused us to love and appreciate her for what she truly was—a woman of God!"

—Vonette Bright
Campus Crusade for Christ

"Dr. Mears was exhibit A of all that is good and fine and wholesome in Christian leadership. She was exhibit A of what a person ought to be as an outgoing, out-reaching personality. I am in complete agreement with a newspaper reporter in Indianapolis. After he had interviewed Miss Mears, he grabbed a phone and called the city editor, exclaiming, 'I've just been talking with God's Number One saleswoman.'"

—Dr. W. Warren Filkin
Northern Baptist Theological Seminary

"She never yielded to the fashion of the day in toning down the atoning work of Christ or the peril of those who live without the gospel....She valued the esteem of the educated world, but in such matters she dared to stand on her own feet. Her ardent zeal for missions, both at home and abroad, communicated to youth with her unique eloquence, probably enlisted more men and women for Christ's service than has any other woman's voice in the history of our Church."

—Dr. Donn D. Moomaw
Pastor,
Bel Air Presbyterian Church
Los Angeles, California

"'Teacher' dead? *Don't you believe it.* She'll live this Sunday in the thousands of classes where her lessons are taught...in the hundreds of pulpits across the United States and around the world where one of 'Miss Mears' boys' stands up to preach...and in every heart like mine where she has had a ministry."

—Dr. Larry Ward
Ambassadors At Large

"If I were to single out one sentence to pay Henrietta Mears tribute, it would be to commend her in the one channel in which far too many Christian workers fall down: she was utterly devoid of professional jealousy. She'd support and promote and build up other speakers with the same enthusiasm that she put into everything else! She was delighted when the Lord blessed their ministry. I think anyone who has ever been in the limelight and is aware of its perils would be quick to recognize that as the hallmark of a great person."

—Ethel Barrett
Author, *Holy War, Our Family's First Bible Storybook, It Didn't Just Happen* and others

*"Youth do not think
into the future far enough.
Therefore, we must encourage them
to dream of great tomorrows."*

                                    H.C.M.

"SHE IS CERTAINLY ONE OF THE GREATEST CHRISTIANS I HAVE EVER KNOWN!" BILLY GRAHAM

DREAM BIG

THE HENRIETTA MEARS STORY

Meet the Woman Who Shaped the Lives of Some of the Most Influential Christians of Our Time

EARL O. ROE, EDITOR

Regal Books
A Division of Gospel Light
Ventura, California, U.S.A.

Published by Regal Books
A Division of GL Publications
Ventura, California 93006
Printed in U.S.A.

Scripture quotations in this book are from the *KJV—King James Version*

Portions of this book were previously published under the title, *Henrietta Mears and How She Did It!* by Ethel May Baldwin and David V. Benson.

Library of Congress Cataloging-in-Publication Data

Dream big : the Henrietta Mears story / Earl O. Roe, editor.
      p.   cm.
   ISBN 0-8307-1254-2
    1. Mears, Henrietta C. (Henrietta Cornelia), 1890-1963.
2. Presbyterians—United States—Biography.   3. Sunday-school
teachers—Biography.   4. Evangelists—United States—Biography.
I. Roe, Earl O., 1927-
BX9225.M397D74   1990
268' .092—dc20
[B]   90-33489
                                            CIP

1 2 3 4 5 6 7 8 9 10 11 12 /X/KP/ 95 94 93 92 91 90

Rights for publishing this book in other languages are contracted by Gospel Literature International (GLINT) foundation. GLINT also provides technical help for the adaptation, translation, and publishing of Bible study resources and books in scores of languages worldwide. For further information, contact GLINT, Post Office Box 488, Rosemead, California 91770, U.S.A., or the publisher.

DR. HENRIETTA C. MEARS
1890-1963

- Born in Fargo, North Dakota, October 23, 1890, youngest of seven children
- Graduated from the University of Minnesota, 1913
- Teacher and Senior Advisor Central High School, Minneapolis, 1915-1928
- Director of Christian Education and Teacher of the College Department, The First Presbyterian Church of Hollywood, 1928-1963
- Founded Gospel Light Publications, 1933
- Founded Forest Home Christian Conference Center, 1938
- Honored with the Degree of Doctor of Humanities, 1949
- Founded GLINT (Gospel Literature International), 1961
- Called to be with her Lord, March 20, 1963

Contents

Foreword

W HAT A JOY TO PUT INTO WORDS, JUST A FEW OF THE MANY, *many* ways Henrietta Mears has touched our lives.

We called her "Teacher"—and so she was.

For along with her colleague, Richard C. Halverson, Miss Mears filled a crucial instructive role in our lives when, as college student and aspiring actress, we both committed ourselves to Jesus Christ as Savior and Lord during the spiritual awakening of 1947. She taught us lessons we needed to learn, that have served us well over years of ministry.

Henrietta Mears impacted our lives spiritually on so many levels. Prayer is just one example. She not only taught us about prayer, as she expounded the Scriptures to us in her powerful way at the midweek gathering of the college department of Hollywood Presbyterian Church. But she also modeled *how* to pray as she opened her home to us every Saturday morning at 6:00 A.M. for an officers and leaders' prayer meeting. We learned there, from her example, to be bold before God, to ask great things on God's behalf and to do spiritual warfare from a bent-knee position.

But Dr. Mears was not only practical as a prayer warrior. As a strong discipler and trainer of others, she was also eminently practical in her leadership style. Sitting forward in her chair with the body language of intensity, her beady eyes peering through thick lenses—more often than not from under some fashionable broad-brimmed hat, she would put to us the question, "And now, who are you training to take your place when you move on?"

Yet, perhaps more than everything else, two things about this elegant, brilliant woman touched our lives at the deepest level: She demonstrated a zeal and an urgency for presenting men and women with the opportunity to respond, by the Holy Spirit, to Jesus Christ; and she lived what she taught. Teacher didn't simply share theory *about* Jesus and His teachings—she *embodied* them.

Because of the credible life Teacher lived before us, our lives since have never been, nor will they ever again be, the same.

Colleen and Louis H. Evans, Jr.
Washington, D.C.
1990

The Vision of Henrietta C. Mears Continues

T HE YEAR WAS 1933. HITLER WAS ELECTED TO POWER IN GERmany and began to shock the world with his infamous concentration camps and tirades against Europe's Jews. Franklin D. Roosevelt was inaugurated America's thirty-second president and enacted New Deal legislation which began with a nationwide bank holiday. Severe drought converted the Great Plains into a "Dust Bowl." Thomas Morgan received the Nobel Prize for discovering the function of chromosomes in heredity. Edwin Armstrong invented Frequency Modulation (FM) broadcasting.

And in that same year, Dr. Henrietta C. Mears launched Gospel Light Press in Hollywood, California, now known as Gospel Light Publications.

Coming to California from Minnesota in 1928, she recognized that Christian education was a primary responsibility of the Church—in fact, its lifeblood. And she was committed to the Bible, the Word of God, as the textbook of the Sunday School.

In the late 1920s, the institutional Church in North America was in decline. European higher criticism and modernism had undermined the authority of the Bible, and mainline churches were in significant decline. A major American denomination would have ceased to exist had the decline continued to the 1950s.

Being a visionary with feet firmly planted in reality, Dr. Mears was determined to do something about the frequent complaints from kids that "Sunday School just gets dumber and dumber." A university student brought up in her church told her that if he had to pass a test in the Bible he would "absolutely flunk."

She started thinking and reviewing the curriculum resources available from both denominational and independent publishers. Either they were liberal and did not teach the Bible as the authoritative Word of God, though they might be educationally sound, or they were of the International Uniform Lessons variety which were biblical but hopelessly inadequate educationally. She recognized early the need for effective curriculum for both teachers and students in her Sunday School so that they would know the Bible as a whole book, the textbook of life. Beginning with the mimeograph in the church office, and cutting and pasting Bible art on the lessons to liven them for children, Dr. Mears and her staff took the teaching of the Bible seriously and began producing their own curriculum materials. Their Sunday School soon became a real school of Christian education.

The growth was explosive. An editorial in the *Sunday School Times* encouraged pastors and leaders who were concerned about their own dwindling congregations to go to Hollywood Presbyterian Church and see what was happening. At first they were given their own copies to mimeograph at home, but when the cost of these free resources became too much for the church to stand, the elders suggested that Dr. Mears move the project out of the Sunday School office and sell the lessons to the church. So Gospel Light was soon a business in a single-car garage behind the Sunday School superintendent's home on Arden Street in Hollywood. The demand then became so large that printing was required, and the first copyright was secured in 1933.

"Teach the Word clearly and correctly," Dr. Mears always said, "to the end that people may come to know Christ as Savior and Lord and to grow spiritually, faithful in every good work."

With the publication of this book in 1990, we observe the hundredth anniversary of the birth of Dr. Mears, and we recognize that the inspiration and vision of this remarkable, dynamic woman remains a vital force in the life and output of Gospel Light. And that vision has now resulted in curriculum and books being adapted, translated and published on every continent in more than 100 languages, through the help of Gospel Literature International (GLINT), a foundation which she launched in 1962 to help meet the exploding needs of new churches and missions all over the earth. Truly the sun never sets on the places influenced by this great lady.

William T. Greig, Jr.
President
Gospel Light Publications

Acknowledgments

To Dr. Cyrus "Cy" N. Nelson for his guidance, encouragement and helpful insights during the early stages of this book. We regret that he did not live to see this project completed.

To Ethel May Baldwin and David V. Benson, whose 1966 biography, *Henrietta Mears and How She Did It!* is the primary source of information for this book and forms the core of this newer account.

To Barbara Hudson Dudley for allowing us to quote extensively with acknowledgment from her 1957 book, *The Henrietta Mears Story.*

To Eleanor Doan who, in preparation for this new biography of Dr. Mears, undertook extensive research into the heritage of Henrietta Mears and into the current histories of the various institutions founded by her.

To all those on the staffs of Gospel Light Publications, Forest Home Christian Conference Center, GLINT and the First Presbyterian Church of Hollywood, California who also assisted with research, documentation and verification.

To Dean Dalton, Bill Greig, Jr. and Peggy Greig Nelson for reading the manuscript and giving valuable input to the author.

To Virginia Woodard, Regal's editorial assistant, who suffered through the various drafts and whose careful reading of the text resulted in a much better book than would otherwise have been possible.

To Pat Zimmerman, Lisa West and Marian Morris, guardians of the Mears' archives, who gave the author access to materials available nowhere else.

To those who made their treasured photos available for inclusion in this volume and, again, to Peggy Nelson for aiding in the final selection of those that appear within these pages.

ONE

Heaven in Her Soul; The World on Her Heart

I have had the thrill of going around the world many times, and practically every place my plane lands—whether it is in India or Hong Kong or the islands of the sea or Africa —I find a young man or woman who has come up through my college department and is there preaching the gospel of the Lord Jesus Christ. How I thank God!"

Greece

Two women stood on the crest of Mars' Hill, as had the apostle Paul long before, and gazed out in wonder over the city of Athens, spread out across the terrain some 370 feet below. Near at hand and soaring another 140 feet above them rose the precipitous rocky mass of the famed Acropolis. Crowning its summit and silhouetted against the azure sky loomed the white-marbled Parthenon, the temple honoring Athena and an assortment of other lesser gods and goddesses.

A little beyond the fabled structure, on the westernmost edge of the Acropolis, nestled the exquisite temple of Athena Nike, the Wingless Victory. A few hundred yards southeast of the templed mount rested the ruins of the once-magnificent Temple of Zeus (Jupiter), still unfinished and roofless in Paul's day.

Looking southwest of the city, they saw the 482-foot Hill of the Muses surmounted by the graceful National Museum. And five miles farther, the blue waters of the Aegean Sea stretched to the horizon.

Spread out to the North of Mars' Hill—also called the Areopagus—lay Athen's Agora or marketplace, with its Temple of Hephaestus or Vulcan, the best-preserved Greek temple in the world today. The modern city with its Olympic Stadium sprawled for miles to the West and North, the narrow streets and gray buildings bathed in the brilliance of a Mediterranean morning.

The sun was hot and there was no shade. But Henrietta Mears, in a white summer dress, and her traveling companion, Esther Ellinghusen, found a stone smooth enough to sit on and rest.

All the history of ancient Greece seemed to pass before them as they sat in silence, each stirred by many thoughts of the city's bygone glories. Here Zeno taught his pupils on the famous Stoa or Porch. Socrates posed his perplexing questions to the youth of Athens and was condemned to drink the hemlock. Plato and Aristotle gave free vent to their theories about God and society—perhaps in this very spot. In old Athens, new ideas on democracy were put to the test.

Henrietta's mind raced with excitement, moved by the sight of the ruins all around her. But thrilling her most was the scene she pictured of that one called Paul, who 2,000 years before had come to this city "so full of idols," had argued with the passersby in the Agora below and then had been led to this same Mars' Hill to defend his teaching about Jesus and the Resurrection. Perhaps he had also rested on the stone they now sat upon as he talked to some of those who expressed interest in his ideas.

As she recalled the story, Henrietta opened the hand-tooled, light brown leather book she carried with her. Lovingly turning the well-thumbed pages, she paused at Acts 17 and began reading aloud to Esther beside her:

"Now while Paul waited for them at Athens, his spirit was stirred in him, when he saw the city wholly given to idolatry..., and they took him, and brought him unto Areopagus, saying, May we know what this new doctrine, whereof thou speakest, is?" (Acts 17:16,19).

Because of her poor eyesight, reading had always been hard for Henrietta. But holding the worn Bible close to her face she made out the words:

"Then Paul stood in the midst of Mars' Hill, and said, Ye men of Athens, I perceive that in all things ye are too superstitious. For as I passed by, and beheld your devotions, I found an altar with this inscription, TO THE UNKNOWN GOD. Whom therefore ye ignorantly worship, him declare I unto you" (Acts 17:22,23).

As Henrietta continued to read aloud to Esther, they were interrupted by a persistent young Greek who was offering his services as a guide. But they did not want a guide. They had come up Mars' Hill to think about the glories of Greece and to read the account of Paul in Athens. So they had no wish to be disturbed. Continuing to read, they at first ignored the young man. But after a minute, they realized that he had seated himself nearby and was listening to them with genuine interest.

"Do you understand what we are reading?" Henrietta asked.

"If you read slowly enough," the Athenian responded.

When they came to the end of the story, she said to him, "Do you know this Christ that Paul was teaching your people about?"

"No," the young Greek replied.

They began to talk about Jesus and before long they were praying together. As the three of them descended the hill, the youth held the Americans' coats and talked incessantly. Near sundown the two women said farewell to him in front of the British and Foreign Bible Society store, where they had bought him a Bible.

The next day the visitors again met the young Greek.

"I could not sleep last night," he told them.

"Were you ill?" the Americans asked, genuinely concerned for their new friend.

"No, I was up all night reading that Book."

That evening, Henrietta Mears wrote in her travel journal:

> *On Mars' Hill we had the glorious privilege of introducing a 23-year-old Greek youth to Jesus Christ as Savior and Lord. What a thrill! On the very spot where Paul had presented this same Jesus nearly 20 centuries ago, we found that preaching Christ's claims brought the same results today. This wonderful experience was one of the highlights of the trip.*

As she wrote, she could not have realized that less than 10 years later, nearly 100,000 Greek youths would be reading her lessons on the Bible in their own language and that they too would be finding the unknown god and claiming Him as their personal Savior.

Henrietta Mears traveled widely and as often as she could. But she was no mere tourist or adventure-seeker. She chose travel as a means of extending her education, for she had a broad appreciation of the beauties of God's creation and man's cultural attainments. Visiting foreign lands gave expression to her enormous energies for she thrived on her experiences among other peoples. But travel served, most of all, as inspiration for her driving compulsion in life—to see Christ proclaimed to all nations.

India

India is a far cry from modern Greece; if Greece awes the traveler with past glories, India oppresses him with present agonies.

Henrietta and Esther had just arrived in Calcutta. A great religious festival was going on, and the streets were jammed with processions carrying fantastic figures of their gods. Beggars of every description were taking advantage of the crowds.

On reaching the railway station, the two visitors were horrified to see thousands of displaced persons gathered inside, huddled in groups, cooking their food and sleeping. Many, coughing and spitting up blood, were in the last stages of tuberculosis. That night the two women were so troubled, they could not sleep.

The next day they visited temples and shrines. At one of them, the notorious Kalighat, a frenzied mob swept Henrietta and Esther along in their human tide. The hot blood of a freshly killed goat ran over the pavement, as pilgrims darted forward, dipped their fingers in it and smeared crimson marks on their foreheads.

A huge Hindu priest, stripped to the waist because of the intense heat, led the two Americans about. The odor from the seething mob was overwhelming and, everywhere around the women, worshipers were giving themselves over to moral license.

Henrietta wrote that night:

> *No wonder the pioneer missionaries to India had their very hearts eaten out by the condition of the hea-then—without God and without hope in this world! Oh that many of us now would match their devotion! We must if we are to do anything about the lostness of this world.*
>
> *India seems so ripe for communism. "Anything is better than nothing," the people say. But if they knew Christ, they would soon do away with the sacred bulls ambling over the streets, eating everything and leaving their dung on the sidewalks, where thousands of the poor sleep with only their cloth wrapped around them.*

Over a hundred thousand human bundles on the streets! This is their only resting place. In the winter they lie down to shiver and die.

And a few days later, in Benares, India's holiest city, she observed:

It is good for one to visit this city with its innumerable shrines and temples to understand the degradation of idol worship. Thousands of pilgrims visit this place every day. If they can only bathe in the holy water of the Ganges and die in this place, they think they will be blessed. They will not come back to this earth again.

About sundown we pushed through the crowds and went down the hundreds of steps through the processions to the water and got into a little boat. We were rowed out onto the Ganges. The water was teeming with boats carrying the images of the gods ready for the water ceremony. Natives dipped gods into the water and left them there.

The sun was setting a brilliant red. Hot steam from the water rose around us. Odors and weird sounds of the worshipers filled one with horror. Ugly buildings —pseudo-palaces of the maharajas—lined the banks.

Burning ghats [pyres on the river banks] were being lighted to cremate the dead. The bathers were dipping their bodies into the filthy holy water, putting it to their lips, then lifting their faces in prayer with locked hands raised in reverence. One can hardly take it all in. I feel satanic spirits in this place.

While Henrietta was visiting India's majestic Taj Mahal, her guide, in order to prove the unusual acoustics of the high-domed structure, stood on the platform in the center of the main hall and shouted, "There is no God but Allah, and Mohammed is his prophet!" His cry rang sonorously through all the chambers of the monument.

Henrietta asked if she too might say something. The guide granted her request and, ascending to the same platform he had, she exclaimed in her low, powerful voice: "Jesus Christ, Son of God, is Lord over all!"

Like peals of thunder rolling through canyons and over valleys of an Alpine mountain range, her words raced from wall to wall and down the corridors of the minareted shrine: "Lord over all, over all, over all!"

The lordship of Jesus Christ was the message of Henrietta Mears, and she never ceased to proclaim it all over the world as long as she lived.

Snake charmers in hotels, thousands of monkeys scampering between temple idols, camel caravans passing by miles of beggars, and starving, naked children lying in ditches—all were horrid scenes that left deep impressions on Henrietta. Her resolve to bring these people the gospel took even firmer root in her mind.

In fact, every country she visited ignited her determination to do something, although at the time she did not always know what it would be. God, in His own time, however, did channel this concern, enabling her to be the means of a gospel witness in lands all over the globe. And frequently, God did so in ways that brought unexpected results—even to Henrietta Mears.

Lebanon, Palestine, Israel

Once, while visiting Beirut, Lebanon, Henrietta was surprised to find herself the guest of honor at a reception given by several missionary families. They were on the foreign field, as four of them pointed out, because of a challenge she had issued to them years before in Berkeley, California. And they recalled 50 more who were either out on the mission field or preparing to go as a result of her challenge.

On another occasion, Henrietta and some traveling companions were attending a service at the site of the Garden Tomb in

In North Jerusalem, Henrietta Mears (center) and friends stand near the site of the Mandelbaum Gate—actually a road barrier erected near a building owned by a Mr. Mandelbaum—that straddled the then-existing cease-fire boundary line between Jordanian Jerusalem and Israeli Jerusalem. Israeli police manned one side of the gate and Jordanians the other. The gate was destroyed in the Six-day War of June 1967. *L. to r.* are Gladys McElroy, Joe Choate, Henrietta Mears, Ethel May Baldwin and Timothy Choate.

Henrietta Mears afloat in the Dead Sea in 1935.

Northeast Jerusalem, a part of the city then still under Jordanian control. A minister from Cincinnati, recognizing her, asked Henrietta to tell of her Sunday School work in Hollywood. Two missionaries from Bangkok interrupted, saying that they had been using her Sunday School materials for years.

After her talk, a minister from Greece volunteered that her translated lessons were being used extensively in his country, even in the royal house. In his Sunday School alone were 650 students using these same materials.

While in Israel, Henrietta met a Mr. Samuels, a Jewish tour guide who had been reading the Bible for 26 years and was well steeped in its history. As the two of them sat in front of their hotel on the shores of Lake Galilee one evening, they talked of Jesus Christ as Messiah. Night came on, and as stars studded the deep blue satin sky, one cast a path of light right up to their feet. Henrietta asked her friend if he would accept Christ as his Messiah.

Tears rolled down the cheeks of the devout Jew as he said, "Yes, Miss Mears, I would like to let Christ into my heart, but do you know why it is so hard? I would be a second Stephen—stoned to death!" They continued to talk on into the night, and when they parted, Mr. Samuels expressed his appreciation for fellowship that he described as being "like Jesus had with His disciples."

A year after Henrietta had returned to California, Mr. Samuels sent a message to her by one of her friends for whom he had also acted as a guide: "Tell Miss Mears I did what she asked me to do."[1]

He died the next year.

Africa

Of the world's several continents, Africa was one of Henrietta's favorites. Her adventures there ran the gamut from spending a few days on the yacht of King Farouk—Egypt's last monarch—and riding camels across the desert to hiking in a rhino-populated reserve while retracing David Livingstone's steps to the mightiest cataract in the world, the thundering Victoria Falls.

Once when her party was braving jungle roads, their car broke down not far from white rhino territory. The day was nearly ended before the engine finally responded. In the semi-darkness, they inched their vehicle along toward their destination, not daring to put on the headlights for fear of provoking a rhino charge. Their safari continued to their next stop in South Africa's Kruger National-al Park, the world's greatest wildlife sanctuary where they could see more game in their natural habitat.

Henrietta's diary on that date overflows with excitement.

> *The next morning we started out for game. There before our very eyes near the road was a giraffe raising its head eighteen feet above the ground. It posed for us like a Hollywood star. We drove along slowly looking through the woody bush which conceals the animals. Stop! A herd of zebras crossed over the road! Impala leaped in front of us, the most beautiful fauna in the world. One of these graceful creatures had been dragged up into a tree by a leopard and left in the branches. Think of a leopard carrying this large beast up into a tree! The Bristol gnu, an ugly black creature, the blue wildebeest, the huge baboon with its young, the sable antelope, the warthog that turns his tail straight up when running, and the duiker were other animals we encountered....*
>
> *But I suppose the most exciting event was the 200-mile plane trip over the game reserve at Victoria Falls. At dawn we flew into the air to begin our search for wild animals. All went smoothly for a time, then our plane banked to almost a 90-degree angle, and we were looking at a herd of giraffe on the ground not more than 75 feet below us. The pilot skimmed along less than 50 feet above the ground. When he saw the animals, he turned quickly, dipping and banking until we could shoot a picture straight below.*
>
> *We saw zebras by the hundreds and all the other animals we had seen in Kruger, but we were searching*

for elephants. Back and forth across the waste and jungle we flew. Everyone was straining for a glimpse of the great beasts. At last we sighted one, then another and another. We had found our game for the day!

On Sunday morning at 6:30, the wings of our plane carried us to Northern Rhodesia [now Zambia], to Livingstone, the city that bears the name of the renowned missionary explorer. A few miles away in Southern Rhodesia [now Zimbabwe] are the Victoria Falls, "the Smoke that Thunders," first viewed by Livingstone on November 16, 1855.

My thoughts were much with this missionary hero when I consider his utter loneliness in these jungles with only the roar of wild animals and a black man for company. Now everything bears his name, but I fear many have forgotten his work.

Later, the travelers visited a missionary station in the Congo (now the Republic of Zaire) set high in the mountains, overlooking a chain of volcanoes. Henrietta thrilled as Mel Lyons, with his arm around her shoulder, pointed out the villages which faded into the foliage, and it warmed her heart to hear him tell of the evangelistic work he was doing there. During the week he was training Bible teachers who would go to villages just like these to expound the Word of God.

How little had she ever thought that this big football player who had jerked sodas at the Forest Home Christian Conference Center would one day be preaching the gospel in far-off Africa. And Mary, whom he had met at Forest Home and later married, helped in the hospital of this teeming compound. They now had four lovely children.

As she did everywhere she went, Henrietta ministered to the missionaries of this station. She always felt that the missionary must be inspired and fed from the Word, since he was constantly giving out. Over 50 of the young people gathered one evening to meet "Teacher" and to hear her.

God had been speaking to her from Philippians 2:13, and she gave them what He had laid upon her heart. "For it is God which worketh in you both to will and to do of his good pleasure."

When she had finished, a young woman came up and said, "You won't remember me, but I was in your college class. I married a doctor and came to the Congo to serve." The surprise came when Henrietta revealed that she well remembered not only the young missionary, but her two sisters as well.

In that group of missionaries was also one Marjory Shelley, who went on to translate and publish Henrietta's Gospel Light Sunday School lessons for those living in the Ivory Coast. She had heard Henrietta only once before, but Marjory remembered well her message on the will of God. And that night, as Henrietta again opened God's Word to them, the missionaries felt the Lord drawing them closer to one another and to Himself.

A Lifeline of Power

Henrietta's deep love for missions and missionaries was as natural for her as it was genuine. When she was still a college student herself, she dedicated her life to God and wondered if missions in the Far East was His call for her. But because He had a better plan for Henrietta, God closed this door so that through her influence, many others would go as missionaries, not only to the Orient, but to all the world.

She bore adventure in her soul. And she overflowed with the thrill of life. But adventure and thrills were not sufficient motivation to propel Henrietta Mears again and again to distant nations. She hiked through jungles in Africa, climbed mountains on Formosa and walked amid the dying in India—all to obtain a more informed view of the world.

Many people who travel to the sordid spots of this earth never really understand the hopelessness of those suffering about them. The attitude of such travelers is frequently one of either complete disassociation from the dying, as though they were not of the same human race, or of a passing pity that never excites the heart to action. Few stand on the hilltop, as our Lord did (see Luke 19:41), and weep over Jerusalem.

But wherever Henrietta went, she was crushed by the black despair of peoples never privileged to hear the gospel. What she experienced firsthand on her many journeys broke her heart and impelled her to even greater efforts in her determination to know Christ and to make Him known. From platforms and pulpits throughout the English-speaking world—in churches, on campuses, at conventions—wherever she was given opportunity to speak, she proclaimed the gospel of Jesus Christ, her Savior and Lord.

Christ's lordship resonated through all her writings, and she enshrined it in the lives of the hundreds of young men and women she trained for the gospel ministry. For though her vision encompassed the world, she encountered her greatest adventures for God in Hollywood, California where—during her 30 years in this city of klieg lights, cameras and stars—she raised an altar to her Lord: the then-largest Presbyterian Sunday School in the world, an endeavor which the late Dr. Wilbur M. Smith declared was "the most significant work among our nation's youth done by a woman in the twentieth century."

She also founded a Sunday School publishing house that continues to place the gospel in millions of hearts and, she pioneered one of the nation's most popular Christian conference centers, where thousands upon thousands are still being won to the Savior.

Wherever and however she labored, she was an open lifeline of power, a divinely chosen instrument for one of the most significant revivals of modern times. Her contribution to the international cause of the gospel ranks as one of the more important in contemporary church history.

The narrative of her life, while a story of adventure and accomplishment, is most importantly a demonstration of unflinching faith in Jesus Christ and a testimony of His power and love in the life of one who appropriated both.

Note

1. Mr. Samuels assisted Rev. Lloyd Douglas in his research for writing *The Robe*. He was invited by Douglas to come to Hollywood and to serve as a technical adviser for the film based on his book. Because of his reluctance to leave Israel, Mr. Samuels declined the invitation.

    Claiming he had questioned every weaver in Palestine, Mr. Samuels told Henrietta Mears he concluded that weaving a robe in one piece was not possible. Rather, he believed, Christ's robe was really the traditional prayer shawl which all devout male Jews wear.

TWO

A Lineage of Faith

G od does not always choose great people to accomplish what He wishes, but He chooses a person who is wholly yielded to Him."

ADVENTUROUS, DARING, DEDICATED, ZESTFUL AND TALENTED, HENRIETTA Mears was a woman who dared to believe in the greatness of her God. That she came so early to possess undoubting faith, spiritual power and great vision is due in part to her heritage, for she descended from a long line of spiritual forebears whose own lives and examples pointed her unerringly to the Person, worship and service of Jesus Christ.

William Wallace Everts

William Wallace Everts, maternal grandfather of Henrietta Mears, was born April 14, 1814 and named William for his uncle, a United States senator. William's father, Samuel, the son of a sea captain, was a natural leader. An officer in the militia, he raised a company for the War of 1812 and was made a brigadier general. After the war, he served his county in Vermont as sheriff. As a young boy, William greatly admired his father's daring and prowess, and he emulated Samuel's military bearing in the way he carried himself.

A devout man and a graduate of Middlebury College, Samuel was careful to nurture his children both spiritually and intellectually. In these respects, he was fully supported by his wife, Phoebe Spicer Everts, a woman of deep conviction and a schoolteacher by training. Between them, Samuel and Phoebe gave their children such stimulus that six later chose to enter professional careers.

William's twelfth year proved unusually eventful. By oxcart and canal boat, his father moved his family from Vermont to Michigan. There Samuel suddenly came down with a fever and died soon after. Phoebe, left almost penniless, then moved her family back East, across Lake Erie, and settled in Clarkson, New York.

Realizing the family's poverty, a doctor and a farmer helped Phoebe in raising William. But she realized that any further molding of her children's spiritual life rested upon her. And she proved equal to the challenge, leading family prayers and continuing to instruct the children in Christian living. As a result, at 13, William responded and was converted during a revival being held at his Clarkson school. Recognizing his mother's influence upon that decision, he later stated, "My mother, more than any other human being, determined my character and destiny."

When William was 15, he and his mother were present at a service where a large number of inquirers responded to the invitation to accept Christ. But when three persons—a Presbyterian minister, a Methodist minister and a Baptist deacon—all declined to pray for the new converts, the meeting's moderator, Rev. Henry Davis said, "William Everts, come up here and pray."

William did so and prayed with such power that a woman turned to Phoebe and asked, "Do you know who that boy is?"

Phoebe replied, "It is a child the Lord gave me."

"Blessed art thou among women, and blessed is the fruit of thy womb," the woman declared in an outburst of feeling. Her words expressed the general feeling of all who were present and had heard William pray that night. Afterward, the Reverend Davis took William into his own home and the next year, with the hearty endorsement of his church, sent William to Hamilton, New York, to study for the ministry.

William arrived at school in the fall of 1831 with just three dollars in his pocket. Despite having to support himself through eight years of school—even having to work in the morning before the 5 a.m. chapel service—he rose to the head of his class and stayed there. And young William's preaching so amazed his contemporaries that they called him the "Boy Preacher." By age 25, the flaxen-haired minister was the most popular young Baptist preacher of his time.

His first marriage, to a Maria Wykoff, lasted only three years. She died, leaving him two daughters, Eliza and Maria. Then, in 1843, while pastoring the Laight Street Church in New York City, he married Margaret Keen Burtis of Philadelphia. She bore him three more children: Margaret, Henrietta and Will.

Like his father before him, William proved to be a remarkable leader; he always saw matters positively when everyone else was being negative. Every church he pastored grew by the hundreds. In 1852, the First Baptist Church of Chicago invited him to become its pastor, offering him a princely salary of $1,000 annually plus moving expenses, if he would accept. And as further inducement, they notified him that their church would soon install both gas lighting and new furnaces in First Church. Even so, William declined the invitation to move to the Windy City with its then 42,000 inhabitants, choosing to serve other churches elsewhere.

Then on February 1, 1853, he accepted a call to pastor the Walnut Street Baptist Church of Louisville, Kentucky. The population of Louisville then exceeded Chicago's by some 8,000 people. But the Walnut Street Church offered William only a half-finished building and a congregation of 50 worshipers.

Within a year of William's arrival, the sanctuary was completed and dedicated. In six years, the congregation was Louisville's largest, and the Walnut Street Church, with a core group of its own members, was already establishing a branch church on Chestnut Street. Also at that time, the trustees of Franklin College of Indiana conferred upon William the honorary title of Doctor of Divinity.

Meanwhile, First Baptist Church of Chicago remained interested in William. In 1858 and again in the spring of 1859, he received calls from First Baptist. At first, he hesitated to accept. His pastorate in Louisville was enormously successful, and the Evertses were happy in the ministry there. But growing North-South tensions over the issue of slavery were making his position increasingly difficult as a Northerner pastoring a southern church.

A pro-slavery faction of five or six in the church then began circulating falsehoods against William in a maneuver to get him to leave the state. At first, he resisted the pressure and stood firm, because the majority of the church wanted him to continue as their pastor. But when he realized that his reputation was at stake and that his continued presence could permanently divide the church, he felt led of the Lord to leave and to accept the call to pastor Chicago's First Baptist Church. He undoubtedly felt as Margaret did, that "life is too short to waste in antagonisms." So in August 1859, barely two years before the Civil War broke out, William and Margaret arrived in Chicago. William's earnestness, enthusiasm, hopefulness and good humor were used by God to inspire growth in First Church to a congregation of 2,000 in just six years. Though he received many calls from other churches, he remained in Chicago for 20 years, even while also assisting struggling churches in many other places across the country.

In his seventh year in Chicago, his beloved Margaret died, her death proving as great a loss to the church as to William himself. Yet his ministry and that of the church never faltered. In the Great Chicago Fire of October 11, 1871, great parts of the city were devastated. Unscathed, First Church provided desperately needed relief to those who were affected, serving more than 12,000 meals in its basement and distributing $16,000 in cash to those rendered penniless by the fire. Tragically, a second fire in 1874 destroyed the sanctuary of First Church—a building considered one of the finest in the city—and ruined many of the church's wealthiest members. Within a year, under William's inspiring leadership, a new First Church building began rising in a new location on the then west side of the ever-growing city.

A gifted fund-raiser, William was heavily involved with other Chicago Baptists in the organization of the University of Chicago from 1857 to 1872, working hard to raise money for it. He was also instrumental in the founding of the Morgan Park Seminary and Baptist Theological Union in 1863 across the street from the University of Chicago campus. The seminary was successful almost from the beginning, and among its first students was Dwight L. Moody.

Another major achievement William brought about was the uniting of then rival Bible societies. He finished writing a book, *The Christian Apostle*, the day before he died, September 25, 1890, less than one month before the birth of his granddaughter, Henrietta C. Mears.

Margaret Keen Burtis Everts

Margaret Keen Burtis, Henrietta Mears' maternal grandmother was born in Philadelphia on August 30, 1817, the second child and only daughter of Mr. and Mrs. John Burtis. John, a Quaker, had come to Philadelphia from New England and worked 25 years for the United States Bank of Philadelphia before becoming the proprietor of a large manufacturing firm. Mrs. Burtis was the daughter of Joseph Keen, a surgeon well-known among Philadelphia Baptists. Though a chair-bound invalid for many years, she was a woman much loved for her gentle, quiet, radiant spirit.

The best qualities of both her parents combined in Margaret who, from her early teens, showed unusual abilities and leadership potential in whatever she attempted. Vivacious, confident and loving, she won the affection of those associated with her. Always unassuming, she was—without realizing it—the center of attraction in social situations and an irresistible influence for good upon others.

As a very young girl, she had loved to wear fine jewelry and beautiful clothes—and she wore them with taste. But after her conversion to Christ and her baptism at age 14, she put away her jewelry and elegant wardrobe and dressed with Quaker simplicity the rest of her life. She used the money she saved by avoiding personal adornment as a benevolent fund for others.

When Margaret was only 16, her mother died, leaving her in charge of the house with it family of seven, along with many guests and visiting relatives as well. While training the young children to do their part too, she ran the household and looked after the rest of the family's personal needs with a calm efficiency that belied her calendar years. And even then, she found time to study music—she proved to be gifted—and to study many scholarly books, keeping a detailed record of all she read. Margaret, with her family, attended Sunday School and church regularly and spent much time in visitation, particularly with those less fortunate than herself, seeking to help them practically and spiritually. At 17, she entered the Collegiate Institution for Young Ladies in Philadelphia.

During a great Bible convention held in Philadelphia in 1836, a theological student named William W. Everts who was attending the convention was offered the hospitality of the Burtis home for several days. While there, William found himself attracted to Margaret and suggested that they correspond with one another after he returned to Hamilton. Margaret was willing, but first asked her father's permission to do so. Fearful both of losing her and of the difficulties she would face as a future minister's wife, he withheld permission, and the matter ended there—for the time being.

By 1842, William was already a promising New York City minister in a successful pastorate. But he was also a widower trying to raise two tiny daughters alone. Quite naturally, his thoughts in time were again of Margaret Burtis. He renewed their acquaintance and proposed marriage to her. Margaret's father no longer opposed the relationship, so William and Margaret were married in the Burtis home in November 1843 and returned to New York together where William was then pastoring the Laight Street Church.

From the beginning of their marriage, Margaret mothered William's infant daughters as though they were her own. She also formed a deep and lasting friendship with the mother of William's first wife, Maria. She and William also had three children of their own: a son, Will, and two daughters, Margaret (who was to become the mother of Henrietta Mears) and Henrietta.

A devoted mother and companion to all her children, Margaret spent long hours entertaining them, guiding their conversations and encouraging each one in developing a sense of personal responsibility. A firm mother, she corrected her children when they erred, but never did so in the presence of others. Greatly interested also in their mental growth, she worked with them as they wrestled with such subjects as geography, grammar and arithmetic. And she won all her children to Christ before each one reached the age of 12.

To her husband, Margaret was both a devoted friend and an unerring counselor. She stood side by side with him in his work and responsibilities, augmenting his efforts with her own. As William himself wrote of Margaret a year after her death:

> *Few women so entirely identify themselves with their husband's life and pursuits as Mrs. Everts did. She*

> *watched his health, not only for his comfort, but as it*
> *fitted him for work. She supplemented his pastoral labor*
> *in making calls and receiving applications.*
>
> *Possessed of a remarkably facile pen, for the last fif-*
> *teen years she carried on most of her husband's corre-*
> *spondence, which, with the certainty of an every-day*
> *mail of from one to five letters, was, of itself, no incon-*
> *siderable labor; but in addition to this, she copied thou-*
> *sands of pages for publication.*
>
> *Every sermon preached was prayerfully listened to,*
> *and afterward discussed with reference to its suitability,*
> *its faithfulness, its probable success in winning some, in*
> *warning others, in up-building all. None of the little*
> *cords of sympathy and confidence that bind pastor and*
> *people were by her unnoticed or uncared for, but held*
> *with a careful hand, and strengthened by every act.[1]*

One day in Louisville, when her husband was pastoring the Walnut Street Baptist Church, Margaret, as was her custom, was out with a lady companion, knocking on doors and passing out tracts. They entered a boardinghouse and timidly knocked on one of the doors, unaware that the occupant inside was the English actor-comedian, Edwin F. Strickland. The actor was busy studying his lines for a new play and trying to create a suitable make-up for his character, so he was in no mood to be interrupted.

When he heard the knock on his door, Strickland assumed some newsman had come to interview him at this inappropriate moment. He angrily flung his door open and was startled to find the two ladies standing there. Seeing the irritated man before her, clutching a wig in one hand and a well-smeared make-up cloth in the other, Margaret exclaimed, "Oh, I must have come to the wrong place."

"Madam, I assure you, you have indeed," Strickland answered, performing a low bow.

"I am distributing tracts," Margaret quickly explained. "My husband is Dr. Everts."

"Madam, I am honored. We have attended his services," the actor replied, mellowing somewhat before the woman he later described as sweet-faced and noble, "her face as beautiful as her disposition and spirit."[2]

Then, though his room was littered everywhere with theatrical paraphernalia, he invited the two women to come in. He informed them that he was an actor of some years standing and currently performing with his wife and a young actor, George C. Lorimer, at a Louisville theatre.

"The soul of an actor is as dear to me as any others," Margaret told him. She gave Strickland a tract and invited him and the others with him to special services then in progress at the Walnut Street Church. The actor told the ladies that he and Lorimer already knew of Dr. Everts and the church, for they passed the building regularly when coming from and going to the theater. In fact, on one occasion seeing crowds pouring into the church, the two men went in themselves, only to find another minister in the pulpit at the time. He assured the women he would visit the church again, and they left.

When Lorimer and Mrs. Strickland later returned from rehearsal, Strickland told them of the visitors he had had in their absence. Though his wife remained disinterested, Strickland and Lorimer both went again and again to the Walnut Street Church and heard Dr. Everts preach.

William Everts returned their interest and stopped by one day to visit the actors in their rooms, only to find the two men carousing with others from their troupe. He refused their offer of wine and warned them, "You have offended against the Lord your God, and your sins will find you out." William's words convicted Strickland and Lorimer both. Before their theatrical engagement in Louisville ended, both actors were converted and baptized by William Everts in his church.

Eventually, both Strickland and Lorimer went into the ministry. Mrs. Strickland was later converted under her husband's preaching. And later, when William eventually resigned as pastor of Chicago's First Baptist Church in January 1879, that church within two months called the Reverend Doctor George C. Lorimer, then pastor of Boston's Tremont Temple Church, to succeed the Reverend Doctor William Everts in the Chicago pulpit. Lorimer accepted.

Lorimer always regarded Margaret Everts as his spiritual mother and wrote these words in her honor:

> *I feel it a sacred duty to her memory, publicly, to acknowledge my indebtedness to her. If I have advanced in the divine life, if I have been useful to the church, if I have been able to overcome spiritual enemies, I confess, freely and candidly, that, under God, I owe much of my success to her. She advised me, when I needed counsel; she encouraged me amid my early perplexities and despondency; and she prayed for me when only the strength of God could support me.*
>
> *She was a mother in Christ, and I shall always reverence her memory as a son. Her influence has exerted an almost angelic power over me, and I hope for good to others, as well as to myself. Shall I not, therefore, arise and call her blessed?*[3,4]

For seven years in Chicago, along with being a wife and mother, Margaret served beside her husband, fully involved in the life of the First Baptist Church and in many civic and charitable organizations throughout the city. Then both family and friends began to notice a growing weariness in Margaret, even though she remained as serene and as active as ever. Though urged to relax occasionally and to get more rest, Margaret felt she could not, explaining that what was to be done must be done immediately.

Margaret had long been troubled by the fate of many young girls who came to Chicago from rural areas in hopes of finding employment. Those who could not get jobs often became prostitutes to support themselves. Concerned for their welfare, Margaret had become active in the support of a home for these victims of prostitution.

One day in September, Margaret attended a meeting of the city council at which she appealed for more funds to expand the capacity of this home. Coming back to her own home that evening just at dark, she admitted she was "so tired she could hardly command her feet."[5] Yet that evening she attended a women's prayer meeting which was followed in turn by another brief meeting on some church expenditure. The next day she was too weary to go out and stayed home, spending the day sewing. Still, she spent that night caring for a sick neighbor.

The following morning, she awoke feverish and ill. A month of fever, delirium and sleeplessness followed, until at noon on October 11, 1866, only 49 years of age, Margaret Burtis Everts died.

Three years later, in an official history of the First Baptist Church of Chicago, a notation appeared that read:

> *The death of our beloved sister, Mrs. Margaret K. Everts, wife of our pastor, Dr. W. W. Everts, on the 11th of October, 1866,...inflicted a wound which is still fresh, and almost incurable. In this last instance, alas! how great was the loss. In the seven year walk of that pious and beautiful woman with this church, none knew her but to love her, and none named her but to praise.*[6]

Margaret Burtis Everts Mears

Growing up in Chicago as the daughter of Margaret Keen Everts and Rev. William Wallace Everts, pastor of one of the city's larger and more influential churches, Margaret Burtis Everts—destined to be the mother of Henrietta C. Mears—came naturally into a rich spiritual inheritance which she, in time, passed on to her own seven children.

For three years following her mother's death in 1866, Margaret—along with her brother, a sister and an aunt—lived in Berlin where she studied music and art. Then in 1869, back in Chicago again, she married Elisha Ashley Mears, a Vermonter who had come to the city to study law. Mears had taken his bar examinations on his twenty-first birthday, joined the Chicago Bar Association and became one of the youngest practicing lawyers in the city.

Born and raised in Ashley Hall on the Mears family estate in Poultney, Vermont, E. Ashley Mears was the latest in a line of bankers and jurists. Ashley also had two sisters, Elizabeth and Cornelia, both of them staunchly Christian women. Cornelia—from whom Henrietta C. Mears received her middle name—was once courted by Horace Greeley, then a young printing apprentice in Poultney. But Cornelia rejected Greeley who later went on to found the New York *Tribune* and to candidate for president of the United States in 1872. Greeley was defeated for the presidency by General Grant. Neither Cornelia nor Elizabeth ever married and both lived out their lives in Ashley Hall.

In anticipation of her marriage to Ashley, Margaret had planned to have a formal wedding in her father's church. But the wedding turned out to be larger than she had envisaged for, instead of issuing formal invitations, her father simply stood up in his pulpit and invited the entire membership to attend. Apparently, most of them did, for mounted police were necessary to control the crowds who attended. Sadly, their many beautiful wedding gifts were burned just two years later in the Great Chicago Fire of 1871. Ashley eventually built a large brownstone house on Michigan Avenue for Margaret.

Margaret Mears was tiny: she weighed only 80 pounds on her wedding day and never topped 98 pounds in her lifetime. But though small in stature, she was a giant force in her family, culturally, intellectually and spiritually. She was strong, yet serene; poised, yet enthusiastic; restrained, yet loving. She was active and involved in the church and in the community, yet she put nothing before her family and its welfare. Margaret rejoiced in the Word and was a power in prayer. And like her mother before her, she won many to the Lord by her winsome witness. She knew both prosperity and adversity and bore both with equal grace.

On December 29, 1910, when Henrietta Mears was just 20 herself, her mother died in Minneapolis, Minnesota where the family was then living. In tribute to Margaret Burtis Mears and to the impact of her life, her pastor, Dr. W. B. Riley, minister of the First Baptist Church of Minneapolis, wrote of her:

> *Margaret Burtis Mears was the daughter of Dr. W. W. Everts, so long the pastor of the First Church, in Chicago, and so well and widely known. Those who knew his wife, the mother of Margaret Burtis, could see in Mrs. Mears a combination of the excellent characteristics of both parents. In intellect she had few equals; keen, inquiring, aggressive, confident. She literally revelled in the word of God, and came as nearly walking according to its sacred precepts as is possible in the sinful flesh.*
>
> *As a Bible teacher she had few equals in the city of Minneapolis. And in "the practice of the presence of God" she had no superiors. Like Martin Luther of old, one and two hours a day she spent upon her knees. When she appeared before a great class of young women on Sunday they gave audience to one they knew had been in the presence of God, believed that her message was direct from the Spirit. When she visited the homes of the poor, or talked with the convicted sinner, they alike understood that a messenger from the Holy One was at work for Him.*[7]

And, at Margaret's funeral, Dr. Riley turned to her youngest daughter, put an arm around her shoulders and said, "Henrietta, I hope the spiritual mantle of your mother will fall upon you."[8]

The mantle was not long in settling into place.

Notes

1. William W. Everts, *Christian Womanhood: Life of Mrs. M. K. Everts* (Chicago: Church and Goodman, 1868), p. 247.
2. Barbara Hudson Powers, *The Henrietta Mears Story* (Old Tappan, NJ: Fleming H. Revell Company, 1957), p. 86.
3. Everts, *Life of Mrs. M. K. Everts*, p. 212.

4. George C. Lorimer's son, George Horace Lorimer, became editor-in-chief of the *Saturday Evening Post* in 1899, after serving the publication initially as literary editor. He headed the magazine for over 30 years and is credited with making it one of the leading periodicals of its time. In leading the *Post* to success, he is recognized as having discovered many writers who later became famous.
5. Everts, *Life of Mrs. M. K. Everts*, p. 335.
6. *History of the First Baptist Church, Chicago* (Chicago: R. R. Donnelley & Sons, 1889), p. 42.
7. W. B. Riley, *Minneapolis Standard*, January 28, 1911.
8. Powers, *The Henrietta Mears Story*, p. 111.

THREE

Like Mother, Like Daughter

I 'm amazed to see how many of my own policies and beliefs trace back to my grandmother. The same thinking, the same ideas and approach. She taught them to my mother, and I was almost unconsciously reared upon these same precepts."

> *One thrilling thing...about the life of Henrietta*
> *Mears is the great spiritual heritage she has received.*
> *The scope of her life has been tremendous; even more*
> *tremendous is the spiritual influence of her forebears,*
> *which can be traced back through at least five genera-*
> *tions, and the spiritual 'mantle' that has been handed*
> *down on the maternal side from one generation to the*
> *next. Truly this is a witness to the scriptural promise*
> *"that it may go well with thee, and with thy children*
> *after thee."*[1]

During the births of their first six children, Ashley and Margaret
Mears knew great wealth and luxury, but they also experienced
much sorrow. Ashley, their first son, died suddenly on his twentieth birthday. Will, their second child, came down with spinal
meningitis at fourteen and was left deaf for life.

The birth of Clarence, their third, was followed by the birth of
Florence, their first daughter, who died at seven of typhoid.
Despite this tragic loss, Margaret Mears renewed and deepened
her commitment to Christ and His work.

Fifth in the family line was son Norman who went on to father
nine sons of his own. Then Margaret, their sixth child and second
daughter, was born. Sister Margaret was already 11 years old and
her mother now 42 when Henrietta, their seventh and last child
was born. "Praise God, it's a girl! I couldn't face rearing another
son," Ashley exclaimed. He also teased Henrietta about her tardy
arrival on the scene, saying that she was "like the apostle Paul 'out
of due season.'"[2]

Margaret and Ashley Mears had already moved their family
from Chicago and were settled in Fargo, North Dakota when little
Henrietta Cornelia was born, October 23, 1890. Ashley then
owned a chain of 20 banks across the Dakotas, and the move West
enabled him to be closer to his holdings. For three years, Henrietta's parents were able to indulge her every need. She even had
her own nurse, Tillie, as a constant companion.

Then the Great Panic of 1893 hit, striking even before the

newly elected president, Grover Cleveland, could assume office. Four years of disastrous depression followed. Railways collapsed; silver-mining and agricultural states, particularly in the West, encountered economic ruin; businesses failed; construction all but stopped; and banks across the country closed, including many of those owned by Henrietta's father. This setback in the family's fortunes caused Henrietta later in life to joke, "I was born with a silver spoon in my mouth, but it was yanked out before I got the taste of it."

Tiny, energetic Henrietta was the delight of her parents and adored by her older brothers and sister Margaret who were themselves already growing in independence and maturity. Sharing her brothers' spirit of excitement and desire to be in on anything happening, she managed to keep the entire Mears household on its toes.

A Rich Heritage

Mrs. Mears' influence on Henrietta reflected the practical wisdom she had gained in the rearing of her other six children. Coupling this knowledge with her own rich heritage, she was able to share with her daughter all the treasures of a deeply spiritual and experienced mother. And with the sensitivity of the very young, her own innate curiosity and keen interest in everything, Henrietta soon sensed that her mother's life was different from any other around her. At first, she wondered why.

Noticing her mother going regularly to her room every morning, Henrietta toddled after her one day to see what her mother did in there. In the room, she found her mother on her knees, her hands folded and her lips moving. Imitating her mother's actions, Henrietta knelt beside her, folding her chubby hands and made her lips move too. Putting her arm around her daughter, Mrs. Mears explained that she was talking to God, that God loved Henrietta and would also hear her when she talked to Him.

The mother then prayed that the Lord would make Henrietta a good girl that day and always be with her. Satisfied, Henrietta jumped up and was quickly off about the many things that filled her busy childhood days. But she never forgot her mother on her knees talking to God, and her great ambition was to spend an hour in prayer, just as her mother did each day.

> *So one morning she got the large alarm clock, placed it in front of her on the bedspread and closed her eyes in prayer. She prayed and prayed and prayed. She prayed for everything she could think of. She paused and thought and prayed some more.*
>
> *Then she peeked at the clock to see how she was doing. Only one minute had elapsed! What did her mother think of to pray for, for a whole hour? Then it was that small Henrietta got her first glimpse and understanding of what prayer consists of.*[3]

Sometime during Henrietta's first few years of life, the Mears family moved from Fargo, North Dakota to Duluth, Minnesota for a brief time before settling finally in Minneapolis. The First Baptist Church of Minneapolis, was then pastored by Dr. W. B. Riley, a man of stature and great influence, a thoroughly evangelical scholar who was destined to become nationally known through his powerful preaching, his many books and his later founding of Northwestern Schools where in 1947 he was succeeded as president by Billy Graham.

Soon the time came for Henrietta to begin kindergarten. She looked forward to attending school with eager anticipation. Because of her natural instincts for wanting things accomplished at once, waiting for the first day of kindergarten was a real lesson in patience for her. When finally the day did arrive, Henrietta went joyfully off to school. But her joy was short-lived. Upon returning home she confidentially told her mother, "Kindergarten is to amuse little children, and I'm amused enough. I want to be educated."

A Child's Belief

Yet Henrietta's hunger for education, even at that young age, did not overshadow her interest in the spiritual. So that her mother would be more likely to take her to evening meetings at church, Henrietta would rush home from school each day and take a nap. Mrs. Mears hesitated at first, for fear that others would think she was forcing her child to attend with her, when, in fact, it was the other way around. But after much persuading by Henrietta, her mother finally gave in and took her along, carrying with her a small hassock to place under her daughter's dangling feet when she sat in the pew.

One Easter Sunday morning when Henrietta was about seven years old, she announced to her mother, who was bathing and dressing her for church, that she was ready to become a Christian and join their church. Because the girl was so young and the matter so serious, Mrs. Mears responded cautiously.

> *"But you are so young, dear. I'm afraid everyone will think that at seven you are too young to understand what it means."*
>
> *"I realize that I'm a sinner. Why, mother, you know how sinful I am! And I know that Jesus is my Savior. You're always trying to get everyone to accept Christ as Savior, and I'm ready. I want to join the church."*
>
> *Her mother was combing her curls around her finger and brushing them. "Well, dear, it isn't up to me. We'll have to talk to Dr. Riley about it."*[4]

A few weeks later, young Henrietta and her cousin, Margaret Buckbee—only four days younger than Henrietta—stood before the congregation of the First Baptist Church and responded to questions put to them concerning faith and doctrine. The girls answered with such clarity and frankness that the congregation broke out in laughter. Henrietta, thinking she was saying something wrong, turned in dismay to her mother. Smiling warmly, Mrs.

Mears encouraged her to continue answering, assuring her that the people were laughing with them and not at them. On a Sunday soon after, Dr. Riley baptized both girls.

Before she could read words for herself, Henrietta loved to listen to her mother read the Bible aloud. Sometimes her mother would attempt to simplify the words—endeavoring to clarify the meaning for the little tyke beside her—but Henrietta would stop her and ask her not to change them, assuring her that she understood them as they were. Surprisingly for one so young, Henrietta's favorite portion of Scripture even then was Paul's mighty classic, Romans, the book she most frequently taught in later years.

A Mother's Example

The Mears household abounded with everyday applications of spiritual truths. Discipline was not an arbitrary parental code, but a godly standard of life governing every relationship. By the parents drawing simple, natural parallels between earthly parenting and that of a heavenly Father, the Mears children easily learned that the obedience and love they gave to their father and mother were human analogies of sonship in God's family.

Forgiveness and retribution, for example, were carefully defined. Whenever a child did wrong and duly expressed his sorrow, he was forgiven. But he also had to learn that repentance was not enough; someone had to pay for the wrongdoing.

To pay the penalty for one of her children's offenses, Mrs. Mears would deny herself butter for a stipulated number of meals. At the dinner table, whenever the children noticed their mother was not taking butter-which she greatly liked—a pall of silence and guilt fell on them all, causing the culprit to cringe in shame. When sufficient time had elapsed for her fulfilling a particular child's punishment, Mother Mears would ask the erring child to pass her some butter. Invariably, the child would scramble to get the butter to her as quickly as possible. Young and impressionable, Henrietta never forgot these incidents nor the lessons learned from them.

Ashley Mears fully supported his wife in matters of family discipline, although his approach often involved a humorous or whimsical touch. When brother Clarence fell into the habit of coming home at night after the approved hour, his father resolved the problem in his own unique way: by hiring a private detective to accompany Clarence on his evening sojourns and to ensure that he always got home in time.

As Ashley explained to Clarence,

> *"I am not going to let my children go to the devil, and I see no reason at all why your mother should have to get up in prayer meeting on Wednesday night and ask for prayer for you on this matter. We'll see if we can't take care of it first."*[5]

Interestingly, after a few outings in the company of the detective, Clarence developed an astonishing sense of punctuality. So did his brothers and sisters.

As evidence of his confidence in his wife's care of the children, Ashley often referred them to her with an "ask your mother" when they came to him with certain requests. Even though mother's word was law, a child—dissatisfied with her answer—would sometimes return to Ashley and appeal for a counter-ruling. Ashley had the ability—even while agreeing with his wife—to mollify the disgruntled child with some humorous comment.

On one occasion Henrietta came to him to complain about one of her mother's "unreasonable" decisions. Her father, unable to hide a smile, comforted Henrietta by saying,

> *"My dear, you'll just have to forgive me this time. I had no idea how unreasonable your mother was going to turn out to be when I married her. But you'll just have to put up with it this time, and the next time I promise I'll try to give you a better mother!"*[6]

Mrs. Mears recognized the balance that her husband brought into the life of the family with his humor, optimism and kind ways. Nothing in life—whether setbacks in his business, poor health or other reverses—ever got him down. As her mother acknowledged to Henrietta,

> *"If the Bible says that every man who bridleth his tongue is a perfect man, then your father is a perfect man. I have never heard him say an unkind word. The Lord knew I needed someone to see the silver lining in every cloud, for I am more serious. He always sees the funny side of every situation."*[7]

Always socially concerned and active, Mother Mears frequently visited, among other places, the Florence Crittenden Home. When she felt Henrietta was old enough to understand that tragedies were part of life, she took her daughter with her to the home where they gave little gifts to the young residents. The experience of coming into contact with these hapless women made its mark on Henrietta's 10-year-old mind. Not long afterwards, she and her cousin Margaret formed "The Willing Workers," their private social service organization "to do good for unfortunates."

Henrietta's later effectiveness as a personal worker was a quality first nurtured in her by her mother. In the Mears home, a stack of New Testaments—each with salvation verses clearly marked—were placed near the front door. Salesmen and other visitors to the home were each given one with a gracious word of encouragement to study it.

Mother Mears would often make some such comment as this to a young man who came to the door to sell something: "I am always so interested in young men. I have four sons of my own, and I am concerned not only with their preparation for this life but for the one to come. I was wondering if you have ever accepted Christ as your personal Savior." From her mother's example, Henrietta learned a kind and sympathetic approach in inspiring people to seek God.

Another lesson passed on from mother to daughter concerned the economizing of time. Mother Mears strove to use every avail-

Henrietta Mears in August 1903 at the age of 12 years, 10 months.

able moment to its fullest, playing the piano for but a moment or two while waiting for the family to gather for dinner or reading a page of poetry while resting from housework. She would not allow her children to sleep late, even on holidays. Summer vacation was not for "running wild all day"—the mornings were spent in reading, memorizing great literature, music practice or the like. During school Mrs. Mears insisted that Monday morning lessons be prepared on the previous Friday afternoon, so that the weekend would not be haunted by unfinished homework.

Henrietta Mears showed the effects of this teaching all her life. A distasteful job was not to be put off. If someone needed to be reminded of his duties, she was there to do the job. If a meeting were called for 9:15, Henrietta was there at 9:13 ready to get started. All of this gave a sense of urgency to her life that was infectious. Others around her soon found that they, too, were anxious to get things done. In spiritual matters this sense of urgency reached its greatest intensity.

Henrietta's ability to concentrate on what she was reading was another quality developed in her early by her mother. Mrs. Mears, when seeing her daughter engaged in a book, would come up to her without warning, close the book and ask the girl to tell her what she had been reading.

Henrietta might remonstrate, "But Mother, I've only been reading for 10 minutes."

"My dear," Mrs. Mears would reply, "if you have been reading that long, you certainly should have learned something. Now tell me what you have read."

Even into Henrietta's teen years, her mother remained the paramount influence in her life. Mrs. Mears' great faith and practical wisdom cultivated both her daughter's spiritual sensibilities and her social graces. If Henrietta returned home from a party, complaining that it was dull and uneventful, her mother asked what she had done to make it interesting: "Wasn't there some game you could have suggested? Even though it wasn't your party, you should have felt an obligation to help the others have a good time."

Mrs. Mears responded similarly when her daughter came home, grieving over an uninspiring church meeting: "But did you give a testimony, Henrietta? Did you offer to help plan the meeting?"

Such reinforcement from her mother produced a sense of responsibility and initiative in the young woman that gave her in later life a readiness to contribute suggestions and create programs in situations where other people were throwing their hands up in discouragement.

Young Henrietta gleaned a wealth of knowledge and training from her family as well as from her formal schooling. Her mother's sister, Aunt Henrietta Buckbee, a concert soprano, encouraged her niece in a singing career. And Henrietta Mears did take voice lessons with an Edwin Skedden who was an opera coach and director of music at the First Baptist Church.

Although Henrietta did give some recitals and served as soloist on many occasions in the church and community, she was not destined for the concert stage. Yet her voice studies and the performances she did give taught her how to use her voice to maximum efficiency. Consequently, when her career as a teacher and lecturer began unfolding, she was able to address large audiences comfortably with a power and projection few others could match.

A Healing Touch

When Henrietta was only 12 years old, she contracted a painful, crippling case of muscular rheumatism. Many other cases were also reported in their region that year. And one of her friends, who contracted the disease at the same time, died from it. In constant pain, young Henrietta was almost completely immobile, having to be carried about from place to place.

Her family feared for her life, for during this siege, she began to suffer repeated nosebleeds. Claiming Philippians 4:19, "But my God shall supply all your need according to his riches in glory by Christ Jesus," Mother Mears took God at His word. She asked Henrietta if she would like Mr. Ingersoll, a family friend and member of a Presbyterian church, to come and pray for her nosebleeds. Henrietta agreed.

> *When Mr. Ingersoll arrived, he said, "Henrietta, do you believe the Lord can heal you?"*
>
> *Henrietta looked up at him and said, in her direct way, "He created us. I see no reason why He cannot heal us."*[8]

Mr. Ingersoll prayed for the bleeding to stop completely. God heard and answered, for the bleeding stopped and never occurred again in her lifetime.

The rheumatism, however, not only continued but became more painful with time. One afternoon, Henrietta, now 14, called her mother to her bedside and asked, "Do you think Mr. Ingersoll would come back and pray for my rheumatism?"

Within a few hours, Mr. Ingersoll was again in Henrietta's room, asking once more for God's intervention. As he prayed, Henrietta was suddenly filled with confidence that she was completely healed. All the pain was gone. Tears of relief flowed down her cheeks as she raised her voice in prayers of thanksgiving.

Her road to full recovery was swift and sure. She regained her strength rapidly and, to build up her muscles, Henrietta energetically took up horseback riding and swimming. Within three months, her body was free of any trace of the illness. And throughout her life, she never had a recurrence of rheumatism.

Henrietta, however, had never enjoyed good eyesight. She was so nearsighted that from her first day in school, when she was only six, Henrietta wore glasses. Then at 16, her vision problem was immeasurably compounded when she accidentally jabbed a hat pin into the pupil of an eye.[9] Her doctors could do nothing for the condition and predicted possible blindness for her.

Realizing the seriousness of this mishap, Henrietta and her mother discussed the situation and decided to ask their friend, Mr. Ingersoll, to return and join with them in special prayer for the healing of the injured eye. Mr. Ingersoll did come to them and joined with them in a time of earnest prayer. Henrietta had no doubt that the God who had made her could also heal her eye.

Specialists who later examined the eye agreed there was indeed a hole in the pupil and shook their heads in amazement that she could see anything out of it. That she was, in fact, seeing could not be explained except that God had stretched forth His hand and healed her eye—even though the hole remained. Henrietta learned from this experience and from her mother to accept all Scripture at face value. For God to touch her body simply meant taking Him at His word.

A Divine Revelation

When still a senior in high school, Henrietta, with her good friend, Evelyn Camp, attended a series of meetings in their church led by Dr. Riley. His closing sermon was such a challenge for full-time Christian service that Henrietta and Evelyn rose as one and marched down the aisle when the invitation was given. They both felt a tremendous sense of commitment to go wherever the Lord wanted them to go, and to do whatever work He wanted them to do. And, like every other young person who has given his life to serve the Lord, they were keen to know where they were to serve.

In time, Evelyn developed a deep concern for Japan, feeling the Lord would have her serve Him there. But, try as she would, Henrietta felt no such urge to go and work with the Japanese people. She saw the need in Japan and felt a deep concern for that country and its people, yet she did not feel led to serve there.

Henrietta prayed, lest something was wrong in her life, keeping her from wanting to go to Japan, too. "Is something wrong with me?" she asked herself again and again. Yet not one to jump into action without divine direction, she waited and prayed, abiding the Lord's time.

Her only solution, she felt, was to search out for herself how she could appropriate God's power and find His direction for her life. For weeks, she scoured the Bible for references to Christ's presence, particularly for those concerning the ministry of the Holy Spirit. She closeted herself with God.

Then a divinely revealed truth began to take shape in her mind, as the object of her search gained focus in her thoughts: It was God Himself she was seeking. In Him lay her call. But how to acquire the full measure of His presence, His will, His power? What needed to be done? What discipline to take up? What efforts of mind and will to reach for?

Then suddenly, a cascading flood of light rushed into her soul, illuminating darkened corners, transforming her questions into understanding and confidence, as the controlling insight of her life dawned upon her: She could do nothing more to obtain God's presence and power than to receive the fulness of His Holy Spirit as a gift. By faith then, she reached out and took what God had for her—Himself.

Notes
1. Barbara Hudson Powers, *The Henrietta Mears Story* (Old Tappan, NJ: Fleming H. Revell Company, 1957), p. 82.
2. Ibid., p. 93.
3. Ibid., p. 98.
4. Ibid., p. 94.
5. Ibid., p. 96.
6. Ibid., p. 102.
7. Ibid., p. 97.
8. Ibid., p. 100.
9. This accident was not related to the eye weakness which constantly afflicted not only Henrietta Mears, but also several others in her immediate family.

FOUR

Trials, Tests and Triumphs

W ill is the whole man active. I cannot give up my will; I must exercise it. I must will to obey. When God gives a command or a vision of truth, it is never a question of what He will do, but what we will do. To be successful in God's work is to fall in line with His will and to do it His way. All that is pleasing to Him is a success."

WITH HIGH SCHOOL BEHIND HER, HENRIETTA LOOKED FORWARD TO ATTEND-ing the University of Minnesota. But first she was forced to make one of the more serious decisions of her life. Because her already poor eyesight was continuing to deteriorate, her doctors advised her to give up any thought of further studies. Otherwise, they predicted, she would be blind by the time she was 30.

Willing to Sacrifice Sight

Deeply concerned, her mother asked Henrietta what she was going to do. Would she accept their advice and forgo further reading and studying? Her unhesitating reply was typical: "If I am going to be blind by 30, then blind I shall be! But I want something in my head to think about. I'm going to study as hard as I can as long as I can."

So she entered the University of Minnesota and proceeded with her studies. Yet aware of the dangers, she carefully disciplined her habits, increasing her powers of concentration during lectures, studying only by daylight and not by electricity. Immediately after a class, she found an empty room and began preparing for the next class. She always finished an assignment while the subject was still fresh in her mind. Her concentration was such that she could fully comprehend a book in a single reading.

Henrietta relied heavily upon her ability to listen and to absorb lectures given in class, so refining her auditory skills that she could remember and repeat almost verbatim most of what she heard. As a result of her disciplined habits, she learned much and retained it while, at the same time, sparing her eyes as much as possible. Consequently, she not only earned excellent grades but also gained a reputation on campus as the student who seemingly never had to study to get them.

When asked about her lifelong struggle with extreme myopia, general eye weakness, irritation and other vision problems, Henrietta would remark, "I believe my greatest spiritual asset throughout my entire life has been my failing sight, for it has kept me absolutely dependent upon God."

Learning to Let Go

Already in her college freshman year, Henrietta plunged into Christian service, serving the Sunday School of her church as superintendent of the junior department. Being responsible for this high-energy age-group was a great challenge for Henrietta, but she proved equal to it. And through the experience, God gave her a genuine vision for service in Christian education.

In Henrietta's second year of college, when she was 20 years of age, her mother fell critically ill. Henrietta remained out of class to care for her, but on December 29, 1910, just a few days after Christmas, Mother Mears died. Following her mother's death, Henrietta went through a period of loneliness and great grief.

> *The one who had taught her so much and had been such a constant spiritual strength and companion was gone. It was a time of great spiritual testing for Henrietta....She who had always been the life of the party wherever she went, loving people and activities, drew apart more and more into spiritual solitude. It seemed as though the Lord was drawing her away from everything, testing her to see if there was anything she would not be willing to yield to Him.[1]*

Her father—who was soon to die himself—and her sister Margaret became concerned about Henrietta. They urged her to socialize more. But she turned instead to spiritual truths for the comfort and comprehension she needed just then. Providentially, through his strong forceful preaching, Paul Rader, then minister of Chicago's Moody Memorial Church and holding meetings at the time in Minneapolis, thrilled her with his messages and deepened her understanding of the believer's life under grace.

Henrietta at this time wrestled with more than just grief. She thought often of Dr. Riley's words on the occasion of her mother's death when he said, "Henrietta, I am praying that your mother's mantle will fall upon you." How, she wondered, could she possibly measure up to such high expectation.

Then one winter night, alone in her room, as she knelt in prayer, she felt she "saw the Lord." In a total surrender of herself and of everything she held dear, she finally experienced closure in the matter of her mother's death and entered into a life of total dependency upon the Lord. That matter was now settled for all time and would never trouble Henrietta again.

The room was still and her heart was quiet before the Lord as she then asked God for spiritual power that she be fully used of Him in the might of the Holy Spirit. Assured in her spirit that her request had been honored, she expressed her gratitude for His goodness to her. "Thank you, Lord. I accept by faith the filling and the power of the Holy Spirit, just as I accepted Christ as my Savior."[2]

She would later describe this encounter with the Lord in this way:

> I [had] felt absolutely powerless from the thought that I could possibly live up to what my mother had been and had done, and I prayed that if God had anything for me to do that He would supply the power. I read my Bible for every reference to the Holy Spirit and His power. The greatest realization came to me when I saw that there was nothing I had to do to receive His power but to submit to Christ, to allow Him to control me.
>
> I had been trying to do everything myself; now I let Christ take me completely. I said to Christ that if He wanted anything from me that He would have to do it Himself. My life was changed from that moment on.

An early evidence of what the Holy Spirit would be doing in and through the life of Henrietta Mears took place during her junior year at the University of Minnesota. In the university's Shevlin Hall, she started a Bible study class for university women that met every Thursday afternoon. The class met for less than an

Henrietta Mears on the occasion of her graduation from the University of Minnesota, June 12, 1913.

hour each time, and she was the sole teacher.

Only a few attended at first. But then those few began bringing their friends. Soon 60 women her own age were studying and praying with her each week. She continued the class through her senior year. Testimony to the spiritual impact of that class was that several women who attended it later went into missionary service.

Henrietta approached graduation in 1913 with an exemplary scholastic record. Had she not had to remain out of class during her mother's final illness, she might have received a Phi Beta Kappa key. As it was, her grades were so high, she was excused from all final examinations. And she was graduated still able to see!

Beginning to Teach School

Henrietta's first public school teaching position after she left the university was in Beardsley, Minnesota, a little town with a population of only 850 persons. She served the high school there as both chemistry teacher and principal, with speech and dramatics as sideline responsibilities. In the course of performing her many duties, she found the morals of the school's students so appallingly low that she commented, "God made the country, man the city, and the devil the small town."

Determined to be a positive influence on her students, she entered into their various activities, coaching plays, organizing choirs, even raising money for new pianos and Victrolas. When she found out the school had no football team, she found a coach and set about organizing a team. Then even though it meant trudging through sleet or mud to get there, she never missed a game, rooting for her school's team from their bench. In turn, her huskies occupied the first rows of the Bible class she taught at the Methodist church, listening eagerly to her spiritual coaching.

Her methods were original, and her enthusiasm infectious. One Sunday night, when she could not get any of her youngsters to stand and give a testimony, she asked the entire group to rise and sing a hymn. They stood. After the hymn, she announced that any who testified could sit down. The humor of what she had done broke the ice for all, and one by one the members of the group began expressing themselves and sharing their faith with one another.

These were depression years, and money was scarce, making it hard to raise even the smallest amount of money. Few members of that Beardsley church had much to give that year when the annual campaign for missions was announced. But Henrietta was undaunted.

She challenged her young people with a plan that inspired and excited them. "I want you to work and earn as much money as you are able," she said. "Do everything you can to bring in money for our missionaries. And I will match you dollar for dollar."

Eager to outdo the other groups and one another, the young people charged out on their assignment. Townspeople marveled at the sudden interest of their youth in running errands, doing chores, tackling odd jobs and every other task they could find that generated a little income. And they all saved their earnings.

When Missionary Sunday arrived, the youth class could barely sit still in the pews as the other classes reported their collections: $1.25, $3.00, $15.50. Then the minister called out, "Miss Mears' Young People's Class."

Charlie—one of the harder working members of the class —leaped to his feet and shouted, "$120!" Such an amount for missions was unheard of in those times, and the young people were jubilant in the triumph of their near-miracle.

Soon after, Henrietta was approached by two of the members of her football team who asked if she would start a Bible class for a number of them. They acknowledged that she had been encouraging them to study their Bibles, but they hadn't been able to do so on their own. Henrietta agreed to hold the class in the parlor of the home where she lived. And she encouraged the two young men to bring friends with them.

The class began that night. As the class continued, attendance grew, until the room, the hallway and the stairsteps were full. Finally, they opened windows in the parlor, so those who couldn't get in could stand outside and listen.

Before Henrietta's year in Beardsley was to end, a Catholic priest called on her to thank her for the amazing changes she was bringing about in the lives of the town's young people and to express the gratitude of the community. They subsequently had many long, interesting talks together on spiritual matters.

One night, a group of Beardsley's teachers were out in the country, attending a corn-husking party at a large farm. While there, Henrietta was introduced to a young man whose parents owned the hotel in town. A handsome Harvard graduate, he was immediately interested in Henrietta. As they talked, they found they had many interests in common and greatly enjoyed each other's company. He asked if he could take her home afterwards, and she consented.

For two weeks afterwards, as their friendship grew, he hovered about Henrietta, seizing every chance to be with her. They went for long drives in the countryside and dined out together. She spoke with him at length about those concerns that were dear to her and shared with him the faith that gave her life purpose and direction. He responded with a promise to attend church with her.

Then one day the president of the school board called on her. Henrietta could tell from the gravity of his manner that he had come on a matter of some seriousness. Coming directly to the point, he questioned her about the man she had been dating.

> *"What kind of a young man is he, Miss Mears?"*
>
> *"Why, just wonderful," she answered. "He is very intelligent, gracious, polite—very charming in every way."*
>
> *"Well, I always knew that someone, some day would find a good side to him," he agreed. "The trouble is that he has such a bad reputation that if you continue going with him the town simply will not believe that you are reforming him, but instead—! You see, he has the worst reputation in town. I always felt he had possibilities, but it seemed there was never anyone to challenge him. But you will ruin your reputation instead of improving his."*[3]

Henrietta was stunned, dismayed and almost disbelieving what she had just heard. Yet, unable to doubt the principal's counsel, she knew she would have to act on what he had told her. That night, when her Harvard man called her, she told him he could not come to see her again. Not easily put off, he told Henrietta that whether she consented or not, he was coming over because he had to talk with her at least once more. He came to the house, and Henrietta agreed to only a brief conversation with him.

> *"I know what you've heard," he said miserably, "and the trouble is, it's true. I know it would be too much to try to live down, so I'm going to leave town. I didn't care until I met you. Now I'm sorry."*
>
> *"It's too bad that you didn't have enough courage to be true to yourself," she said gently.*

> *"I know. I want to make a fresh start. At least I want*
> *to thank you for making me want to start over again*
> *somewhere else."*[4]

And then he was gone, leaving town abruptly. Some days after he left, his mother visited Henrietta and thanked her for giving her son reason to change and for inspiring him to become something better. Henrietta was grateful to God that He had used her to make a difference in a genuinely promising life.

The next school year found Henrietta in North Branch, Minnesota where she once more served the local high school as both chemistry teacher and principal. While there, she again attended the Methodist church, assisting with the Sunday School and the youth groups. She walked to the church from her room in a boardinghouse, each time passing an impressive brick house on a hill, surrounded by vast lawns and an ornate wrought iron fence.

Henrietta was intrigued by this home—owned by a wealthy lumberman—if for no other reason than the fact that no one on the high school faculty had ever been invited inside. The lumberman had five children, and one was Everett, an incorrigible boy who was a terror to the teachers, and none had been able to tame him. They warned Principal Mears that Everett and his pranks were the scourge of the school.

Armed with determination and a pocketful of spitwads, Everett quickly set himself to unnerving his new principal. But to his initial dismay and wonder, she remained unperturbed by his harassments. This was going to be no fun at all!

Henrietta "treated Everett as if she didn't have a doubt in the world but that he had very good reasons for being the most difficult pupil in the class but that the two of them together would just have to be brave about the whole thing and rise above the problems. She swept him along in a manner of expectant comradeship."[5] And she went out of her way to introduce him on an equal footing with others to all the activities in which she expected her students to take an interest.

Her friendly and determined attitude began to have effect. One day Everett delivered to his principal an invitation to their home. When she met Everett's family they expressed their gratitude that she had been able to win the boy's admiration and respect. He had also ceased to be such a problem to them.

Henrietta was invited back to the home many times, giving her numerous opportunities to talk to them about Christ. Years later, Everett's sister called on Henrietta and said, "Oh, those wonderful days when you were with us in our home! We will never forget them. You revolutionized North Branch. Our whole family was changed because of your influence on our lives."

Choosing to Obey God

Henrietta's life during this time in North Branch was not devoid of romance. Her vivacious personality, keen sense of purpose, spontaneous humor and immense capacity for appreciation drew many men to her. But she loved only one seriously enough to consider marrying him.

He was tall, handsome, black-haired, intellectually challenging and a delight socially. A graduate of Dartmouth and widely traveled, he was now a banker in this small Minnesota town. And because the town was small, they were constantly meeting on the street, in the post office, in the drugstore.

A friendship developed between them that soon grew into love. But as his attentions toward her increased, fear struck her heart, for he was of a different faith. Sooner or later, Henrietta knew, she would have to end the relationship.

When the young banker went out of town on a business trip, the town dentist asked Henrietta out. She dated him several times and was sure her doing so would discourage the banker's ardor, thereby sparing her having to terminate their friendship directly. But her seeing the dentist only brought matters to a head more quickly.

When her banker-suitor returned, he asked Henrietta to marry him. He tried to make her see that he admired her religious convictions. He tried to persuade her that they could establish their home, that she could go on and believe and do just as she wanted to and not have to change in any way.

Henrietta agonized over his proposal. A home had always been very important to her. She loved children and companionship. She loved entertaining and the social life. And she loved this persuasive young man. Yet wouldn't she be compromising her faith, her beliefs, to share her life with someone who had a different faith from her own?

As the months slipped by, Henrietta could not escape this thought: Marrying this man, fine though he was, would be like establishing a home and deciding that each night the husband would dine in one room and the wife in another. They would both have an excellent meal, but they would have no fellowship together. If, in the matter of their faith, they could not sit together at the same table and have fellowship, their relationship would be an impossible one.

Her inner conflict was great, for this was the time of her greatest decision. In the solitude of her room, she prayed: "Lord, you have made me the way I am. I love a home, I love security, I love children, and I love him. Yet I feel that marriage under these conditions would draw me away from you. I surrender even this, Lord, and leave it in your hands. Lead me, Lord, and strengthen me. You have promised to fulfill all my needs. I trust in you alone."

For Henrietta, the matter was now settled. She knew what she had to do and she did it. She terminated the friendship.

Ever assured that she was in the Lord's hands and totally surrendered to His will for her, Henrietta knew God ordered the events of her life so that only what was best for her ever came to pass. Consequently, she was always able to make light of her singleness and to joke comfortably about her never having married. Her most frequent explanation whenever the subject came up was to say that St. Paul was the only man she could have married, and he didn't wait for her! And when teaching about the woman at the well who confessed to Jesus that she had had five husbands, Henrietta would chuckle and say, "Now she must have been a real glamour girl. She could get five husbands and I couldn't get one."[6]

But in honest sincerity, she also wrote:

> *The marvelous thing has been, that the Lord has always given me a beautiful home; He has given me thousands of children; He has supplied every need in my life, and I've never felt lonely. Since I am a very gregarious person, I thought I would have a feeling I didn't belong. But I've never had it, never! I've never missed companionship.*
>
> *Through one experience after another the Lord has shown me that He had something special for me to do. After I went through that final door, where it was just the Lord and I, into wide open spaces of people and things and excitement, life has been one great adventure. It has been a tremendous thing to see how the Lord has filled my life so abundantly with lovely things, and I want to tell everyone that wherever the Lord puts you—even alone on an island—He absolutely satisfies you.*
>
> *So often young people will say to me, "Oh, Miss Mears, I want to be just like you! You are so happy! I, too, never want to get married."*
>
> *And I say to them, "Nonsense! The Lord intends for you to marry; that is the way He has made us. It just so happens that in my case that wasn't His will."*
>
> *But it has pleased me to know that young people have been able to see my happiness and my complete satisfaction in the life that God has given me.*

Adhering to Fixed Goals

Henrietta had contracted to serve in North Branch for just a single year, so as the school year came to an end, she prepared to return to Minneapolis. But North Branch was not prepared to let her go so easily. As she arrived at the railway station to her train for the city, a delegation from the school board intercepted her and made a final effort with a tempting offer to keep her in their town. They offered her both a renewal of her contract and a bonus if she would remain. But certain that her career was leading her elsewhere, Henrietta declined their kind offer and returned to Minneapolis.

Despite her two years of successful teaching on the high school level in Beardsley and North Branch, the Minneapolis board of education denied Henrietta a high school teaching appointment. Saying she was too young a woman to teach high school chemistry, the board offered her a position in the junior high school instead. She accepted the post on a substitute basis only; she had trained to teach high school students and that was what she wanted to do, so she would not accept a permanent position on any other level.

The next fall, she was offered a teaching appointment at Central High School, but to teach mathematics, not chemistry. Still it was a high school teaching position, so she accepted. Then on the first day of school, the principal announced that the regular chemistry teacher had been drafted into the armed forces and asked for names of others qualified to teach the subject.

One of the older teachers on the staff responded:

> *"One of my former students has joined our faculty as a newcomer this fall. Knowing of her work in the university, Miss Cohen, head of the chemistry department at the University of Minnesota told me that this former student of mine had the most brilliant mind of any student she had taught, and I agree. I suggest that we could find no better candidate than Miss Henrietta Mears!"*[7]

All the other teachers supported the suggestion with applause, and Henrietta became Central High's new teacher of chemistry and head of the department, a position she was to occupy for 10 years with distinction.

Teaming Up to Serve Christ

Now that Henrietta had returned to Minneapolis, she and Margaret chose to make their home together, an agreement that was to last until Margaret's death in 1951. Sensing God's hand on Henrietta's life and realizing that her younger sister was marked for great ministry, Margaret devoted the rest of her life to her sister's care, "encouraging her, supporting her, running the household, making a place of hospitality for Henrietta to share with others in her Christian work."[8]

> *Margaret was always a wonderful contrast to Henrietta. She was a very successful businesswoman in her brother's firm and in other establishments for over 20 years. Her keen practical approach to everything kept all projects on a solid foundation. She had a sharp, dry wit, and a stimulating humor that kept everyone intrigued....She could meet anyone in any stratum of society. She was interested in everyone, had no inhibitions, and immediately established a rapport with the person with whom she talked. Her sly sarcasm in good-natured fun kept everything on an even keel.*[9]

A delightful hostess and a superb cook, Margaret took complete charge of their home, providing the necessary physical setting for her sister's spiritual concerns and needs.

> *Margaret took every physical responsibility from Henrietta: she paid the bills, did the shopping, ran the household, bought all of Henrietta's clothes, hats and accessories, shoes, gloves and purses. Henrietta never had to give a thought as long as Margaret was alive for*

*what she "should eat, or drink, or wherewithal she
would be clothed." Margaret would never marry, for she
felt that her responsibility was to Henrietta, to help her
devote full time to her unique Christian ministry.*[10]

Notes
1. Barbara Hudson Powers, *The Henrietta Mears Story* (Old Tappan, NJ: Fleming H. Revell Company, 1957), p. 111.
2. Ibid., p. 114.
3. Ibid., pp. 119-120.
4. Ibid., p. 120.
5. Ibid., p. 117.
6. Ibid., p. 114.
7. Ibid., p. 122.
8. Ibid., p. 120.
9. Ibid., pp. 120-21.
10. Ibid., p. 121.

FIVE

Go West, Young Lady, Go West!

L ook to the horizon.
   Do you see the slightest change?
The slightest speck? If you do, follow it."

HENRIETTA MEARS WAS DESTINED FOR SUNDAY SCHOOL WORK FROM HER earliest years. She taught her first Sunday School class at the age of 11 when her brother Norman asked her to help out at the Berean Mission in Minneapolis by teaching a Sunday afternoon class of beginners. By the time she was a freshman in university, she was already superintendent of her church's junior department.

While she was an undergraduate on campus, she introduced Bible classes for women. And in each town where she taught school, she affiliated with a local church and assisted in the Sunday School, touching scores of lives. Her teaching ministry eventually encompassed tens of thousands of boys and girls, men and women, all of whom she won to Christ through the steadfast teaching of God's Word.

A Loyalty to Scripture

Throughout her life, Henrietta Mears remained absolutely loyal to the Bible as the authoritative revelation of God. Her proficiency in teaching the Bible and her ability to quote long passages of Scripture from memory grew out of her deep commitment to the Word and her intensive study of it. She knew her Bible and loved to teach it to others.

Her study methods were simplicity itself, nothing beyond what the average believer is equally capable of doing. She possessed several Bibles in various translations, but her favorite was a leather-bound King James edition which was well marked and somewhat tattered. That particular Bible was her friend for almost a lifetime.

While listening to others expound a passage, she would jot in the margins their thoughts or her own. And in private study, she scribbled ideas that helped her summarize a whole passage at a glance. She usually worked with a notebook at hand, but when one was not available, any sheet of paper would do. Some of her observations were even committed to the backs of envelopes.

But the form of writing was not significant, the intensity of concentration was. The technique, therefore, was not the important aspect of her Bible study; it was the avidity with which she devoured every truth in it. Her devotional hour was not a routine with her, nor a discipline born of fear or habit. She opened her Bible with eager anticipation in the sacred silence of personal fellowship with God.

"If you would be pure," she advised others, "saturate yourself with the Word of God." And she seized every opportunity to show how it could be done.

An Opportunity to Teach

Not surprisingly then, when she returned to Minneapolis from Beardsley, Henrietta was soon involved in teaching Sunday School again. At the First Baptist Church, her sister Margaret had been teaching a group of 18-year-old girls. The girls called themselves "The Snobs" and would not permit a newcomer to join their class. Margaret was in despair over them and implored her younger sister to take over the class and teach it for her.

Henrietta did so. Within a few months under her teaching, the girls stopped calling themselves "The Snobs." Then when the Sunday School was subsequently reorganized, every one of the regulars answered a call to serve in the church. Henrietta was left with just one girl, a visitor who had been in class only once before.

The two of them set out on a canvas of the neighborhood. They called on every home within a mile of the church where a young woman lived. The following Sunday 55 girls were present to form a newly organized "Fidelis Class."

The class met at first in a small room, but the attendance soon doubled and they moved to a larger room. Over the years they pushed out the walls of every room they occupied. Within a decade, the Fidelis Class numbered over 500 members, and a special hall was built to contain them.

As Henrietta taught, sister Margaret acted as greeter, standing in the church door and inviting passing young women to come inside and hear her sister teach the Bible. One of these women later said, "Margaret invited us in to see her sister's hats, and they were something to behold. But we soon learned that there was more to Henrietta Mears than just her hats, as we found Christ as our Savior."

One afternoon while calling on members of the Fidelis Class, Henrietta stopped in front of a large brown house. She secretly hoped that Virginia would not be home or would be busy, for this young woman seemed so uninterested in spiritual matters. Finding Virginia's fiancee with her, Henrietta was greatly relieved, thinking it would not be appropriate now to talk with her about the gospel.

After a few moments of pleasantries, Henrietta left the couple. But as she began to drive away, she felt God was speaking to her: "Henrietta, why didn't you talk to Virginia about me? Wasn't that why you came here in the first place?"

Henrietta drove around the block, parked her car and once more rang the bell. Virginia and the young man were surprised to see her again and asked if she had forgotten something.

"Yes," their Bible teacher replied. "I failed to do the very thing for which I came here in the first place—to talk to you about your relationship to Christ."

"Oh, Miss Mears," Virginia exclaimed. "George and I were just saying how we wished you had stayed, so you could talk to us about God."

Within half an hour the young couple met the Savior.

As an outgrowth of the Fidelis Class, Henrietta organized the "Dorcas Group," made up of young married women from the class. Their purpose was to sew and give to missionaries as well as to discuss problems and spiritual aspects of their lives as young mothers. The group met in different homes, soon becoming one of the established fellowships in the church. Both groups remained an ongoing part of the life of the church.

A Call to Leadership

About this time Henrietta's old friend, Evelyn Camp, returned home on her first furlough from Japan. She shared her ministry experiences with Henrietta's Fidelis Class. Later, when Evelyn returned to Japan, the president of the class went with her. And other class members also went into missionary service.

As Henrietta observed one after another of her Bible students answering the call into Christian service, she realized God was speaking to her. He was clarifying her own calling in the Christian field by confirming what she was already doing for Him:

> *She had been called to train leaders and to nurture the spiritual growth in thousands who could go in her place to penetrate the world with the Gospel of Christ. Only* one *Henrietta could have gone to Japan*[1]*— or to anywhere else.*

Instead of sending her, God was asking her to multiply herself in the lives of the many others whom He would then send out in her place.

An Invitation to Honor

One Sunday soon after, Margaret and Henrietta arrived at church to find that their pastor, Dr. Riley, was out of town. Occupying the pulpit was a Dr. Stewart P. MacLennan from the First Presbyterian Church of Hollywood, California. A magnificent figure of a man, Dr. MacLennan preached eloquently, fearlessly and movingly. His sermon on "The Love of Christ" made a profound impact on the two sisters.

Margaret and Henrietta customarily invited visiting ministers to Sunday dinner, but this time Henrietta said to one of the deacons, "I don't think it is fair for us always to have the privilege of fellowshipping with these guests. Why don't you take Dr. MacLennan to your home today?"

But the deacon refused, saying, "Now Henrietta, you know that they always have a better time with you and Margaret."

So Dr. MacLennan went to Sunday dinner with the Mears sisters. After an amiable two hours, Henrietta suggested to Dr. MacLennan that they should drive him back to his hotel so he could rest and prepare for the evening's service.

"Do I have to go?" he asked. "You see, I am writing a new series of sermons on the person of Christ, and I would like very much to go over them with you."

And so, through the afternoon, they listened to this man talk about the Christ whom he knew and loved so deeply. Before their time together was over, Dr. MacLennan told Henrietta that she and Margaret would have to come to California. The idea was so unexpected that the two women just laughed. But their guest finally made them promise to return his visit if they ever came to California.

A Decision to Make

When 1927 arrived, and Henrietta took a sabbatical year off from teaching at Central High. She had critical career decisions to make, and she needed time to think them through. She was certain now just what the Lord wanted her to do for Him. But less clear was whether she should continue ministering in Christian education as something separate from teaching public high school. Or was God calling her from her present profession into full-time Christian ministry instead?

If she was to remain in the academic world, she felt she should go on to Columbia University and take postgraduate work in school administration. But if God wanted her full-time in His service instead, where and in what capacity did He want her? And when?

A Chance to Travel

As Henrietta sought the Lord's will in these matters, He began ordering events to give her the direction she sought. Dr. Riley, aware that Henrietta was seeking to know whether the Lord wanted her to remain in public school teaching or to move into full-time Christian work, suggested that, since this was her sabbatical year, she and Margaret travel. "It may give you a vision of this world that will determine the direction of your life."

So Henrietta and Margaret left for Europe. They returned to the United States with some of the sabbatical still before them, so they decided to spend the winter in California. They remembered Dr. MacLennan's preaching in their home church two years earlier, so they decided to look him up and attend his church on the corner of Gower and Carlos in Hollywood.

They were delighted with all they saw at Hollywood Presbyterian Church. Dr. MacLennan had taken a once-little country church near Hollywood and Vine and had built it up into one of the most influential Presbyterian pulpits anywhere. Evidence of the church's visionary outlook was the 1,500-seat sanctuary that the pastor and his congregation had erected for their then 400 members. Already hundreds attended Wednesday evening prayer meetings. And some 500 to 1,000 men met in a special Bible class called "Macsmen."

The sisters were pleased that the church emphasis was on the young and 400 or more were in the church school. They tingled with excitement as they observed this work for God being carried on in a city bursting with the strength and bluster of its youth.

An Offer to Consider

Dr. "Mac" was delighted to see them and invited Henrietta to speak on several occasions, and the response to her messages was immediate. Just before the Mears sisters ended their visit to Hollywood, Dr. MacLennan offered Henrietta the position of Director of Christian Education. But how could she accept? All their ties and associations were back in Minneapolis, and whatever successes she had had were there.

Besides, Margaret was involved in business in Minneapolis. They owned their own home. And Henrietta was already scheduled to resume her teaching at Central High. What should she do?

In a few weeks Margaret and Henrietta were back in Minneapolis. But Henrietta's thoughts gave her no peace—and neither did Dr. MacLennan. He wrote—he telegraphed—he telephoned! But was this God's leading?

A Need to Choose

The letters and telephone calls from Dr. MacLennan indicated that he wanted her for his young people, and he painted glowing pictures of what they could accomplish together with the youth that were pouring into this "city of make-believe." But other opportunities to serve had also opened up to her while she had been in the Los Angeles area. What of these? Not wanting to make a mistake and still not knowing what she should do, Henrietta returned to Hollywood.

One noon, she and Dr. MacLennan went to the Pig 'n Whistle restaurant on Hollywood Boulevard for lunch. As they approached the entrance, the door opened silently before them. Never before having seen a door controlled by an electric eye, she was genuinely amazed and impressed. As they ate their lunch and talked about the possibilities of the work that could be done in Hollywood, Henrietta, without realizing it, found herself saying, "If I were going to do such-and-such, I'd...." Finally, she saw that her own door had opened as silently and effortlessly as had that electric-eye door when she entered the restaurant.

A Problem to Solve

Yet there was the matter of her teaching contract and the fact that school was to open shortly. And, of course, there was their house; property just wasn't selling at this time of year. Would they be able to get their money out of the house?

Trusting that God would reveal His plan for her, she returned to Minneapolis to see what could be done about the teaching contract and the selling of their home. The home appeared the most improbable of solution. So she decided, as had Gideon (Judg. 6:36-40), that she would put out a fleece to ascertain beyond doubt that God was leading in the step she was taking. Her fleece was placing an additional $2,000 into the asking price for their home.

The first person to come and see the house dashed through

with his head down, seemingly seeing nothing at all. As he left, Henrietta said to Margaret, "Well, he's certainly not interested." Actually, the man had been so interested and so afraid that someone would get to the real estate agent before him that he had rushed through the tour in order to close the deal quickly at the price quoted.

A Time to Act

The challenge of the fleece was met, and so positive a demonstration of God's leading gave to Margaret and Henrietta their final incentive. In 1928, bidding farewell to family and friends, they moved to Hollywood. As her sister worked at establishing their new home—getting the furniture uncrated, hanging drapes, setting up the kitchen, supervising the garden—Henrietta began her work at the First Presbyterian Church of Hollywood, realizing that as she walked through its doors, many other doors of opportunity would open as well at the impulse of an unseen hand. And through those same doors would march a multitude of redeemed boys and girls, men and women, singing praises to God and glorifying the Christ whom she had taught them to know and believe—and love.

Note

1. Barbara Hudson Powers, *The Henrietta Mears Story* (Old Tappan, NJ: Fleming H. Revell Co., 1957), p. 125.

SIX
Making Dreams Happen

*T*he Sunday School which lays
small plans will measure its
accomplishments accordingly."

IN 1928—WHEN HENRIETTA MEARS BECAME DIRECTOR OF CHRISTIAN EDU-cation, the Sunday School of the First Presbyterian Church of Hol-lywood had 450 enrolled. In two and a half years, the enrollment grew to 4,200. A dream come true? Yes, because the church's new director knew that people would come to Sunday School if there was something worth coming to.

"Dreams do come true," Henrietta Mears affirmed. But she spoke as no abstract dreamer. Rather, she spoke as a down-to-earth doer, a pragmatist who knew that dreams come true only for those who work hard enough to make them happen. Consequent-ly, she was always quick to transform her visions into concrete plans.

Set Down Objectives

"The first thing I did in Hollywood," she said, "was to write out what I wanted for my Sunday School. I set down my objectives for the first five years. They included improvements in organization, teaching staff, curriculums and spirit.

"I wanted a closely graded program, a teaching material that would present Christ and His claims in every lesson, a trained teaching staff, a new education building, choirs, clubs, a camp program, a missionary vision, youth trained for the hour."

Henrietta was also wise enough to know that her primary objectives as the director of Christian education were not numbers but quality, not mere busyness but purposeful action:

> *The work of the director of Christian education is too often thought of in terms of output or activity. It is to be admitted that productivity is the logical end for which a director is secured by a church, and it is toward this end that he must apply himself. This cannot, however, be measured by volume of action. It is accomplished only through purposeful action. Only that which is directed toward definite goals, which in turn are founded on sound educational philosophy, can be ulti-*

Henrietta Mears at about age 38 when she joined the First Presbyterian Church of Hollywood as director of Christian education in 1928.

mately meaningful. The principles must always precede the activities.

Henrietta also insisted rightly that Christian education worthy of the name must be Christian. And being Christian meant that every lesson must honor Christ. And that, in turn, meant that every teacher must be faithful to the Bible. "Christian education recognizes the inspired Word of God," she would say, "not only as its text and the sum of its message, but also as the source of the principles by which successful Christian education must be carried on."

In Minnesota, Henrietta had been a successful teacher, but now as a director of education in Hollywood, she would have to organize and train others to teach. With reliance on God and allegiance to His Word, she mapped out the course she was to take. What she often said to her fellow teachers thoroughly characterized her own ministry:

> *Two things Joshua had to do to qualify him for his great work: to be strong and of good courage, and to make the Book of the Law his continued study. God's Word must be our only infallible guide. In keeping it, there is great reward. To reject His Word is to be rejected.*

Developed Staff Rapport

Strengthened then with the courage born of her convictions, emboldened by her study of the Book of the Law and aflame with the love of Christ, Henrietta Mears walked into the first teachers' and officers' meeting she had called at the First Presbyterian Church of Hollywood. They came eagerly, for word had already gotten around about the new director. Some had heard her teach on her earlier visits and were anticipating great things for the Sunday School. Others were doubtlessly skeptical, thinking, "No one could be as good as they are making her out to be!"

Speaking in soft, friendly tones, her eyes dancing with enthusiasm and goodwill, she said, "I believe I know just what you are thinking. I think I might feel the same way if I were in your place:

'Another director of the Sunday School—new plans, new ideas, her way of doing things! Now everything is going to be changed again!' 'If I have to reorganize my class once more or try out some fancy new theory, I'll just die!' 'What does she know about Hollywood anyway?'"

Her audience broke out in laughter, probably more at themselves than at their new leader, for she had caught them offguard. "You don't like changes and neither do I," she continued. "You've been getting along without me up to now, and it would certainly be a great burden for me to have the responsibility of rushing in here to try and reorganize everything overnight.

"So here is what I thought we might do: We'll relax for six months and use the time for observation, and then we'll sit down and evaluate the situation and decide together what we need to do. You undoubtedly will have some ideas, and I might just possibly have a suggestion or two myself."

Those present could hardly wait for her to close the meeting before they rushed to the platform. "Oh, Miss Mears, we can't wait six months! Our department just has to have something done about the teachers. We are having a terrible time. No one wants to teach three-year-olds."

And on and on. She had won the first round. For now they had invited her into their departments themselves.

Provided Personal Example

Henrietta's aggressive and positive attitudes toward her new job ignited the imaginations of those about her. "Many of the Sunday School rooms need painting," Henrietta reported to Dr. MacLennan one day. The following Sunday he announced from the pulpit that members were to come on such-and-such a day, bring hammers and paint brushes and be prepared to work.

On hand to greet them, attired in their work clothes, were Dr. "Mac" and Henrietta. To the surprise of some, she chose to paint the women's rest room off Fellowship Hall. Her doing so showed them that she would never ask them to do something she was not willing to do herself. At the same time, her action was not contrived to make such a point; for her, it was just a matter of a job to be done—and the quicker the better.

If any had retained reservations concerning the new director, these fell away quickly as they watched her demonstrating genuine love and unbridled enthusiasm for whatever she did—whether painting, cleaning, talking with collegians or going home to study, with books piled up to her chin. She soon won the loyalty of all along with their willingness to undertake any task she asked them to do.

Utilized Latent Talent

And that was Henrietta's genius—the ability to get others to serve and to work where needed. She never waited for teachers to come into her Sunday School from some other church to assist her. Her principle was to train her own leaders. Her enthusiasm and challenge and drive broke down resistance even in those adamantly convinced she had overestimated their capabilities for particular jobs.

In her estimation, during the early days of the college department, only one individual showed any promise of becoming a good song leader. So Henrietta told him one day that he was to lead the singing for the meeting that evening. The lad, panicked by her suggestion, said, "No, absolutely no. I will not do it."

As he continued to protest, she pushed him out of the office and told him to go practice and learn how to lead singing. Through the closed door, his voice could be heard, "I won't do it! I'm not a song leader! I don't even know how!" But he led the songs—and eventually went into the ministry.

Years later, Dr. L. David Cowie said of this incident: "Teacher puts you on your mettle to produce. You had to do it, and she wanted you to be able to do it, and to feel the sole responsibility, and not to have any feeling that she would do it for you. She literally forced me into being a leader. She pushed me into responsibility."

During the many years she served as Christian education director of Hollywood Presbyterian Church, Henrietta Mears took several trips around the world. Among her traveling companions were her sister Margaret; curriculum writer, Esther Ellinghusen; and her personal assistant, Ethel May Baldwin. Henrietta traveled not just as a tourist but as one seeking to gain a better perspective of other peoples that she might excite and inspire the imaginations of the young people in her church. Here in Egypt, at the pyramids, she takes a donkey ride.

And here, Henrietta *(l.)* and Ethel May continue their tour of the pyramids, observing these ancient wonders of the world from their lofty viewpoint atop a pair of camels.

Recruited Personal Assistant

When Henrietta Mears had visited the Hollywood Presbyterian Church during her winter sabbatical in California, she had taught the youth group and had taken time to meet the class members, shaking hands with them individually. In that group was a young Ethel May Baldwin who was greatly impressed by the power of Henrietta's teaching and by her unassuming friendliness.

"She was the first leader that I didn't put on a pedestal and then was afraid to go near. It wasn't until years later that I discovered why," she confided. "Henrietta Mears shunned pedestals. She would never permit a person to place her on one. She was not going to have anyone disillusioned by her falling from some great height."

The Lord had already been speaking to Ethel May and had planted in her heart the desire to serve in Christian education. She had dedicated her life to Him and had indicated her willingness to serve wherever He wanted her to. Then about six months later, Henrietta joined the church staff. During the launching of a membership drive to get young business women into Henrietta's Tuesday Evening Bible Club, Ethel May overheard her exclaim, "I'm just going to have to have a secretary."

Ethel May was quietly determined to find out if this was where the Lord wanted her. It was, and a month after Henrietta took up her new position as director of Christian education, Ethel May became her secretary. As Henrietta discovered Ethel May's many abilities, the secretarial position quickly grew in responsibility to that of assistant director of Christian education, personal companion and a host of other assignments.

Henrietta was able to place such confidence in Ethel May that she said of her assistant, "If Ethel May should leave at 12:00, I would leave at 12:01." But Ethel May did not leave and neither did Henrietta. Both stayed and gave the church a lifetime of service, building together the great work in Sunday School ministry that touched and won countless lives for Jesus Christ.

Maintained Family Emphasis

Though she was a single person herself, Henrietta Mears built a family emphasis into her Sunday School at every stage from the nursery department through the adult department. Her Sunday School always offered something for every member of the family, from the infant to the senior citizen.

She was particularly aware of the concerns and needs of young marrieds with small children. She did not believe Sunday School was a place where parents dropped off children to be picked up later. She wanted these parents to bring their children and stay for Sunday School themselves.

Yet she recognized that no couple was going to leave their baby in facilities that were inadequate, unattractive or untidy. Nor were they likely to entrust that baby into the keeping of someone insufficiently competent or caring to meet their child's needs while it was apart from its father and mother.

If a couple felt they could not leave their infant in the church nursery, the father and mother would either have to take turns coming to church or—more likely—not come at all. In any case, they would be unable to attend as a family. And the same would be true of parents with older young children for whom the Sunday School failed to provide appropriate, inviting facilities and programs.

"Don't try to build a bigger Sunday School," she would advise. "Don't have a visitation campaign to get more people. Build a better Sunday School. Have a place for every person, every age. If you don't have rooms for junior highs, you cannot invite them. If you don't have a place for young marrieds, you won't have them. If you don't have a place for the babies, they will not be there."

After some years, when all her plans and programs for the Sunday School of Hollywood Presbyterian Church were in place and she had the necessary facilities for implementing them, she said:

> *We have just finished an educational building for*
> *our babies, including children up through the primary*

department. We spent half a million dollars on babies. One of the elders raised his eyebrows and asked if such a building was necessary "just for babies."

I told him that such a building was the most necessary structure in the world; for if the parents have a place to put the babies, they will come with their children and, in turn, go to the young marrieds' class. Thus, we have a Sunday School atmosphere from the very beginning....

Do you have a place for every age in your Sunday School? And do you have a program for every age? Think through the age characteristics of each group and gear your program to them. And is your program as good as it could be?

In her capacity as head of the Sunday School, Henrietta always considered herself as serving the whole church of which that Sunday School was a part. And a Sunday School that ministered to every member of the family, thereby ministered to the larger body. For, she believed, by building godly lives in individual members of the family, the family as a whole was being built up and strengthened in its faith. And families, strong in their faith made for a stronger church that, in turn, made stronger the whole Body of Christ.

Established Graded Classes

Back in 1923 when the present church edifice was completed, construction was to begin right away on an education building. But this project had to be set aside because of the Depression, causing Henrietta to say, "I guess the Lord didn't give us an educational plant for years, in order to prove that it isn't buildings out of which a Sunday School is created, but rather a program that presents Jesus Christ. If the children and youth and their parents are coming, you'll find some place to hold the classes."

So for 22 years, the Sunday School grew and thrived, and a

generation went out never having had the advantage of the facilities of Education Building No. 1 that was finally erected in 1950.

"God closely graded children, I didn't," Henrietta would say. From the moment she came to Hollywood, one of her dreams was to have a department for each age, at least through age eight She believed it was best, in fact, to group children during their earliest years into classes at age intervals of every six months, and this grading was accomplished as the years moved along.

One June the superintendent of the kindergarten department explained that the four-year-old (or almost four) graduates from the department for two- and three-year-olds were not sufficiently prepared for her age group. The reason why was easy to see: Of necessity, the program for the two- and three-year-olds was geared down to the twos, and the threes were not learning all they were capable of.

So four months before graduation the next year, the older ones who were to graduate—those about to turn four—were taken to separate classrooms, and a program was implemented just for their age. The difference in their comprehension and grasp of things was so tremendous that Henrietta was determined to continue to do this—at least for four months—until a permanent place could be found to create a new department. And so a step was taken toward forming a department for each age.

Naturally, with such Sunday School growth, the incidents which took place were often laughable—though perhaps more so in retrospect. Over the years, Henrietta and the Craig family, the church's wonderful Scottish custodians, would laugh about the many times she had chased them out of their home to make room for her ever-expanding classes. The Craigs initially occupied a nice bungalow with five big, square rooms. But these rooms were ideal much-needed space—in Henrietta's fertile mind—for the Sunday School classes, clubs, Vacation Bible School and the like that were already under way.

So the chase began. The Craigs moved from the "Bungalow" to a place next door, occupying one-third of an apartment building. And before long, the other two-thirds of that apartment house was

converted into the junior department, with drapes on wires forming class space after the worship service and the upstairs bed-
rooms serving as excellent classrooms. The juniors soon discovered that from the upstairs porch of the Junior House to the roof
of the "Bungalow" was an easy jump, so a chase of another kind
was also soon in vogue.

In time, growth and overcrowding caused Henrietta to look
with longing at the Craig's remaining third of Junior House. Thinking that this time, they were getting out of the line of chase, they
moved out and into a building on another street. "Now we're
safe," the Craigs thought.

But Henrietta was still close on their heels. She gave them time
to settle in, catch their collective breaths, relax and think, "Well,
that's all behind us now." But then the phone would ring and the
now-familiar voice would say, "Mr. Craig, do you think you could
move upstairs? You know that apartment would give you an extra
room."

The never-complaining Craigs moved upstairs, and their former
downstairs apartment just north of the church became the department for two-year-olds. Then it was needed for a club; the junior
highs held their meeting in it on Sunday evenings. After that it was
turned into offices for two of the ministers.

Eventually, when Henrietta could be persuaded to vacate the
main church building, that same downstairs apartment became the
Christian Education Department. She had always believed that when
anyone came to the church to see a minister or the director of
Christian education, that individual should be found in the church
building. Also, she wanted to be in the "main line of traffic."

Now, how would people ever know to come to a "house" for
an office? Well, they came all right and they found her. That office,
the entire time she occupied it, was "Grand Central Station" and
there was "always room for one more."

One morning Henrietta and Ethel May arrived at work to hear
sawing and hammering going on in their building. Since they were
usually the ones in the thick of such activities, they wondered
what could be going on. To their horror, a large section of the

kindergarten department was being walled off to give the office more floor space. All agreed that the church office needed to be enlarged, but what then was to be done with the 125 kindergarten children who were present each Sunday morning? Since no other room was large enough to hold all the four- and five-year-olds, the department was divided into separate age groups. As a result, another step was taken toward Henrietta's goal of a separate department for each age.

During those early years, a room on the second floor of the church was occupied by the primary department—kids in first through third grades. This room had been designed as a ladies' parlor—long and narrow. The question each time then was whether to arrange the chairs the length of the room with the children facing the doors and being disturbed by the late-comers? Or to reverse the chairs with the kids facing the bright light streaming in through the windows. Of course, if the superintendent could hold the attention of the children in the last rows some 56 feet away, he could seat the kids across the width of the room in many short rows, one behind the other to the distant wall.

As the primary department began pushing out the walls of their room, they quickly took over similar rooms on the third and, eventually, on the fourth floors of the church building. Other departments previously occupying those floors had to be relocated, necessitating having to find new space for them. The advantage was that the move got the high schoolers off the fourth floor, but what about having all those eight-year-old third-graders on the fourth floor? In case of fire, how could they be gotten out? The fire escape was too scary for them. The solution was to build an enclosed outside stairway and for all children from the upper floors to use this new stairway when exiting and to meet their parents at the foot of it. That way they would not get mashed in the crowds of adults pouring out of the balconies at the close of services.

After many Sunday mornings with equally many changes, Henrietta wondered what kept the superintendents and teachers from descending upon her in a body and resigning enmasse. To their credit, they were not serving Henrietta Mears, but like her, they were serving the Lord who ruled and overruled in every situation.

Introduced Worship Services

Henrietta Mears did not have "opening exercises" in her Sunday School. But she did have "worship services," a far more elevating term. Even the youngest child was being taught and trained to worship the living God, not just to sit through some opening exercise. No single place could accommodate every man, woman and child for that initial half-hour worship service, the various departments each held their own.

Not that all the age groups would willingly have met together anyway. Henrietta was mindful of the teenagers who wouldn't be caught dead in Sunday School with a lot of babies—any age under their own—or with adults. Yet those young children deserved to learn to worship, too. Henrietta would often say, "If you are having problems at the junior high level, begin your training earlier while the mind is eager to grasp new thoughts and everyday living can form good habits easily."

Expanded Educational Facilities

As the existing classrooms in houses and buildings filled up or otherwise became unavailable, additional classrooms had to be built. And they had to be temporary, as big plans for permanent education buildings were already afoot. After some ardent persuasion of the building code enforcers that involved making them aware of the church school's phenomenal growth, the resultant classroom shortage and the eagerness of the congregation to build, they began to look favorably upon the church and its immediate problem.

The authorities granted permission for the construction of temporary classrooms, and some portable "rabbit hutches"—as they came to be known—were built. Some wondered later whether the officials would have granted permission for these temporary classrooms to be built, if they had realized just how portable these structures were to become. For the "rabbit hutches" were shifted from place to place whenever they got in the way of newer development.

Even so, eventually the junior department had no place to meet. What to do? The board of education of the public schools came to the rescue, renting the church a grammar school auditorium only two blocks away along with as many classrooms as possible. Yet, even with these magnificent accommodations, several classes had to hike back to the church and into the famous rabbit-hutch classrooms for their sessions.

Attracted Young People

Henrietta Mears had a positive attitude toward the requirements of today's youth. Rather than bemoan their delinquency, she offered a program to meet their interests and ambitions. And she never blamed the youth for not wanting to come to church. Instead, she looked to see what was lacking in the program, what failed to attract them.

She knew the necessity of having more than just the Sunday morning Bible hour to compete with the attractions that would draw them away. Youth have to be kept busy, she believed; they must have a total program to satisfy their total personalities. She knew their needs and interests well, so enormous value was placed on activities throughout the week: clubs, interest groups, socials, camps and choirs. Even so, everything she did began with the teaching of the Bible.

So when Henrietta arrived in Hollywood, she had already planned to have a suitable place for youth to gather, where a program of activities under sound leadership could be designed to meet their spiritual, physical and social needs. In her youth and college departments, her programs enabled young people to become involved in Bible study, to participate in worship, to enjoy a social life, to form lasting friendships and so on. And she saw to it that every detail of every event was carefully planned and executed to be the best possible. The parties and recreation were always on a high plane and full of good fun.

"Miss Mears thought anything worth doing should be done in the best way possible and done for Christ. That included parties as well as prayer meetings," Ethel May affirmed.

The principle behind the planning of Henrietta's youth programs was that school friends move away and change, but church relationships grow and grow. She also understood that quality programming brought in parents as well. Her goal was to make the youth program so attractive that it could be said, as one collegian expressed it, "I would rather bring my fraternity brothers to parties and functions at the college department than those on the 'row.' They are always the greatest."

Erected Education Plant

Finally, after some 22 years of service as Christian education director, the day came when Henrietta was asked to present what she wanted in the way of an education building. "What shall I include?" she asked William S. Porter, chairman of the building committee.

"Include everything you want," he replied instantly, expressing his confidence in her and in her program.

"And I did that very thing," she often remarked later. "I included all the dreams we had had for the junior highs and high schoolers. And do you know, they gave us everything we asked for!" "Dream big" was always her motto, and dream big she did.

So hammers pounded and saws buzzed until, late in 1950, Education Building No. 1 stood as a living testimony to the faithful congregation who had erected this building for their youth. At the dedication ceremony on Sunday, January 7, 1951, the senior minister, Dr. Louis Evans, Sr., described the new youth education building as "our Annapolis or West Point for God for training of our youth as they march toward the tasks of the Kingdom tomorrow."

During the next seven years, two more magnificent education buildings materialized to meet the needs of the nursery, the

In Henrietta Mears' Sunday School, the growth of classes often outstripped the capacity of the church to accommodate them. But the ministry continued, even as construction progressed. Classes in the high school department meet here in the open air as a new building rises around them. In the course of Teacher's career as director of Christian education at Hollywood Presbyterian Church, three new education buildings were completed.

preschoolers—the two-, three-, four- and five-year-olds—and the primary.

Flags waved, horns blew and drums beat, as the members of these age groups formed a parade and marched to the ground-breaking ceremony. They could be heard coming long before they could be seen. As they swung into view, the congregation thrilled at the sight of the future generation marching to the house of God and, Lord willing, from there one day into the service of God.

As the work proceeded, the remaining houses along the block were either razed or relocated. A long-awaited moment arrived when the building chairman, Robert T. Hunter, decided that the "rabbit hutches" had fulfilled their purpose and ordered their demolition. With their demise, a colorful chapter in the history of the church came to an end.

Finally, Education Buildings Nos. 2 and 3 were completed and ready for use. On Sunday morning, September 16, 1957, a service of thanksgiving and dedication was held to express thanks unto God and to dedicate the new education buildings:

> *In the name of God the Father, God the Son and God the Holy Spirit, for the teachings of His holy Word, the practice of prayer, the joys of Christian fellowship and the missionary advance into the world; for the winsome presentation of Jesus Christ to all; for the Christian enrichment of community and world; for the eternal purposes of God as they include all children who serve and are served.*

Already Henrietta Mears' years of ministry with Hollywood Presbyterian Church had resulted in the erection of a large Christian education plant, the development of a successful Sunday School curriculum and the evangelization and discipling of tens of thousands of young people and adults.

More and more of Henrietta's big dreams were coming true.

SEVEN

The Secret of Her Success

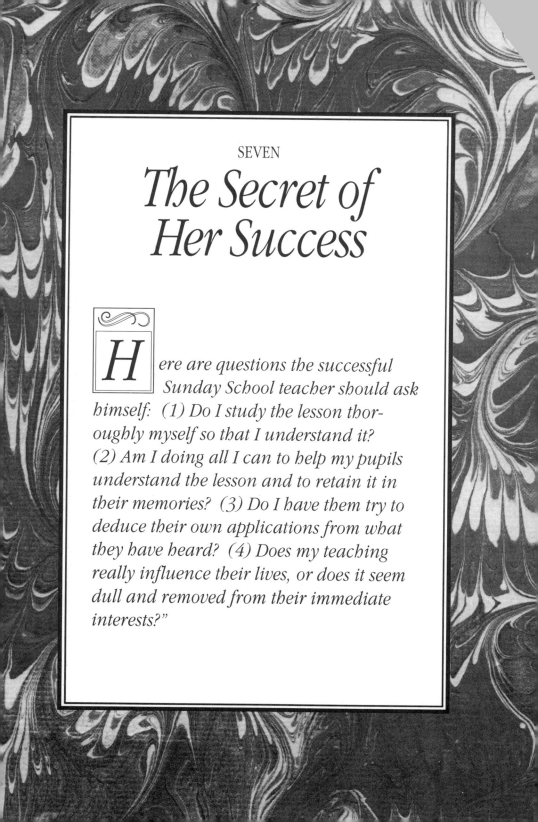

Here are questions the successful Sunday School teacher should ask himself: (1) Do I study the lesson thoroughly myself so that I understand it? (2) Am I doing all I can to help my pupils understand the lesson and to retain it in their memories? (3) Do I have them try to deduce their own applications from what they have heard? (4) Does my teaching really influence their lives, or does it seem dull and removed from their immediate interests?"

MANY WHO OBSERVED HENRIETTA MEARS IN ACTION WONDERED IF SHE possessed some kind of magic formula for the phenomenal growth that took place in her Sunday School. Visiting teachers, Christian education directors and pastors, seeing new education buildings going up to accommodate ever-growing classes implored her to divulge her secrets. Letters came from everywhere requesting information on how similar successes could be repeated in other churches.

How did Henrietta Mears do it? What was the secret of her success? Her answer may have been a disappointment to some, but to those who worked with her over the years, the answer was obvious and unsurprising. For Henrietta's success as a Christian education director could be summed up in two words: energy and excellence.

Energy

Henrietta seemed to thrive on work. The more she undertook, the more she could do. And the more she did, the more she succeeded. "The key," she would often say, "is in one word—work. Webster spells it W-O-R-K, and it means just what he says it does. Wishful thinking will never take the place of hard work."

When asked by others for ideas that work, she would quickly answer, "There are no ideas that work unless you do!" And she would tell her young people, "You don't know what you can do until you try it."

She herself was capable of exhausting those who worked with her while she remained willing to go on, tired but gripped by boundless enthusiasm for the many tasks before her. She was always seeking to build a better Sunday School, not just a bigger one. For her, the matter of what the pupil was learning was pre-eminent, yet a curriculum could not be developed at the sacrifice of teacher training, student visitation, classroom preparation, office management or the teaching and directing of the college department with over 500 on the active roll.

Only once, after she had been in Hollywood about three years, did the pressure of work get to Henrietta and almost overwhelm even her legendary powers.

> *One day in early summer she reached a point of near-exhaustion, and just put her head down on her desk and wept. "It's impossible. Nobody can do it!"*
>
> *To see Miss Mears give up the struggle was too much, and Ethel May rushed her up to Dr. Mac's office. He was out, but Miss Mears sat there in quiet for a while reading the Bible on his desk. She found the verse, "As thy days, so shall thy strength be," and sitting there in the quiet study she realized the great truth that the Lord will never ask you to do one more thing than you are able to do.*
>
> *She learned to tend to the task that the Lord has for today, trusting Him to give the needed strength, but knowing that if tomorrow's task is heaped upon today's burden, it will be calamity.[1]*

The lesson was well learned. Her faith and strength were renewed, and Henrietta Mears was once again unstoppable. Despite her responsibilities as administrator and teacher, she accepted speaking and teaching engagements elsewhere that involved much preparation on her part. And to take on her subsequent roles of writer and editor as well took both courage and forethought, for she had been reared from a child to believe that she must finish whatever she undertook.

Yet she appeared to do it all with true aplomb, endless drive and unabated zest. Ted Cole, one of her collegians, recalled Henrietta's energy in this way: "It didn't matter how youthful or athletic one was, no one could keep up with Miss Mears." And she had been going strong for years before he even arrived on the scene!

Actually, Henrietta's incredible energy was activated by a combination of factors: she was convinced of the purpose and value of the Sunday School; she was motivated by the assurance of her call and mission to the Sunday School; and most of all, she was inspired by a dynamic faith in the power of God to build that Sunday School. She expressed her "secret" in this way:

> *If a church is really determined to increase its Sunday School, it will find ways and means to accomplish its purpose. The need is primarily for a greater faith in a wonderful God. Jesus said that He could not do many things among those of His day because of their unbelief. The building of a Sunday School is a long road, and there are many turns and climbs, but the rewards are worth the effort."*

Henrietta likened the empowerment she and her co-workers received to that which kept the old-fashioned trolley cars operating. As long as the trolley car kept the grooved wheel at the end of its roof pole pressed upward in rolling contact with the overhead power line, the car received the current it needed. Just so did God energize them, enabling them to move ever forward in God's omnipotence, riding on in His everlasting power.

Excellence

Henrietta's fabled high energy level was not the only reason new education buildings rose and Sunday School classes grew. For coupled with her ceaseless drive were her demands for excellence on every level and in every facet of Christian education. Paramount was her call for the highest possible standards throughout and her insistence on trained teachers in every class and department.

High Standards

Henrietta frequently spoke about the need for standards of excellence in our Sunday Schools:

> *Our Sunday Schools must be vastly more efficient institutions. Their sessions must be carried over to a*

weekday program, for no child can receive all the Christian instruction and training he needs in one hour on Sunday morning. The church must be prepared to reach out and get the many millions of boys and girls who are still without religious instruction of any sort.

And to meet this challenge we must have educational plants that are adequate. Compare the glazed halls of our modern school buildings with the worn-out carpets of the Sunday School department; the up-to-date, well-bound books on every school desk with our ragged songbooks and Bibles; the fine hardwood study chairs with the dilapidated ones so often relegated to Sunday School departments.

No wonder young people feel that the three Rs [reading, 'riting and 'rithmetic] are more important than the fourth—religion. When the student goes on Sunday to a room poorly lighted and miserably furnished, what else can he think?

He sits at the feet of teachers five days a week who have had the finest training for their work, but on Sunday the lesson from God's Word is taught by a teacher who has accepted the class because there is no one else to take it. Sunday School is, in fact, the only teaching a person will undertake without training.

We must change our standards. Everything we offer youth must be excellent. Their association with the gospel must be of the very finest in every way.

High standards of excellence, Henrietta believed, were no less possible in the Sunday School than in the public school. But they would not be achieved without effort. And she reminded those who thought otherwise, "There is nothing easy about Sunday School; it demands everything we have. It is a labor of prayer. It is a labor of intelligence. It is a labor of muscle."

Similarly, she pointed out that excellence was necessary for success and that neither was achieved without effort: "Success in this great enterprise of teaching the Bible for fruitful results, like success in any other great undertaking, must be purchased at the price of effort."

Trained teachers. At the same time, Henrietta Mears understood that no matter how strong the desire for success and no matter how great an effort was made, excellence was not possible with inexperienced, untrained people attempting to do the job that needed to be done. As she often made clear:

> *This whole process is called Christian education. It is a very comprehensive field, indeed, and cannot be run by the inexperienced. We are too willing to let the Sunday School be managed by a few willing but untrained enthusiasts.*
>
> *It is a hard task, because it is endless. We can never rest from this gigantic evangelistic and educational program. It means a marathon of physical endurance, of mental acumen, of moral courage and spiritual strength. It is a task for strong men, not babes.*
>
> *There was a day when men like the great merchant prince John Wanamaker devoted every moment outside of business obligations to the Sunday School. That kind of investment made spiritual history.*

Inevitably, a Sunday School stands or falls on the quality of its teachers. And firmly believing that quality teachers were trained teachers, she lamented the prevailing attitude in Sunday Schools generally that God can use anything—or anyone, whether trained or not. Perhaps He can, but should He have to? Henrietta thought not.

> *How seldom the Sunday School teacher is asked for his credentials. A public school teacher is not ques-*

> *tioned as to whether he will teach, but rather can he teach. Our request in securing Sunday School teachers is invariably, "Will you take a class?"*
>
> *And good-natured men and women, much against their wills, answer, "I will keep the class going until you can find someone else."*
>
> *If an algebra teacher is absent, can you imagine the principal going out in the neighborhood, ringing door-bells and asking a housewife, "Will you come over and take a class in mathematics because the regular teacher is sick?"*
>
> *Absurd! He notifies the superintendent's office of his need, and a trained person comes.*

Because Henrietta believed that God deserved only the best we can give Him, and because the best teachers are trained teachers, she kept an eye out for the public school professionals in her church, always assessing their potential for service in her Sunday School. Consequently, some of her most gifted associates were instructors, principals and counselors in the Los Angeles city school system.

But being realistic, Henrietta knew she could not expect that the public schools through her church would supply her with all the trained teachers she would need for her continually growing Sunday School. So the training of teachers became one of the great compulsions of her life. And knowing what made a good teacher, she determined to translate the knowledge she had gained herself through public school teaching into the life of her Sunday School, so that her teachers might be adequately prepared for their tasks.

And Henrietta never doubted for a moment that a church—any church—could develop its own trained leaders. "Every church should produce its own leadership," she would say. "Something is wrong if we are not. There are plenty in the church. They need to be enlisted and trained."

To those who would suggest that not everyone is born with

teaching ability, Henrietta responded, "Is there such a thing as a born teacher? Yes, if we mean one who is born to be made a teacher and who is willing to pay the price of teaching."

She emphasized:

> *Teachers are not born; they are made. However, a person must have the natural desire to be taught. A good teacher is first of all teachable himself.*
>
> *We must train workmen in our Sunday Schools that need not to be ashamed. A teacher must know his subject, observe his pupils and then do something about them. The more a teacher depends upon the Holy Spirit, the more will he wish to make himself an instrument fit for His use.*
>
> *He will want to know how God made the human mind. He will desire to probe the depths of the human heart. He will seek to know the laws that govern his approach to this pupil who was created to be a temple of the living God.*
>
> *But failure to work according to God's laws and lack of definiteness have characterized much that has been done under the name of Sunday School teaching.*

Despite an ever-present need of trained teachers, Henrietta was never hasty in choosing teachers for her Sunday School. Wholesale announcements regarding needs for teachers in such-and-such a department were taboo. For, she emphasized, one bad choice might take years to undo, whereas a little cautious foresight could avoid such a situation.

So what governed her selection? In every prospective teacher, she sought certain qualifications.

An evident and productive relationship with Christ. Knowing Christ, of course, was essential. But for Henrietta, a prospective teacher must also have a track record, demonstrating previous productive service for the Lord.

As Christian education director, she did not want to have teach-

Henrietta Mears, "a teacher in Christ's college."

ers who habitually failed in other areas of life. In fact, her policy was just the opposite. She invariably sought after busy men and women who were already putting out for the Kingdom.

One day she called up an elder of the church who was also a successful automobile salesman in Los Angles and heavily involved in a myriad of other activities. She asked him to take over a twelfth-grade class of boys.

"But, Miss Mears," he argued, "I am already so busy with my other tasks that I wouldn't know how to squeeze this class in."

"That's the reason I am calling on you, George," she answered. "I want you in my Sunday School because you know the value of time and because you have proven yourself in other fields."

George accepted.

A willingness to spend time in lesson preparation and in training classes. As Henrietta knew well from personal experience a teacher's training and skills were necessary. But they alone would never compensate for a lack of adequate preparation before each class. "Don't display your ignorance and bring disrepute upon Christianity by speaking out in your...classes," she would admonish all. "Study and know whereof you speak, and then open your mouth."

When it came to the importance of her teachers investing sufficient time for solid preparation, Henrietta pulled no punches:

> *I have had so many people say to me, "Oh, Miss Mears, I wish I could do all the things you do. Why, I would give anything if I could have the result you have in your Sunday School!"*
>
> *Well, let me tell you right now that I don't believe you! You watch the organist play so beautifully at your church, and you say, "I would give anything to be able to play as she does!"*
>
> *But your mother and father spent hundreds of dollars on your music lessons when you were a child, and you were too busy to practice. Instead, you went out to play with your friends.*

> *So it is with your Sunday School class: You don't have results, because you don't take the time or make the effort to do anything about your teaching or to learn more about your students. I tell you truthfully that I have never seen a teacher who was willing to invest time and effort in his class who was not successful—that is, if he was teaching the right age class.*

While Dr. William Evans was the church's interim pastor, he gave her a teaching suggestion which she faithfully followed herself and which she gladly shared with her colleagues:

> *When you are preparing a lesson, first list various members of your class on one side of a page, and under their names write out their spiritual needs. Write down on the other side how you are going to meet those needs in your lesson.*

This method was always used in her teaching. Her lessons were a part of her personality, the expression of her heartfelt concern for her students. In this respect, Henrietta Mears was an excellent example of one who applied to herself the same demands she made of others. She spent many hours in the preparation of each lesson and every message.

Often, after an arduous day of work and counseling, she would be seen heading toward her car with an armload of books. One young fellow or another would disengage himself from those who would be around at the time and without a word take the books out of her arms. Invariably someone would ask, "Where are you going with all those books, Miss Mears?"

"Home to study for those lessons you are going to hear next Sunday and Wednesday," she would reply.

Even after long periods of preparation, Henrietta would rise early in the morning to meet the Lord in prayer and in the reading of her Bible. This availability to the Lord for new instructions or strengthening of other thoughts gave her a spiritual authority for which her teaching became known.

Henrietta had a long-standing rule that she would do nothing on Saturday nights except prepare for her Sunday responsibilities. The only exception to that rule which she ever permitted was for the weekly meeting of the Life Work Recruit group. This group came into existence after she began challenging her youth to open themselves to the will of God for their lives, whether as Christians in the business world, in the professions or in the ministry.

One particular Saturday evening meeting ran very late, and Henrietta finally dropped into bed exhausted. Her secretary, Ethel May, was spending the night. Just when it seemed as though they had just gotten to sleep, the alarm clock went off.

Ethel May managed to get one eye open. It was still dark outside, but by the light of the street lamp, she could make out a ghostly figure, still dizzy with sleep, reeling about the room. From the depths of her pillow, Ethel May called out to Henrietta, "Get back into bed. If you don't know the book of Romans by now, you never will!"

Soon deep breathing came from Henrietta's side of the bed, and Ethel May knew her colleague had taken the advice. But "I never got by with that but once," Ethel May said later. "Wasn't it lucky she was teaching the book of Romans that she had loved to have her mother read to her as a child and she had taught so often?" In the morning, even Henrietta had to laugh at what had happened in the night.

Her spiritual preparation continued right up to the moment she stepped onto the platform. Her college department always had a pre-prayer session for a half an hour before each meeting. Henrietta was unfailingly present to participate. With 20 or more of the college students kneeling and praying with her, she would ask the Lord to bless the lesson and sometime included its points in her supplication.

To no one's surprise then, she could freely declare, "I have discovered that if the Bible is taught the way it should be that it will be like a powerful magnet drawing youth unto the Lord Jesus Christ. What a supremely superb Textbook we have!"

A desire to model Christian living as well as to teach God's

Word. "Your pupils are not bowls to be filled, but torches to be lighted," Henrietta Mears often reminded her teachers. "You are not only training minds, but souls."

With such statements, she was affirming that religious training involved a man's will and his emotions, not just his mind. She wanted teachers who would instruct their pupils not only to know, but to feel and, finally, to do. "I am convinced that learning is more than the ability to repeat the sayings and ideas of another; rather, it is a dynamic development of the conduct and character of the pupil," she declared.

Similarly, she would say,

> *Every child is born with a great capacity for knowledge. We cannot make capacity, but we can cultivate that thing which is God-given.*
>
> *We grieve because children remember so little of what we have taught them from God's Word. There is a reason for this. Not enough attention is given to other phases of religious education.*
>
> *Learning is more than the ability to repeat the ideas or writings of another. There are real evidences of learning. We must face this fact: When a child has learned, we find there is a change in his behavior. His life is different. He places different values upon things.*
>
> *To tell him the story is not sufficient. The purpose of the teacher is to "draw out," not to "cram in." We must create an interest in the heart and mind of the child that will make him reach out and take hold upon the things he is taught.*
>
> *Whenever an interest is created, there is at the same time a great desire to learn as much as possible about that thing.*

Henrietta knew that by association a child begins to see lived out in his teacher's life something he has been telling his pupils in class. So she urged her teachers to do whatever was possible in the way of extracurricular activity that would enable them to share themselves with their pupils.

> *Real teaching should help the student to demonstrate an increased ability to meet the problems of life and to act on his own initiative. As he comes in contact with the experiences of others, his own experiences are enriched. This is learning one's lesson.*

Among her teachers were many who tried to bring total learning into the lives of their students by modeling Christ before them in real-life situations. One of the ninth-grade teachers was an officer on the police force, later to become an inspector. Besides teaching his class a Sunday morning lesson, he frequently took his pupils swimming in the police center's pool and escorted them through its various buildings, explaining the functions of each one. His students greatly loved this Christian man, and he deeply influenced their young minds through the association he built up in them between living a godly life and respect for law.

An instructor in Henrietta's high school department was a leading researcher in an aircraft plant. His scientific training spilled over into his teaching of the Bible with the result that his students, beset with intellectual problems, felt confident in taking their questions to him, for he spoke with a precision that they admired.

By their lives inside and outside the classroom, these and other teachers in the Sunday School of Hollywood Presbyterian Church demonstrated what Henrietta Mears described as "contagious Christianity." "A true Christian's enthusiasm for the Lord Jesus Christ should be so exuberant that it would be far more likely to set others on fire than to be extinguished by worldly influences. Have a Christianity that is contagious!"

And to all her Sunday School teachers and to those who taught Sunday School elsewhere, she gave this word of encouragement and affirmation:

> *Don't ever say, "I'm just a Sunday School teacher." If you were a professor at Harvard or Oxford, you would*

be proud of it—proud of the great responsibility.

Teacher, you are a professor in Christ's college. As a Sunday School teacher, you can be equally proud—not the sort of pride that exalts self, but the warm joyful glow of humble satisfaction that comes to those who serve the Savior in His strength, not theirs.

What a responsibility you have—to teach an immortal soul to have fellowship with God! To fulfill this responsibility, you must be wholly dedicated to the Lord and to the task He has for you to do. Christ was a teacher. He told you and me that our commission is to teach (Matt. 28:19,20).

Don't ever say, I"m just a Sunday School teacher." You are a teacher in Christ's college. Know your subject matter. Be proud that you teach!

Was Henrietta Mears a successful Sunday School administrator and teacher? She was indeed. And the secret of her success? In her own words, "If you will present God's Word so that it meets the needs of young and old alike, you will have a successful Sunday School."

Note

1. Barbara Hudson Powers, *The Henrietta Mears Story* (Old Tappan, NJ: Fleming H. Revell Co., 1957), p. 136.

EIGHT

"Thank Mr. Falconer"

Our message is the Word of God.
   Our field is the minds of people.
Our missionaries are the teachers
   of the world.
Our tools are paper and ink."

ONE DAY HENRIETTA PICKED UP A STUDENT'S MANUAL IN THE PRIMARY department and read the lesson title: "Amos Denounces Self-indulgence."

"What?" she thought. "How can any child grasp that?"

Other lessons showed her how irrelevant this primary Sunday School material was to the six-, seven- and eight-year-olds. At the same time, she learned the publisher was discontinuing the lesson material she used in her junior department. Henrietta moved quickly to resolve the problem.

Since type was then cast from molten metal, she asked about the possibility of buying up the type used to print the manuals for juniors. Then they could print their own copies. But the lead had already been scrapped and melted down.

Her next resort was to purchase as many lesson manuals as were still available. But this gave her only a three-year supply of material for the juniors. Now was the time to explore other options while they still had lesson material on hand.

Grasshopper Methods and Carrots for Paul

Henrietta went immediately to Dr. MacLennan and asked, "Do you mind what materials we use in our Sunday School?"

"Use anything you want as long as it teaches the Bible," he replied.

She requested and received sample curricula from various Sunday School publishing houses. Then she gathered the educators of the church together to survey the Sunday School literature then available to them in 1929. Most of the materials were biblically sound, but all were unattractive. They had no pictures for children and were not graded for any particular age, so all would have to be adapted.

And in none of the materials was the subject matter presented chronologically. On one Sunday, a child would study about Saul the King, and the next week study about Saul of Tarsus. The lessons jumped from the acts of Abraham to the Acts of the Apostles in what Henrietta termed "the grasshopper method." And in the most widely used curriculum, the story of Creation was presented only once in a single lesson over a span of several years. If a child missed that Sunday, he or she would have to find out somewhere other than in Sunday School how the world began.

Henrietta had sat on the curriculum committee for the public schools of Minneapolis and was keenly aware of the necessity to grade materials to students' abilities. She was appalled then to find Sunday School literature so deficient in this respect. She came to the conclusion that the Bible was the most poorly taught book in the world.

Two comments made to her soon after she came to Hollywood remained in her mind:

A young junior boy had once said to her, "I don't wanna go to Sunday School anymore. All they do is tell you the same old story over and over and over again. Only it just gets dumber and dumber."

And a young man with a Phi Beta Kappa key asked her, "What's wrong, Miss Mears? I've gone to Sunday School all my life, but if I had to take an examination on the Bible today, I'd flunk."

Finally the supply of old curriculum for juniors ran out. As the books for a new course arrived on her desk, Henrietta opened the package herself to review the materials. One lesson read, "Paul survived his shipwreck because he had eaten carrots and was strong."

She rewrapped the books and returned them, explaining that she could not use any material in her Sunday School which denied the miraculous in Scripture. She knew now what she had to do—write the lesson materials for her Sunday School herself.

Hand-written Manuscripts and Mimeographed Books

Henrietta sat down with her fellow educators and worked out a prospectus, determining the accomplishments expected at each age level. Then she began writing. To keep ahead of the week-by-week demand for lesson materials in a Sunday School growing astronomically was a full-time job in itself. But Henrietta still had all her administrative tasks in addition to speaking and teaching

The first Gospel Light Bible lessons were born in the mind of Henrietta Mears. In those embryonic days, she and Ethel May Baldwin were the sole staff.

responsibilities with their corresponding hours of preparation. The only explanation of the fact that she found the work load bearable is that God in His might and power intervened on her behalf.

As page after page of Bible lessons came from Henrietta's pen, Ethel May took them, then typed, mimeographed and stapled them into books. Due to the amount of space needed for type-written copy and the thickness of the books themselves, the women produced only four lessons at a time, instead of the usual 13 for a quarter. Desiring to make the lesson books as attractive as possible, they collected out-of-date religious calendars, then cut out the beautiful pictures of Bible themes and pasted them on the covers.

Then because mimeographing rubbed off on nice Sunday clothes, the woman purchased fancy fonts of type for an old Multi-graph machine, so they could print handset titles on the book cov-ers. These first homemade books don't look like much alongside the beautiful Sunday School books on the market today, but they were way ahead of anything else available in their day.

As the need grew for greater production of the lesson books,

Esther A. Ellinghusen, a gifted junior high teacher in the Los Angeles public school system and superintendent of the junior department of the First Presbyterian Church of Hollywood, shared all the curriculum writing and editorial responsibilities with Henrietta Mears during the early days of Gospel Light Publications (then Gospel Light Press).

Henrietta inquired about the possibility of having them professionally printed. But she was constantly told that the costs of doing so were completely out of her reach. So she resigned herself to continue mimeographing as attractively as possible her closely graded, biblically based lesson books.

Henrietta then recruited Esther A. Ellinghusen to join her in preparing the lessons by writing for the juniors. At the time, Esther was teaching in a Los Angeles junior high school and superintending the junior department of the church. Before beginning to write, she interviewed the head of the remedial reading department of the Los Angeles public school system, studied vocabulary charts and compared school textbooks for size of type, vocabulary, sentence structure and illustrations.

Now, with the knowledge she gained from her extensive research, Esther wrote constantly. She was consumed by one thought: How can I best teach these children about God's love?

Many whom she enlightened through her lessons, reflecting back later, knew she had taught them well of God's love.

The demands on the Sunday School's production department —Ethel May—increased enormously with two writers turning out more pages of handwritten Bible lessons. So Ethel May increased the production department staff to include her parents. And because of her mother's growing concern that Ethel May would develop cancer of the hand from stapling hundreds and hundreds of thick lesson books, her father took over that job entirely.

Inquiring Visitors and Long-distance Commuters

By 1930, the Great Depression was rampaging across the nation. Necessity forced the church to cut every possible corner when making up the budget. So the take-home Sunday School papers were among the first items to go. To compensate for this loss, Henrietta and Ethel improvised word puzzles, mazes and crossword puzzles and added them to their mimeographed lessons. And their work grew.

"You know, I believe everyone gets to California at least once in his lifetime," Henrietta would say, as visitors came from far and near to visit the Sunday School and to observe what was being done. As they looked and listened, they began to realize that the children here knew a great deal of Bible and were able to answer questions concerning it intelligently, enthusiastically and with understanding.

Invariably, the visitor would ask Henrietta, "What lesson material are you using, Miss Mears?"

With a tip of her head and slight shrug of her shoulders, she would matter-of-factly reply, "Oh, just some mimeographed material that some of us are writing and putting together here."

Yet that same mimeographed material was the reason that parents were driving their children from neighboring towns to Sunday School in Hollywood, some driving as far as 50 miles, passing up many other churches on the way. And they were commuting these distances in 1931 when money was still scarce and before anyone had even thought of freeways.

Visitors frequently asked Henrietta how they could obtain her lesson materials, and she would patiently explain, "Such a thing would be out of the question, as we are hardly able to produce it fast enough for our own use."

By mail and in person, the requests for copies of her lessons continued. And always, Henrietta kept answering, "I'm just producing it for my Sunday School and have no way to do more.

An Immovable Object and an Irresistible Force

As Henrietta was invited out to various churches to speak, she felt that she must accept and do her part, so that she, in turn, could invite pastors and workers to come to Hollywood. And so, in the course of this exchange of speaking engagements, a Mr. Marion Falconer, a druggist in Anaheim, California and Sunday School superintendent of a Presbyterian church, invited her to speak to his teachers. She did, and they soon became well acquainted as both attended other Christian education workshops in the area, intent in their desire to have the best for their respective Sunday Schools.

Then one Sunday morning, Marion Falconer came to visit Hollywood Presbyterian Church. Before leaving home he had already decided that he would once again ask Henrietta to publish the lesson materials she was writing for her Sunday School. While waiting for her to finish her responsibilities, he went to various departments to observe.

They met, exchanged hearty greetings, and Henrietta moved to go on. But Marion would not step aside. "Miss Mears, I have been asking you repeatedly through the months for copies of your Sunday School literature. I must have copies of your lessons."

Henrietta had a delightful little laugh of incredulity which she gave to turn aside inquirers when she felt confronted by something that—to her way of thinking—bordered on the impossible.

In most cases, that laugh was all that was necessary to bring about a change of conversation. But not so with Marion Falconer.

Determined, persistent and persuasive, he presented Henrietta with strong reasons as to why her lesson materials should be printed and made available to many Sunday Schools. In near desperation, he declared, "Miss Mears! I will not leave this church until you give me some copies of the material or until I have your promise that it will be printed."[1]

Something in the earnestness of his plea struck a responsive chord in Henrietta, and she gave him a promise. "Well, I'll tell you what I'll do, Mr. Falconer. I could not possibly say that I would print the material as of this moment, but I will look into the matter of printing once again."

Many were the times in years to come that Henrietta would say, "Thank Mr. Falconer for making me print the Sunday School lessons. He just wouldn't take no for an answer."

Harry Rimmer and Cary Griffin

Sparked by her commitment to check printing costs yet again, Henrietta's mind began to turn over ideas. She thought of Dr. Harry Rimmer, an eminent scientist and lecturer and an active member of Hollywood's First Presbyterian Church. "I wonder how Harry Rimmer gets those scientific paper-covered books of his printed. He doesn't have a lot of money. Ethel May, let's call up Harry Rimmer."

Henrietta and Harry Rimmer were old friends from Minnesota days, and when he heard her request, he said, "Henrietta, go see my printer, Cary Griffin. He'll take care of you."

Henrietta contacted Cary Griffin in nearby Glendale, and that was all it took. He threw in his lot with "the ladies" and determined to help them. But never one to rush into anything without counting the cost in both time and money, Henrietta asked Cary what would be involved financially. Could the books be sold and then the bills paid?

Though previously strangers, Henrietta and Cary engendered a rare mutual confidence in one another. Cary agreed to hold his bills, except when he had to make a layout of cash, as for engravings, and then he would have to have the money up front. Financial matters settled, Cary then turned to the task of educating Henrietta in the graphic arts.

Henrietta liked to tell how Cary would sit on her davenport, attempting with patience and understanding to "educate" her in the various aspects of production and printing. But he was never successful in educating either Henrietta or Esther in printing. Neither ever grasped the composition of a page. Cary recognized a lost cause and gave up the effort. The women wrote, and he paged.

If they wrote too much copy, he added another page or cut the copy. Writing and editing nine books a quarter, in addition to manning a growing Sunday School, played havoc with that thing printers call a "schedule," but they all stayed with the project. Esther and Henrietta wrote as hard and as fast as they could, and Ethel May proofread as quickly as she could.

They decided to leave the lessons undated. That way the courses could be repeated every year for each particular age. Then churches would not have to throw away cupboards full of outdated manuals, as Henrietta had to when she first came to Hollywood.

Books and Half-books

Esther Ellinghusen always caught everyone up in whatever she was doing, so naturally her teachers in the junior department heard often about the new lesson materials being printed. This being the case, no one thought it odd when one Sunday morning, D. Stanley Engle, one of her teachers, asked, "Esther, who is going to ship these books and take care of the accounting?"

That was a good question, and Stanley Engle, being an accountant with the Union Oil Company, was the right one to ask it. Stan answered his own question by volunteering to handle the distribution and accounting operations. His offer was enthusiastically accepted.

The first printing of 1,000 copies of the junior lesson book arrived in the Christian education building and were stacked everywhere. When Stan assured Henrietta of his confidence in the future of the book, she looked at the stacks of them around her office and replied, "It is not the future that concerns me as much as it is what we will do with them now. We stumble over them every time we turn around."[2]

"Put them in my garage," Stan answered. And so his garage became the first warehouse and distribution center of Gospel Light Press. A small desk in his dining room served as the first head office.

Stan recalls that when Esther wrote a check for $84.74 to pay for the engravings in that junior pupil's book—their first book off the press—her mother commented, "Well, that's money down the drain!" Time quickly proved her wrong, for with no advertising and only word-of-mouth recommendations to promote the book, orders soon poured in for this book—and for subsequent books as well.

When Henrietta's book for juniors appeared in print and she saw her first copy, she became so excited that she immediately decided to prepare and print a junior high book. But she faced a major problem: It was already June, and the book would have to be finished and printed by mid-September so as to be in the hands of those using it for the Sunday School quarter starting in October.

Henrietta had long wanted a course on the Christian life that would ground the new junior highs in the Word of God and confirm them in their faith, since many of them had received Christ in their junior years. Working at all hours of the day and night, she had both the pupil's and the teacher's books ready in time to meet her deadline. When that next quarter began, the Christian life course was ready and waiting for all who would need it.

Over the years, Henrietta tried to get back to redoing the books for that course, feeling they were too simple and elementary. But it seemed that each time she thought of revising them, some mother would come to her with a story of how she had found her son on his knees beside his bed, doing exactly what was asked of him in the lesson. To Henrietta, these responses

The first warehouse and distribution center for Gospel Light Publications (then Gospel Light Press) was this garage behind the Hollywood home of D. Stanley Engle, one of Henrietta Mears' Sunday School teachers. The Engle dining room became the first Gospel Light office.

were evidences of God's seal on the books. She never redid them.

Behind all the writings of Henrietta Mears lay her firm conviction that Sunday School students should be taught the Bible sequentially at their own level of understanding, progressing through the Bible four times from two years of age until they finished high school. She declared, "If the Bible is taught the way it should be, it will be like a powerful magnet drawing children and youth unto the Lord Jesus Christ." And everything she wrote conformed to those convictions.

The year 1933 was pivotal for Henrietta and her colleagues. They obtained their first copyright that year. And with writers and publishers working as a single team, they published 12 full courses before year's end, officially launching Gospel Light Press as a publisher of Sunday School curricula—the first Sunday School publisher to provide closely graded Bible lessons.

As Henrietta had believed, having a Sunday School with a curriculum that was Bible-based, Christ-centered, child-centered and closely graded for each specific age level would prove magnetic in its drawing power. By the fall of 1933, enrollment in her Sunday School topped 6,000, eventually topping at 6,500, making it then the largest Presbyterian Sunday School in the world.

Not only was the new curriculum having an impact at Hollywood's First Presbyterian Church, but also in the Engle dining room. Orders for the new courses were now coming in from numerous churches everywhere. By the end of 1933, 13,366 copies had already been sold to 131 Sunday Schools in 25 states, surprising even the writers with their undoubting belief in the miraculous.

Throughout 1934, sales tripled, as more new books and even flannelgraphs were added to the Gospel Light line. By this time, the Engle home had become an annex to their garage. Books were piled high in corners and under tables. Stan's wife was constantly on the telephone taking orders or at the desk processing the mail. In the evening, her husband kept the accounts, tied up bundles and shipped the literature to an ever-increasing number of churches in more and more states.

The new publishing venture proved to be of mutual benefit to both publisher and printer. Cary Griffin helped put Gospel Light Press on the map. But likewise, Gospel Light helped make Griffin-Patterson Printers. And both of them kept Henrietta hard at work, writing furiously to meet relentless deadlines and demanding schedules.

One day as she and Ethel May worked together on a course, Henrietta stopped in mid-lesson, put down her pencil, leaned back in her chair and said, "I can't write another word! What's going to happen to it after it is written?"

Ethel May responded, "God only asked you to write. He will promote the literature." Assured that God was more than ready to meet His responsibilities if she met hers, Henrietta picked up her pencil and returned to writing the lessons.

As 1935 approached, Henrietta decided she would like to take

By 1936, three years of spectacular growth had forced Gospel Light Press to move its operations to a second, larger location, a store at 1443 N. Vine Street in Hollywood. Here the company's four pioneering partners—*(l. to r.)* Ethel May Baldwin, Esther Ellinghusen, Stanley Engle and Henrietta Mears—pose with pride outside their new company home.

a trip around the world. But how to take three months out of her writing and editing schedule and still get all those books done that she needed to do? So she asked her printer, "What's wrong with publishing half a book?"

Questions of this sort had not arisen in his line of endeavor before, so Cary Griffin decided he would have to come over and further educate Henrietta about the business side of printing. After they did some figuring together, he said, "Well now, as far as I can see, it would cost you an extra cover for the run." An extra cover sounded just fine to Henrietta. The trip was on!

Sometime later, as Henrietta and Ethel May walked up the gangplank of their ship, galley proofs for their half-book were pressed into their hands with instructions to read them and send them back promptly. Fearing to mail the proofs from a foreign port, the women hurried through the proofreading, so they could send them from Honolulu. Unable to find wrapping paper and string, they somehow got the proofs packaged and off to Cary. In the corner of their parcel, in lieu of a name and return address, was written, "Paper and string have we none but such as we have send we unto thee! Hezekiah 3:2. HCM and EMB."

North Vine Street and Campbell's Soup Boxes

Through the early 1930s, the country was staggered by poverty, but Gospel Light Press continued to increase its sales every year. The little company started with no capital and, for its first three years, had no rented facilities or full-time employees. But by 1936, Gospel Light Press either had to find a store for its operations or move the Engles into another house.

Gospel Light Press moved, and the Engles stayed put. On Thanksgiving Day, 1936, the four partners—Henrietta Mears, Esther Ellinghusen, Ethel May Baldwin and D. Stanley Engle—held a special thanksgiving service in their new location, 1443 North Vine Street, only two blocks away from the flashing lights of the film capital's most famous corner, Hollywood and Vine.

Providentially, Stan then discovered that Campbell's Soup boxes were just the right size for shipping the company's books in. He came up with so many of these boxes that his store staff often accused him of walking to work through alleys to find the Campbell cartons. But before long, all the employees—clerks, typists and shippers—were caught up in the game of "Find the Campbell's Soup Boxes."

About that time Esther Ellinghusen took a year's leave of absence from her public school teaching so she could finish several new courses she was preparing. Completing these early, she spent the rest of her leave traveling through the Pacific Northwest, holding workshops, visiting churches and demonstrating the new Sunday School curricula. Thousands of pupils were introduced to Gospel Light materials and sales rose significantly through her efforts to acquaint pastors and church educators with the new Sunday School materials, demonstrating what personal contact could do.

By the end of 1937, over a quarter of a million books had been sold.

Clifton's Cafeteria and Convention Platforms

Henrietta's area of greatest weakness had always been her poor eyesight. Nevertheless, God had now called her to be an author and writer, a service that made the greatest possible demands on her eyes. Yet He balanced those demands with enormous blessings, enabling her to find genuine fulfillment in this new endeavor, despite her visual infirmities. And more than that, as a direct consequence of her writing, He was opening up to her a new outreach on a national and international scale.

For, by 1938, due in large measure to the new curricula she had introduced, burgeoning Sunday Schools everywhere were begging her to provide them with much-needed leadership training for their teachers. In response, Henrietta, with her associates, launched a Christian Education Training Course at Clifton's Cafeteria in downtown Los Angeles. For the first meeting, she optimistically made reservations for 200 people.

But when Henrietta arrived, she could hardly make her way through a crowd so large that many of the guests ate their supper standing up. From all over the city, Sunday School teachers had come to learn how they could better teach God's Word. These classes were held for several years in a series of Monday night workshops that met on the second floor of Clifton's.

Yet when over 500 people began to crowd into the cafeteria for each session, the manager had to ask Henrietta to find another location. Eventually, these teacher training workshops grew to such dimensions that they were moved to the Forest Home Christian Conference Center in the San Bernardino Mountains. There teachers and pastors from all over the country were invited to come for a week of intensive instruction and exchange of ideas.

A generation ago such workshops and conferences were a unique phenomenon. For after the First World War, America's interest in spiritual matters reached low ebb. This lethargy depleted the Sunday Schools of teachers and students alike. Many even believed the Sunday School was terminally ill and could not be revived.

Henrietta and her co-workers, along with others, were used of God to fan these dying embers into a flame of revival. The meetings that began in Clifton's Cafeteria developed into conferences, rallies and Sunday School conventions across the North American continent. Henrietta Mears' reputation as both author and leader grew, opening doors for her to address tens of thousands of people every year on the "romance" of the Sunday School.

Evangelical Christians found in this movement what they had missed for decades. Many of them remembered that at the turn of the century such conventions were commonplace, even to the point that Congress would adjourn and the President would arrange his schedule in order to attend Sunday School rallies in Washington.

But liberalism in the Church had taken its toll. Now, in the 1930s and '40s with Henrietta Mears and others in the lead, Christians were again inspired to take the gospel to the youth of the world.

Henrietta became a cofounder of the National Sunday School Association, and her appearance on convention platforms in America and Canada struck courage in the hearts of thousands of leaders from every denomination. Innumerable churches regained their composure after the onslaughts of debilitating liberalism and now stood with conviction when presenting the message of salvation to the oncoming, questioning ranks of youth.

Statistics and Transformed Lives

Statistics are exciting when behind them are seen transformed lives. Twelve years after Henrietta Mears came to the First Presbyterian Church of Hollywood, Gospel Light Press was one of the

Eva Cornelius, director of the Greater Chicago Sunday School Association (GCSSA) welcomes Henrietta Mears to the 1949 convention of the GCSSA.

Henrietta Mears appears here with Eva Cornelius and the entire GCSSA board of directors in 1949.

One of the prime movers in reviving interest in the work of the Sunday School in America, Henrietta Mears inspired church leaders across the country at rallies such as this one held in Chicago's historic Moody Memorial Church and sponsored by the National Sunday School Association which she helped to found.

Two pioneers in Christian publishing enjoy a moment together at the 1961 convention of the Greater Chicago Sunday School Association: Henrietta Mears *(l.),* founder of Gospel Light Publications, and Mrs. Bernice Cory, cofounder with her husband, Victor, of Scripture Press.

four largest independent publishers of Sunday School literature in America. Orders were being received from every state but one in the Union. To expedite shipments, 13 depositories were located across the country with 53 bookstores handling the literature. And Gospel Light then serviced 2,126 churches directly, with 736 of them in California.

Gospel Light increased its sales 120 times over the first year's record. Hundreds of thousands of youngsters were being taught that God had a plan for them. Men and women who thought they could never teach were now being trained and equipped. Sunday Schools in hundreds of churches multiplied far beyond expectation. Pastors took heart, parents were won to Christ by converted children, and young men were once again looking upon the ministry as an honorable calling.

To all, wherever Henrietta Mears went, her message was unchanging:

> *We are standing on holy ground. The Lord said to Moses:* Put off thy shoes from off thy feet, for the place whereon thou standest is holy ground (Exod. 3:5). *This is the place where God meets men, and today He is looking for those who will do His will.*
>
> *Does not God want us to be concerned with the youth of our age? What am I to do about taking the gospel to them?*
>
> *I must stand at attention before the Lord of Israel. I can hear Him speaking to me, as He did to Moses: Go, deliver my people.*
>
> *What does God want you to do? Meet Him face-to-face, and you will find out.*

Notes
1. Barbara Hudson Powers, *The Henrietta Mears Story* (Old Tappan, NJ: Fleming H. Revell Co., 1957), pp. 149-150.
2. Ibid., p. 150.

NINE

Beloved Teacher

A s I travel around the world, I
meet scores of people who say to
me, 'I love that old pile of bricks on the
corner of Gower and Carlos: It was
there I met my Savior, my friends and
my wife, and there I found my life's
calling.' I have tried to create in our
college department an atmosphere that
God could use to draw young people
unto Himself and to train them for His
service."

WHEN DR. CLARENCE RODDY, THEN PROFESSOR OF HOMILETICS AT FULLER Theological Seminary, once was asked whom he considered to be the best preacher in Southern California, he immediately replied, "Henrietta Mears."

Yet Henrietta did not like to be thought of as a preacher or minister. She believed these roles were for men only. But she loved to be called "Teacher." She had a reverence for that title, always giving glory to Jesus, *The* Teacher.

So Henrietta became Teacher to the thousands of college students who sat under her teaching at the First Presbyterian Church of Hollywood. It was not uncommon at all to see 300 or more university students from the campuses of greater Los Angeles listening to Teacher in the college department on a Sunday morning. And they came because they knew she would feed them with the Word of God.

Henrietta's success with college-age students bordered on the phenomenal, yet teaching that age group had not been her plan when she came to Hollywood. She had arrived there with an early intention of teaching the high-school class, the age group she had always taught in the past. But a single encounter brought about a change in her plans that was soon to become permanent.

During that first trip to California when she was just a visitor at Hollywood Presbyterian, she was asked to teach a group of people that happened to include several college students. On that particular Sunday she arrived to teach wearing a pink silk dress and draped in white furs. Her ensemble was topped off by a big pink picture hat covered with white roses. Despite her frothy exterior, she immediately plunged her class into a solid study of Romans 12:1,2. Both her appearance and her lesson held the class spellbound.

David Cowie, later to become a Presbyterian minister, was one of the college students present in the class that first Sunday. He said, "Not only do I remember the pink silk dress and the pink picture hat with white roses, but I remember her lesson practically verbatim. We had never seen such a vision of worldly beauty giving forth such spiritual truth."[1]

After Henrietta arrived in Hollywood as the church's director of Christian education, David and several other collegians met with her and insisted that she take over the college class. She consented to do so but only until another teacher could be found. She remained the college department teacher for the rest of her life. She loved the collegians with a special love—and they loved her. She was their Teacher, and they were her beloved college department.

As soon as Henrietta took over the class, the young people began bringing friends who soon brought other friends. Despite the many concrete challenges she set for the students, the class grew in time from a few dozen students to over 600. They came from several different colleges and universities and included many young people who, though of college age, were already pursuing careers in various professions.

A Bold Approach

Henrietta had a bold approach to God, to people and to ideas. She had the courage to venture into difficult realms of thought and doctrine, even when she couldn't fully comprehend them herself. This willingness to tackle intellectual and theological difficulty attracted the inquiring minds of her young people.

One day she sat in her office with a college student talking about the Bible. Teacher asked the student what Paul meant in Colossians 1:20 where he says, "to reconcile all things unto himself."

The student gave her an initial answer, but Teacher replied, pointing again to the verse, "You still haven't taken into account the word 'all.' What does Paul mean, 'to reconcile all things?'"

The student was taken aback by her emphatic query and admitted he didn't know.

"I'm not sure I understand either," she responded. "But I thought we could come to some conclusion together."

Her adventurous attitude toward the deeper truths of Scripture, her openness in admitting her own questionings to her students and her readiness to dig with them for the answers to such questions awakened the imagination of many young collegians who later went on to seminary. Her boldness with students and her intellectual honesty with them sprang from her confidence in Christ. "I may not be able to answer all their questions and doubts," she would confess to other teachers, "but I can introduce them to the One who can."

One rugged chap who had grown up in the Sunday School and was now in Henrietta's college department was also a star football player and an *A* student. He brought Teacher question after question about the Bible and science. She was at no loss to answer the questions that perplexed him, for she had a science background herself and had kept abreast of the current intellectual problems troubling college students.

But as soon as she would answer one of his questions, he would raise another—and another. These question-and-answer sessions went on and on, but seemingly without meeting his needs. Henrietta decided to go to the root of his needs.

"Bob, as soon as we finish discussing one question, you raise another, and you have hundreds more," she reminded him. "This is going to get us nowhere. I want you to meet a Person who can answer all your questions and do much more than that for you."

Shortly after that exchange, Bob accepted Christ as his Lord and Savior and went on to become a Presbyterian minister. Everything in the college department was for this end—to introduce students to the One who would answer their problems. It was not by accident that the motto of Teacher's college department was: "To know Christ and to make Him known."

A Solid Organization

With nothing loose or sporadic about it, the organization of the college department would have been a credit to a good-sized business firm. As much authority as possible was placed in the hands of the students, and they were expected to run things efficiently.

The inner directorship of the department was made up of all the top elected officers: the president, one or two men's vice presidents, a women's vice president, the College House (Sunday evening program) chairman, the social chairman and the chairmen of the committees for personnel, new members, evangelism, and deputation. Officers representing other areas of concern were also often included on this board of directors, so that it sometimes numbered as many as 15. These directors met once a month officially, but usually every week unofficially. Collectively, their responsibilities covered every area of the department.

Next in authority came the general cabinet whose members were appointed by the directors. This larger body was made up of the committee chairmen and their workers. Under the director of socials, for example, were committee chairmen for the Christmas banquet, the Easter breakfast, each of the bi-monthly socials, the recreation nights, the summer beach parties, swims and so on. And each of these chairmen in turn had his own staff.

The responsibilities of the director of personnel were as vital as they were interesting. The entire membership of his department—as many as 600 to 800 names—was broken down so that under one personnel director would be four or five captains, representing the major geographical areas of the members. And under each captain would be as many as 15 to 20 lieutenants, under each of whom came the various individuals living in his area.

On this one committee then were sometimes as many as 60 to 100 people working. And they worked indeed. They had to keep tabs on every member of the department.

If someone had not been in the group for two weeks, a phone call was made. If one had been absent for a longer period, he was called on in person. For special occasions, every member of the group was given an invitation by phone.

This committee had to keep the rolls up-to-date and report any changes of address or status. The director was kept busy meeting now with one captain and his team, now with another. All this labor had an enormous effect on those individuals who otherwise would have felt lost in such a large body, and many students came back to the department again and again because someone knew they existed and was willing to give them a phone call to say hello and let them know they were missed.

A Complete Program

Sunday morning worship. With so much personal attention given to individuals and so much loving care directed to personal needs, it was no wonder that the college department on Sunday mornings bubbled with infectious excitement and a manifest joy in God's goodness. Scurrying feet and whole-hearted enthusiasm were evident among the collegians hurrying to Teacher's class. Strangers were greeted with warm, hearty welcomes as cheerful receptionists asked members and guests to sign the roll. Everything and everyone is animated. And every detail—the announcements, the singing, the soloists, the prayer and the challenge—was geared to both first-time visitors and to more mature Christian members.

The Sunday morning meeting—the most formal of the three main meetings of the week for the college department—was set apart for the teaching of the Word. When she rose to teach, Henrietta became a commanding presence. She began each session with a prayer encompassing the nations, remembering by name several of the alumni of the class serving in far corners of the world. In this prayer, she would lead her students to the very throne of God and ask Him, right at the beginning of the lesson, to command their hearts and minds.

Her lessons were challenging, informative, logical—and always biblical. Certain books of the Bible, particularly Paul's epistles, were her favorites, the chief of these being Romans. Her mind revelled in the great doctrines Paul presented. She loved to emphasize Christ's death for sinners, the power of the Holy Spirit and the majesty of God.

When Teacher expounded Romans to the students, she stressed the doctrine of justification, but not as a mere intellectual inquiry. "Paul says that we are not justified by our own works but by faith in Christ," she would say. "Now, students, have you been trying to earn God's favor? You can't do it. You must believe in Christ."

Henrietta was fond of presenting Paul's sense of indebtedness—expressed in Romans 1—to preach the gospel and his love for his countrymen that they might know Christ. Paul's enthusiasm for preaching Christ stimulated Henrietta and inspired her students as she taught Romans to them. No wonder that Romans also became the favorite book of many of Teacher's students who went on to become Bible teachers themselves.

When she came to Romans 9—her blackboard already overflowing with Scripture references—she would unabashedly assert, "People ask me if I believe in predestination. I must admit that I see many problems with this doctrine. But the great question is, What does the Bible say? If St. Paul teaches predestination in these chapters, then I must believe it."

Then as her powerful voice turned to thunder, she would emphatically declare, "But one thing I do find in this passage—and that is the greatness of God. I believe in a sovereign God."

As she extolled the greatness of her God, she managed to fill the chapel with the presence and glory of God, and the collegians listening to her were sure they also heard the amens and hallelujahs of angels.

Other Bible book series she taught her college department were on the Gospel of John, the Acts of the Apostles, Genesis and Isaiah. She also taught a survey course of Scripture that took the better part of the year and provided them with a grand sweep of the entire Bible. She included a general introduction to each book as part of the survey study.

Henrietta was also a serious student of prophecy. She taught several series on the subject and took her students through the book of Daniel a number of times. Once, after coming back from a trip to Israel and excited over the return of Jews to their ancient homeland, she spent many weeks exploring the prophecies dealing with Israel's restoration.

But always prophecy was made relevant to the practical needs of her audience. She saw in prophecy the actions of a divine Christ who was controlling history. He was always at the center of her lessons.

Wednesday night meeting. At the center of the college department's activities was the midweek meeting, held on Wednesday nights, a time when Teacher most clearly presented the claims of Christ and invited students to accept Him as their personal Savior. Henrietta was ever mindful that college young people must think matters through for themselves, face and resolve challenges for themselves and, coming to their own conclusions, make their own decisions. So the Wednesday night meetings were always geared to thoughtful decision and Christian growth.

Nothing was ever allowed to interfere with the college Wednesday night meetings. They were never combined with other meetings, nor were they dropped for any reason, even during exam weeks. No one ever had to call up and ask, "Are you going to have a meeting tonight? Everyone *knew* there would be a meeting."[2]

While the Wednesday night meetings were primarily for prayer, they were also times of Bible study and personal sharing. "Let the redeemed of the Lord say so," Teacher admonished, encouraging young men and women to give testimonies to the presence of Christ in their lives. The nature of the Christian walk was always stressed, so the songs, the mood of the meetings, even the Bible passages to be discussed were all chosen with the Christian's practical needs in mind.

Since prayer was the essence of these meetings, at least 20 minutes were devoted to prayer at the end of each meeting. The lights were turned low as the collegians knelt together on the asphalt tile floor of the hall, as sentence prayers came from one side and then the other of the darkened room. Teacher would often suggest what should be prayed for—helping some frustrated young person to find Christ.

Sometimes she would begin singing a favorite chorus, familiar to those present. She would lead out with her low, sonorous voice and, as others took up the melody, she would slip into the harmony. Her kind voice moved some to tears as God spoke to them through her gentle promptings.

Prayer not only climaxed the evening but began it for the leaders of the individual groups into which the Wednesday evening meetings were divided. An hour before the rest of the students arrived, the group leaders—sometimes as many as 25—met in Teacher's office. After reviewing the passage to be discussed, these leaders joined Henrietta on their knees, exalting the Lord, confessing their weaknesses and imploring the Holy Spirit to empower them in their responsibilities and to clarify for them the passage of Scripture they were about to teach.

They prayed for the visitors, that they might accept Christ. And they prayed that their department would experience a deep moving of God's presence. Teacher was present with them, for the greatest effectiveness of her ministry was generated in these and similar prayer times. After prayer, the group leaders entered into the main meeting with a sense of expectancy and confidence, for God had revealed to them what He wanted them to do for Him.

Bible study on Wednesday nights differed from those on Sunday mornings. Teacher's approach on Sunday mornings was straight lecture without discussion. Wednesday evenings were based on discussion so that the collegians themselves got involved in the Word. Her whole purpose was to get people directly involved in the Bible, to get them talking about God's Word.

After a brief song service and opening prayer, the students moved into small discussion groups with not over 15 people in each. Sometimes they would meet around tables. Occasionally, she sat at a desk at the front of the room and set the tone by going over the general outline and discussion questions that had been distributed to everyone.

Then the discussion leaders took over. Each group leader's task was to get the students in his group to find the answers in the Bible for themselves. The students were to do the digging; the discussion leader was not to give any sermons of his own—a hard rule for some group leaders to follow as they were pre-seminary students who enjoyed sharing their own views. The better discussion leaders were those who, lacking confidence in their own ability to speak, were more willing to listen to the others in their groups.

Henrietta devised several techniques for keeping the discussion going:

- Have someone read the passage and give a summary of it.
- Have someone else give a brief outline of the passage.
- Ask what the passage teaches about God, Christ, the Holy Spirit, man and his responsibility.
- Find the key verse.
- Read another passage that sheds light on this one.
- Have specific questions ready on the passage itself.

No leader who understood how to use these devices ever complained of not having an interesting group. Most of the discussion leaders were distressed that they did not have time to let their people finish everything they wanted to say.

When 40 minutes or so had elapsed for the group studies, Teacher would call for everyone's attention and then ask the leaders to stand and summarize the essential points their groups had gleaned. This practice then led easily and naturally into an inspiring testimony time. Testimonies were the third purpose of Wednesday nights, always evolving directly out of the Bible study.

After absorbing themselves in what God had done for them, as recounted in His Word, the students were ready to tell what God had done in their lives during the previous week. Usually one of the students led the testimony time, someone sensitive and capable whom Henrietta had chosen. She knew a fine meeting could be ruined if the testimonies ran afoul.

Sometimes when the testimonies did become self-centered and trivial, Teacher would take command of the situation and bring it back to a more Christ-centered emphasis. And when necessary, like a sergeant dressing down his troops, she would address her students in a way that left no doubt in their minds what she meant:

This has been the most ridiculous testimony time I think I have ever heard! All we have been talking about is silly little things that don't amount to a hill of beans. Have we lost sight of why we are here?

There hasn't been one word about winning the nations for Christ. How about these great campuses in this area? Hasn't anything been done out at UCLA [University of California, Los Angeles Campus] this week? Hasn't anyone witnessed to a student at USC [University of Southern California]?

God weeps over these lost students, and we come here to talk about trifles. St. Paul dreamed about the kingdoms brought to Christ. Knox cried, "Give me Scotland or I die." Luther wept over Germany.

The tide of testimony often changed as the young people were made to see what God could do through them. After all, His omnipotence was the key. Nothing of importance had happened in their lives during the week because they didn't honestly believe that God could do it.

But how did this kind of talk affect visitors to the department. As Teacher would be dealing with the Christian students, many an unconverted newcomer sat up and took notice, often accepting the Lord right then and there. The visitors knew that this woman meant business, that Christ was real to her—and they loved it. They were sick of trivialities in their empty lives, and they wanted something dynamic and vital for themselves.

Her older students often squirmed under Teacher's fire, feeling that their testimonies had failed because they weren't in fellowship with Christ. That fact was true, but they hated to admit it. Teacher, however, knew how to crack the whip over those leaders who supposedly held the reins of the class.

"Where are the leaders of this department? Don't they have anything to say tonight? This class will never go beyond the leadership. Don't expect anyone else to have anything to testify if you don't. You are the key."

At the close of the Wednesday night meeting, the class would have refreshments. The object of this refreshment time was to continue the fellowship—fellowship either around the Word, prayer, testimonies or punch and cookies. An hour after prayer meeting ended, most of the students were still hanging around, talking.

Teacher was usually off to the side, leading someone to Christ. At times a little room in the back of the hall would be filled with students seeking the Lord. A group always gathered around the piano, singing hymns. And some of the officers might already be planning the next social or deputation project.

When locking up the church for the night, patient Tom Craig, the Scottish custodian, would leave the college chapel to the last, waiting until Teacher had finished counseling the last student. Sometimes he would encourage the students to leave by turning off the lights, but conversations would continue in the dark.

Henrietta was usually the last to leave; she always had someone else to talk to. Few realized that she had been going at top speed all day and was completely exhausted. But no matter, these were her sons and daughters. She loved them and, through them, she intended to change the world.

After another hour of fellowship around coffee cups and apple pie at Coffee Dan's or some other restaurant on Hollywood Boulevard, one of her students would finally drive Teacher home. Even then, still buoyant and ebullient, she would be talking nonstop about someone she had prayed with and who had accepted Christ. Or perhaps she was stirred by some young fellow who had decided to go into the ministry. For Henrietta Mears, Wednesday nights were thrilling experiences because her students then came face-to-face with Jesus Christ.

Sunday evening College Hour. The Sunday evening meeting for college students was entirely different from the other Wednesday night and Sunday morning meetings. Sunday morning was for the teaching of the Word and Wednesday night was aimed at enriching the devotional life. But Sunday evening—known as the College Hour—was reserved for forums, panels, musicals, testimonials and whatever. On Sunday nights, the collegians could say what they wanted to say and give vent to their spiritual energies. Teacher encouraged anything that allowed the students to interact with what they were doing and learning.

Some of the most interesting Sunday evening College Hour programs were given over to the department deputation teams where the students who had been witnessing at the jails, camps, colleges and hospitals could report on what had been happening in their outreach endeavors.

Occasional College Hour programs were nothing short of amazing. Once, after their beloved Teacher had returned from a trip to the Far East, brimming over with enthusiasm for missionary work in Japan and Formosa, the collegians organized a program around an Oriental motif. They removed all the chairs in the hall and replaced them with some 300 or more cushions which they scattered about the room. Chinese lanterns and travel posters completed the decor.

As soft Chinese music played in the background, girls of the social committee, wearing kimonos, served tea and Chinese cookies. Suddenly, with no warning, all the lights went out. And then a single spotlight in the rear of the hall came on.

There, in the glare of the spotlight, sitting in a rickshaw (courtesy of a local movie studio), dressed in a fancy kimono and waving a paper fan was Teacher. After the initial surprise, a roar went up from the crowd, when two college men, dressed as coolies, stepped between the shafts and pulled the "Dragon Lady" through the back doors, down the middle of the room and up to the front of the hall as a gong sounded. Though her inept and inexperienced coolies nearly dumped her in transit, Henrietta swept the length of the hall in the grand manner of a dowager empress, fanning herself with all the hauteur she could summon.

Once the clamor had died down, she laid the fan aside and delivered a moving, challenging missionary message. That night, her collegians beheld as never before the plight of a needy Orient, facing eternity without Christ. A few months later, two doctors and two nurses were sent to Formosa from the college department to help the missionaries there. Many other Sunday evening College Hours also focused on missionary themes.

The collegians put on one missionary program where all those who were interested in some specific overseas field took part, but they did so in the languages of those countries that were the concerns of the participating students. Only the announcements and final message were in English. The Scripture readings were in both Spanish and Russian, with testimonies in Japanese and German. The music was sung in an African dialect and poetry read in Korean. This multilingual program puzzled much of the audience, but they recognized that those involved in it were committing themselves to a life calling—and doing so before those who knew them best, their college friends.

Many Sunday evening programs gave the creative people in the college department opportunities to show what they could do. And a department as active and large as this one had an abundance of live talent, plus two pianos, a Hammond organ and a stage to work with. On several occasions, they even assembled a small orchestra.

A group of students interested in drama staged plays, complete with costumes, on biblical themes, including one on Paul in Athens. They held literature evenings when Christian poems and prose works were read to the accompaniment of a harp. And at special seasons of the year, especially at Christmas and Easter, their programs, often musicals, were unequalled and glorious.

Four of the college fellows organized a quartet with an outstanding accompanist, and they were in constant demand, not only in the department, but up and down the West Coast, even appearing for several months on television. The group's lead tenor at the time was the student body president of Occidental College. He eventually married the quartet's pianist, and together they went into the ministry.

A regular college choir was a part of the music program of the church, but the same young man who organized the quartet also formed a second college choir that performed only in the department. It lasted for over a year and sang nearly every Sunday morning and on many Sunday evenings. Good by anyone's standards, this choir could do anything from Negro spirituals to classical anthems. Many musically inclined students found in this choir a further attraction to come to the department. A few years later another similar choir had its own radio program for several months.

On certain Sunday evenings, the class frequently had a whole program devoted to a single campus, everyone participating on that program being from the same school. Of course, the rivalry between the schools added to the fun, as all the students from each campus tried to get the most people out. This friendly inter-campus competition further helped to attract students from the various universities, and Teacher heartily encouraged anything along this line.

Monthly youth night. When Dr. Louis Evans, Sr. was the pastor, the church held a youth night once a month on Sunday evenings. This meant that the entire Sunday evening service was run by and for the youth. The college department, along with the high school students, organized these successful youth nights in every detail, except the sermon, which Dr. Evans himself preached. A thousand or so young people gathered for these Sunday evening church services, listening attentively to Dr. Evans' dynamic challenges.

The presence of all these young people in the regularly scheduled services of the church—not just in those they led—was no happenstance. They were excited about going to church and looked forward to being there. But the degree of their commitment to and involvement in the total life of the church was due in no small measure to Teacher's own example.

The Sunday School was Henrietta Mears' domain, but she never for a moment thought of it as a kingdom apart. Though a strong and capable leader in her own right, she never considered herself a rival of the ministers with whom she served. Her Sunday School was the educational arm of the church, not a substitute for it.

She was transparently loyal to the whole church and served her Lord through it. She instilled this sense of loyalty and responsibility in her young people with the result that they never looked upon their own programs and activities as alternatives to that which comprised the congregational life of their church. Consequently, it was as natural for the youth and the collegians to be present in all the worship services of the church, not just those for which they were responsible. They loved their Teacher, but she taught them a higher loyalty to their Lord and to the whole Body of Christ.

A High Standard

So how did the College Hour chairman—as the director of Sunday evenings was called—work with such a variety of demanding programs week after week and keep up the pace Sunday after Sunday without wearing himself out? The trick lay in getting others to do the work. At the beginning of the year when the new officers were taking over, the entire executive staff and all those who thought they might have ideas for Sunday evening programs were invited to a brainstorming session.

With 50 to 100 people at this meeting, everyone contributed as many ideas as he could without too much discussion of details. All the suggestions were carefully recorded by the program chairman's secretary with a note on who showed the initial interest. On the basis of these raw ideas, the chairman then appointed subchairmen who would be responsible for one or more specific meetings. These subchairmen then set up their own committees and saw to it that good programs resulted.

People who already held leadership posts in the department were expected to have one or two nights per year when their committees would take over. As a result, individual programs were put on by the deputation teams, the membership committee, the music committee, the pre-seminarians and so on. In this way, the program chairman was assisted by nearly the entire cabinet, though he still had to be a very strong leader with a great deal of time to spend on his job.

The program chairman's office was second only to the president's in importance. Teacher was always willing to discuss his problems with him and to offer suggestions. But she never made the mistake of taking over his responsibilities. She simply made sure that the program chairman did his job.

Henrietta Mears built into her students a sense of their own responsibility by making them do the work themselves. And because she expected her young people to reach as high and as far as they were able, she charged her students to maintain the highest degree of excellence possible in all their programs. For she was incapable of lowering her own standards when she knew that she or those working with her had not done their best.

The students were introduced early to Teacher's demandingly high standards for them and the college department.[3] During a rush to get out some mimeographed announcements for a special meeting of the college department, several students stayed up most of the night getting the job done. And they were pleased with the job they had done.

> *In triumph they brought the finished product to Miss Mears, who took one look at them and dropped the whole batch of cards in the wastebasket.*
>
> *"Why, Miss Mears, what do you mean? Look how hard we worked!" Even the men were almost in tears.*
>
> *Very firmly Miss Mears replied, "But look how poorly the job has been done. I would rather they didn't go out at all. People will think that is the standard for all our work. We must be Christ-honoring in all that we do."[4]*

Many at first did not understand Henrietta's attitude. Some found her high norms a mind-stretching experience. But for some youth, it was hard to resolve the differences between Teacher's high standards and their need to be trained up to them. For what were they to do when they were expected to put on a class program of excellent quality and were still green at what they were doing?

She still expected all her leaders to do their best, and she knew how to reprimand any who knew better than to offer excuses for less than the best. Intense and energetic with enormous reserve of mental and emotional strength, Henrietta unquestionably demanded as much of her young people as she did of herself.

Dale Bruner, who later became a missionary to the Philippines, was among those young people who grew to appreciate the fact that

Teacher modeled excellence by her example even as she demanded it of them: "If I were to single out a dominant impression of Miss Mears, in addition to those perhaps most obvious: indefatigable energy, her absorbing interest in individuals, her lust for life (symbolized significantly by her hats), it would be her all-consuming passion for excellence.

"Whether by requesting a coat and tie for dinner, or a lesson, or the use of time, Miss Mears always demanded of herself and enjoyed in others, excellence. What so many of us owe to Dr. Mears will never be adequately brought to expression, except at the mention of her name and in her presence, we shall always 'rise up and call her blessed.'"

An Intense Love

Yet her love for them was no less than her demands—and the young people knew it. They were her family, the sons and daughters she had never been permitted to bear physically. So she lavished on them all the emotion and ambition normally reserved for one's own. The students were important to her, not only personally but potentially—for the cause of Christ among the nations.

Still, her love for her "sons and daughters" never allowed her to fall into the trap of parents who can see no wrong in any of their children. Teacher knew well the weaknesses of the young, but she also knew to what noble purposes they could rise when challenged to do so. In rare fashion, her balance of gifts enabled her to combine demanding standards with warmhearted acceptance.

Because none of her qualities obscured the other, Teacher could challenge or counsel, instruct or inspire as the needs of her young people required—and they responded to her accordingly.

Somehow, her students knew and understood the magnitude of Teacher's love for them, an understanding they reflected and returned, as they grew—no less intently—in their love for her and for her Christ.

Notes

1. Barbara Hudson Powers, *The Henrietta Mears Story* (Old Tappan, NJ: Fleming H. Revell Co., 1957), p. 139.
2. Ibid., p. 141, adapted.
3. In 1951, the Ambassador Class was formed in the Sunday School to receive the college department graduates. Dick Halverson was the teacher for this group which also included the young singles of postcollege age. Within a few months the class was averaging 400 for the Sunday programs. Many outstanding projects were sponsored by this group, particularly those involving missions, teaching, assisting with special undertakings in the church and the like.
4. Powers, *The Henrietta Mears Story*, p. 131.

TEN

The Personal Touch

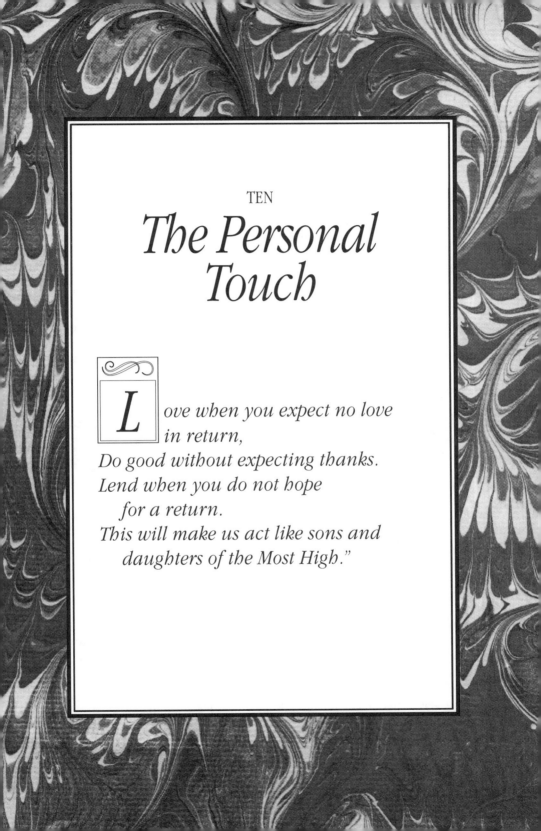

L *ove when you expect no love*
  in return,
Do good without expecting thanks.
Lend when you do not hope
  for a return.
This will make us act like sons and
  daughters of the Most High."

"PERSONAL WORK IS ONE PERSON FINDING ANOTHER PERSON AND BRINGING him to the personal Savior," Henrietta Mears often said. And everything she did to win others to Christ was very personal and much work. Because of her regard for the individual, her witness to people always reflected her genuine personal concern for them. And because she labored tirelessly in the cause of Christ, she did indeed work hard at winning souls.

Underscoring Henrietta's emphasis on the personal approach was her belief that men and women should be won to Christ one by one. This principle was the foundation of all her work, and the thousands of people in the Sunday School of Hollywood Presbyterian Church were evidence of her commitment to it throughout her career. No groups, programs, drive, committee meetings, office routine were ever more important than the individuals in them.

She Was Loving

Henrietta never looked at other people merely as potential converts or as walking decision slips. To her, they were people for whom her Christ had died. And by allowing Christ to love each person through her, she was able to manifest a genuine love for each one who came her way.

"One of the amazing facts about love is that the more you love others, the more they will love you," she said. Christian love was not simply a doctrine or an abstraction, but a way of life, a part of her character that radiated to others and drew them to her.

She Was Wise

Henrietta Mears could hold her own in debating theology or in discussing difficult points of doctrine. But she knew that a show of cold, detached intellectuality was not the approach to use in winning others to the Savior: "A person who is all brain-power with no feeling is as unbalanced as one with no intellectual control over his emotions." Cerebral as she was, she recognized that anyone she was witnessing to was invariably self-concerned in some way. So she advised:

> *If you talk theory, self does not see where self is concerned or where self is going to benefit or where self is in danger; so interest is lost.*
>
> *A sermon on the deity of Christ might not arouse the slightest interest. But it will if you begin with this question: Had you been the thief on the cross, what would your reaction have been to Christ's death? And if He had said to you, "Today thou shalt be with me in paradise," what would you have thought?*

She Was Caring

Every individual was important to Henrietta; she had the gift of making each person feel essential. Small wonder then that people constantly came to her, seeking friendship, counsel or prayer, for Henrietta had a wonderful gift of listening, not just talking. And in conversation with someone, she always tried to discover what interested the person with whom she was talking.

One day a lonely young girl from a family of considerable wealth came into Henrietta's office. The girl was so desperate for friends that she was in tears. As she confided in Henrietta, she acknowledged how her family had tried to buy friendship for her by purchasing tickets to various events for their daughter and her acquaintances. Her parents even financed outings and trips for their daughter and her young associates, yet no lasting friendships had resulted.

"Even though my parents have done all these wonderful things for my friends, they desert me and leave me alone. And I'm so lonely," she lamented. "You don't understand how it is to be lonely; you have so many friends. Everyone loves you, Miss Mears!"

Henrietta felt the girl's distress and knew this was no time to give a lecture on the futility of trying to buy friendship. Instead she proceeded to "busy" herself with some papers as she said, "I do understand how much true friendship means. Now, I'll tell you what, I have some important work to do that I just must tend to, so while I do this work, you take this pencil and paper and sit down on the couch over there and write down every single quality you would like in a friend of yours. Then we'll see what we can do when you've finished your list. I know every girl in this church, you know."

The girl sat on the couch and worked on her list while Henrietta "worked" on her papers. When the girl had finished writing, she showed Henrietta a thoughtfully prepared list of qualifications for the perfect friend.

> *Henrietta studied the list carefully and then asked, "This is the kind of friend you are looking for?"*
>
> *"Oh, yes," replied the girl fervently. "Where can I find someone like that?"*
>
> *"My dear," said Miss Mears gently, "do you realize that everyone is looking for a friend just like that? Now, why don't you go out and be this kind of a friend and let others find the friend in you that they are looking for?"*
>
> *"But you don't understand, Miss Mears; I'm looking for a friend like that!"*
>
> *"And so is everyone else. If you are this kind of friend, everyone will be so happy to find someone like you that you'll be swamped. When you start thinking of others, others will start thinking of you.*
>
> *"And you know, the most important and wonderful thing for you to remember is that you have the Perfect Friend, Christ the Savior, in your heart. You need never be lonely, no matter how alone you may happen to find yourself temporarily."*
>
> *"All right, Miss Mears, I'll try, I really will!" said the girl with a bright smile. "It will be a game. I wonder how long it will take someone to find the perfect friend that they are looking for in me?"*[1]

Cupid and Henrietta Mears worked closely together in her college department, nurturing budding romances into full bloom. So weddings of her young people were milestone events for her as well as for the couples themselves. She is pictured here at the weddings of Kathy and Dale Bruner, who later became missionaries to the Philippines, and with Jean and Don Botsford. At the time of their wedding, Don was then associate manager of the Forest Home Christian Conference Center.

Radiant and excited, the young lady fairly burst out of Henrietta's office, already excited about the friendship possibilities that lay before her as she set about becoming the perfect friend for someone else to find.

In the college department was a lonely, rather nondescript fellow who did not have much money and was frequently in dire financial difficulty. His chief talent was making a nuisance of himself, so others in the department tried to ignore him—usually without success. But Teacher went out of her way to be nice to him, and he realized that in her he had found someone who truly cared about him.

Then, during one of Henrietta's illnesses, this same young man sent her a dozen roses and a box of candy. Touched by this unexpected gesture, Teacher exclaimed, "Why, bless that dear boy's heart! He is such a wonderful fellow!" And she meant every word.

A former collegian, in commenting on Henrietta's caring attitude, declared, "I was impressed with Miss Mears remembering my name when she approached me one Sunday morning in the college department. I didn't think she knew me. Little things like this distinguished her. She always made us feel so important, so crucial to the kingdom enterprise, even if we were not."

Her ability to empathize with the joys and sorrows of others was boundless. She was usually the first to hear of someone's new job, the birth of a baby or a success at school. And she often was the first to hear simply because others recognized that her interest in them was honest and unselfish.

She Was Accessible

Her staff members were often greatly amused when someone would burst into Henrietta's office to share with her some news she had already heard. Yet she would sit and listen to the entire story as if she were hearing it for the first time. When one of her colleagues asked her why she didn't tell the person she had already known of the matter, Henrietta explained, "Why, that would be like pricking a child's balloon. I want people to feel that

One of Henrietta Mears' strongest supporters in her ministry to the collegians of Hollywood Presbyterian Church was Charlotte "Mother" Atwater, the previous superintendent of the college department. Mother Atwater often accompanied Teacher when calling on collegians and personally won many of them to Christ. This elderly saint appears here on Teacher's immediate right at a birthday party given in 1929 by Henrietta to honor her mentor and friend.

it is fun to tell me things. In this way I can keep my contact with them."

Anyone seemed to have access to Henrietta. No matter what the time of day or night, she could always be reached. At the Forest Home Conference Center, she would allow her schedule to be filled up far past midnight with those wanting counseling. Yet she was up in time for the faculty prayer time before breakfast.

Even when she was ill and needed rest, she was reluctant to unplug her phone to prevent people from using up her strength before she had time to regain it. On one occasion she obeyed her doctor's order to stay in bed, but she allowed her college department cabinet to hold their meeting in her room. Then, as they knelt, she placed her hand on each one's head, praying for him.

Always mindful of the needs of the sick, Henrietta tried to visit them in their homes—or at least by phone—to pray for them. One Sunday afternoon, after she had taught twice and had presided through a long committee meeting without lunch, she was obviously weary. When one of her college boys volunteered to drive her out for a late lunch, she asked him instead to take her to the home of "Mother" Atwater, her old friend who was now bedridden.

"Mother Atwater hasn't been able to come to church for several weeks," said Teacher, "and I want to pray with her and let her know we've been thinking about her."

Henrietta's friendship with Mother Atwater illustrates another aspect of Teacher's personal work. When Henrietta took over the college department, Mother Atwater was superintendent of the group. "I'm no superintendent," Mother Atwater confessed. "But if I can help in loving these dear young people and being a 'mother' to them, I'll do it."

Henrietta and Mother Atwater became close friends, and Teacher leaned on this saintly woman for encouragement, especially for prayer. Frequently Henrietta would phone her concerning some urgent spiritual need and ask her to intercede.

Besides prayer, the two of them spent every Thursday afternoon calling on students and winning them to Christ. Rain or shine, they consistently devoted this one afternoon to calling, with the result that the college department grew rapidly—not because of any membership drives—but through the weekly influx of new collegians who had been introduced to Christ.

Mother Atwater was on her knees at five every Sunday morning, praying for two hours or so for Henrietta and the college department. Her ministry continued throughout Teacher's 35 years at the church, and the two of them died within a year of each other.

She Was Positive

Henrietta saw potential in everyone she met. She knew what Christ had done in her life, and she thoroughly believed that with God all things are possible. She loved to emphasize what Jesus did for the woman of Samaria:

This fallen woman was the most unlikely candidate for anything spiritual, but the Savior saw her potential. Her salvation was evidenced by her running off to tell others of the Messiah. This one revolutionized life started a revival in Samaria. It came about by her carrying Christ's power to everyone she met. She was magnetized for service.

Jesus had a way of touching and changing a man, then using the changed man to touch and change someone else. The change that came to the village of Sychar came first to one person in that village. The Reformation that shook Europe first of all shook Luther.

When sharing Christ with someone, Henrietta never played on that person's weaknesses by stressing the don'ts of the Christian walk. She preferred to present the do's and delighted in pointing out that the children of Israel were saved out of Egypt and into Canaan. "I don't want to talk about Egypt," she would say, "for that is only what we are saved from. I want rather to discover all the privileges God has for us in Canaan, the place of blessing."

She Was Direct

Her loving, yet no-nonsense approach was demonstrated one evening during a campfire commitment service at college camp. One young fellow, standing before the fire to give his testimony, pulled a package of cigarettes out of his pocket and threw them into the fire. As he did so, he said, "Well, I guess Miss Mears wants me to get rid of these."

To the astonishment of all, Henrietta reached into the fire, grabbed the scorched pack and handed the cigarettes back to the startled youth. Then looking him squarely in the eye, she said, "Harry, God doesn't want your cigarettes. What would He do with them? He wants you."

Her logic was inescapable: Once Harry found Christ, smoking would no longer be a problem.

This photo was taken of Henrietta Mears *(second from left)* and Ethel May Baldwin *(far right)* on board a ship during their first world tour together in 1935.

She Was Fun

Henrietta Mears knew how to have fun. Once while sailing the Caribbean, she was invited to a costume party on board ship. The party was well underway, and her fellow voyagers were all decked out in colorful, spectacular costumes of their own when Henrietta made a hilarious entrance as a zany Roaring Twenties flapper girl. Several ostrich plumes floated over her enormous picture hat. And she was swathed in a brilliant red frock with several feet of beads draped from her neck.

As she sashayed into the salon, the other guests broke up in laughter. The hit of the evening, she entered into the gaiety of the occasion with her usual gusto and thoroughly enjoyed herself.

Finally, unable to stand it any longer, one of the passengers said to her, "This is utterly amazing, Miss Mears. I know you don't drink liquor, and yet you are having more fun than the rest of us!"

And that was Henrietta's point—a Christian can have more fun than anyone else.

Wearing a quickly borrowed coat and hat and preaching from the *Book of Numbers*—the telephone book, Teacher entertains a group of collegians with her hilarious "sermon" on "Old Mother Hubbard."

She could make people of all ages laugh, but especially the college folk. During fellowship times with them, the students often urged her to give her famous sermon, "Old Mother Hubbard," from the *Book of Numbers*. When she could be persuaded to give this "sermon," she enjoyed the occasion as much as they did.

At such times, someone would run for the nearest telephone book, another would find some old hat, and a third would offer his coat or jacket. With her glasses pulled down to the end of her nose, and with the coat turned backwards, she would stride in, hat down over her eyes and the telephone book under her arm.

With feigned dignity, she would open the book, bend low over the text and, supposedly following along on the passage with her finger, would read, "'Old Mother Hubbard went to the cupboard'—I want to read this passage clear through so you can get the full meaning, and then I will come back, and we shall look at it statement by statement."

And on she would go, her pseudo-exegesis prostrating her listeners in laughter.

"'Old Mother Hubbard went to the cupboard.' Can't you see the pathos of this o-l-d, o-l-d woman going to the cupboard?

"'To get her poor dog'? No! She didn't go to get her poor dog, but that's the way some of you read Scripture. You stop right in the middle of a thought.

"What did she go to get? What is the object of her 'wenting'? You've all seen an old woman 'wenting,' haven't you? She's all bent over low, with furrowed brow...."

And so her exposition of the nursery rhyme proceeded until her listeners were limp from laughing, tears rolling down their cheeks and stitches in their sides.

A former collegian, remembering the fun times enjoyed with Henrietta, wrote back to her and said, "I love to remember the fun over the chocolate malts late at night...a wild moonlight ride the wrong way on a one-way road up Mount Rubideaux with the lights off...hilarious times with you at an occasional two-hour lunch on the Boulevard when coffee was five cents a cup...sharing with you our first joy when I became engaged."

As one of her college boys, later a minister, said of Teacher, "Her mind, her heart, her humor were captivated by Jesus Christ. She was serious about the gospel, yet she had a fabulous sense of humor."

She Was Colorful

In the early 1930s, before two-toned paint jobs were the vogue for cars, Henrietta had her two-door Ford painted canary yellow and kelly green. The paint on this eye-popping color combination had barely dried before the Carnation Milk Company came out with the same colors on all its milk trucks. So Teacher's car was quickly dubbed the "Milk Wagon" by her students.

When someone asked her why she had chosen that particular color combination, she replied, "My college boys like it."

Henrietta in person was no less colorful than the car she drove.

One of the great fun times at the Hollywood Presbyterian Church was the night when George Hendricksen, one of Henrietta's Sunday School teachers, mimicked Teacher in a hilarious spoof called "Miss Mears in Action." No one enjoyed his comedic performance more than did Henrietta herself. Perhaps the other gentleman is impersonating Ethel May Baldwin or Esther Ellinghusen.

In describing her, one of those college boys said of Teacher, "Miss Mears was not beautiful, but she dressed flamboyantly. Her glasses were extremely thick. She carried a handkerchief in one hand, in the other a *Thompson Chain Reference Bible*. But it wasn't long before I was absolutely captivated by the simple profundity of the former chemistry teacher who had a deep commitment to Jesus Christ and a knowledge that God had harnessed her mind for a purpose."

So what word best described Henrietta Mears visually? Was she beautiful? Flamboyant? Or was she just a plain Jane who wore bottle-bottom glasses? Whatever else she had or didn't have, Henrietta Mears had presence. And whether with flamboyance or flair, no one questioned that she had class.

Much of what Henrietta was reflected her richly cultured background and her own love of beauty. She reveled in color, particularly in pinks and reds, her favorite colors. But nothing captured her exuberant style and love of color more than did her hats.

> *She loved hats. She had big hats, small hats, a big red cartwheel, a small red one with a big red rose, but always at least one red hat. There was a beige hat with violets dripping over the brim that has bobbed through many a spiritual challenge.*
>
> *On a trip to South America she went to a famous hatmaker in Buenos Aires and at a very small cost he made ten different hats for her. One was a fuchsia hat with plumes and another was white egrets. She has always said, "I wear my hats for my college boys, and they love them...."*
>
> *But her whole motive was to serve the Lord, for to paraphrase Paul: "Whether you wear a hat with plumes or flowers, wear it unto the Lord." And Miss Mears wore hers unto the Lord.*[2]

Henrietta had no desire to be known as a clotheshorse. Like

everything else she did in life, she dressed with a purpose in mind. Often the occasion or setting dictated what she wore.

> *"If you are properly dressed according to the stan-dard of the group you are in, you can forget yourself. You will attract attention to yourself if you are not abreast of the fashion of the times. If you are over-dressed you will feel conspicuous. Be sure every detail is right and then forget your appearance," she says.*[3]

But, more than that, because of her love for both, she dressed to honor others and to honor her Lord.

> *When people invite you to dinner, honor them and wear your best. Let them know you think it is an impor-tant occasion. They have been working hard all day to make the meal a lovely occasion, so don't act as though you didn't think it important by wearing a sloppy old outfit. I think Sunday clothes are a good idea. Why not look your best when you go to church on Sunday? Hon-oring the Lord should be the greatest occasion of the week.*[4]

Not only in dress, but in decor, Henrietta lavished color and demonstrated beauty, even in her Sunday School rooms.

> *Sunday School rooms were painted light, fresh col-ors. Old, dark upright pianos were painted the same light shade of the walls, colorful curtains blossomed immediately at any window that caught her eye, and any pictures used were attractive and of good quality, suitably framed. Flowers were everywhere.*
> *Nothing could look old or drab or run-down, shabby or unkempt in any nook or cranny utilized by Miss Mears in her ever-expanding program. Everything always had to be pleasing and attractive and as invit-*

ing as possible, so that the setting would be proper in which to lift up the Lord and Savior.[5]

She Was Hospitable

Her home, presided over by sister Margaret, was a place of great grace and style—and open to all. She enjoyed handsome furnishings, lovely china and crystal, antiques and *objets d'art*. And she filled it with the treasures of a lifetime of travel for the enjoyment of all who entered her home. She believed in sharing the beauty and hospitality of her home in equal measure.

> *She had always felt that the beautiful things in a home can be graciously shared by all. So few homes are open in hospitality to large numbers of people that she felt she wanted to have her home gracious and beautiful so that all who came would have a sense of joy in sharing its beauty and a sense of possession as they brought their friends to see her home and show them around with almost a sense of sharing ownership. Of course, this fulfilled two purposes: all enjoyed the beauty of her hospitality, and it brought newcomers within reach of the Christian testimony of the meetings. A social gathering was never ended in her home without a closing prayer.*[6]

She Was Winsome

Henrietta Mears won men and women to Christ by her life. Her vital and vivacious personality, exuding good will and zest for life, appealed to the citizens of the movie capital, just as it did to other alert and energetic people. In this city, known for its moral corruption and superficiality, her life was an open window on the holiness of God, through which many frustrated souls saw beyond the empty materialism of their own empty lives. To them, she represented the highest and the best of Christian virtue.

Henrietta Mears believed in and practiced a ministry of hospitality. Her large, beautifully appointed home was open, not only to family and friends, but also to groups of all kinds from the church, the campus and the community. She presided as a charming hostess at numerous dinners, parties and meetings—times of fun, fellowship and study—occasions when many found Christ or were strengthened in their resolve to live for Him.

But Henrietta Mears also won men and women to Christ through her love, for her godliness of life was crowned with an unreserved love that never degenerated into a stifling legalism in her relationships with them. She loved people for their own sakes and she showed it. Yet her utmost desire for all she met was to love them into the Kingdom of God by the winsome witness of Christ loving them through her.

That manifest love, the essence of her personal work, radiated Christ to those about her who were looking for someone, not something, to believe in.

She Was Witnessing

Coupled with her consistent witness was the skill of a well-trained personal worker who had studied the art of winning the lost. She led many classes and institutes to help others become more effective witnesses for Christ. Sometimes these classes had as many as 300 people enrolled. She had syllabi mimeographed for her students' use.

Each person was required to talk to others about Christ during the week and then be prepared to report at the training sessions. This dynamic approach involved everyone in practical experience, and many who had always considered themselves incapable of leading someone to Christ gave joyous testimonies week after week of the successes God had given them.

But the great triumph of these classes lay in the new Christians who enrolled in the course and then began bringing their own converts. At the end of a personal workers' series, it was not unusual to see several generations of new believers sitting side by side.

Three fundamentals underscored Teacher's classes:

First, a personal worker must thoroughly understand what the gospel is and is not. "A religion," she would say, "is what man does for his God. Christianity is exactly the opposite; it is what God has done for man."

To emphasize her point, she would expound the doctrines

dealing directly with salvation: the holiness of God, the effect of sin, the atonement of Christ, faith, regeneration and so on. She did not want people going out as personal workers who had an inadequate comprehension of what they believed. "Christians are salesmen for Christ. A salesman must understand his product."

Second, the personal worker must be absolutely committed to God. He must be a channel through which the Holy Spirit can flow. "God converts people; the personal worker is merely His instrument."

Third, the worker must have confidence in his product. "If I put wheat into the ground, I must have confidence it will come up; so I must believe that if I put the gospel into a pair of ears, it will bring forth its fruit."

One of her picturesque illustrations was: "If you come into a room and sneeze, everyone will get your germs. The gospel is contagious; go out and sneeze in people's faces."

Faith in the effectiveness of God's Word was at the heart of her work, a faith she underscored with one of her most frequently quoted passages, Isaiah 55:10-11:

> *As the rain cometh down, and the snow from heaven, and returneth not thither, but watereth the earth, and maketh it bring forth and bud, that it may give seed to the sower, and bread to the eater; So shall my word be that goeth forth out of my mouth: it shall not return unto me void, but it shall accomplish that which I please, and it shall prosper in the thing whereto I sent it.*

Her confidence fed on this promise, and every time she learned of someone finding Christ through her ministry, she was spurred on more than before to reach the lost. She developed some guidelines—each point illustrated from the Bible—to use in helping others get started in personal work. And she urged her students to memorize key verses for use with these guidelines:

Ask a man if he is satisfied. Most people are not content with their lives.

A person must understand that he is a sinner. After he sees this, show him what he must do about his sin. Give him the facts about salvation. The sinner must come to the Savior. There must be a personal encounter.

Never pronounce a person saved. Show him that everything is based on the Bible, and let him draw his own conclusions.

Point out that his salvation depends on God's ability and faithfulness. And make sure he realizes that God will not cast him off if he sins. Also, show him what to do when he sins as a Christian.

Urge him to begin confessing his faith before others immediately. Point out that Christ demands all of his life. The Lordship and Saviorhood of Christ should go hand in hand.

One of her illustrations in dealing with men and women about salvation was that of a soldier enlisting into the army:

First, a soldier is not inducted on the basis of feeling, but of absolute allegiance. The new convert must realize that anything less than total commitment will not do.

Second, the soldier is required to make his enlistment known. He is fighting for a public cause. So the Christian must not be afraid to tell others about his faith.

Third, a soldier is called unto a job; so the Christian is supposed to get busy in God's work. Our faith must put on shoes.

Teacher's favorite text in dealing with young converts was, "Lord, what wilt thou have me to do?" (Acts 9:6). Answering this question, she taught, implied an absolute commitment to the Lord

Jesus, a necessary ingredient for spiritual success. Such a commitment involved an absolute surrender in every area of life; nothing was to be withheld from the Savior's control.

Henrietta believed—and taught—that surrender to Christ also meant service for Christ. Salvation as an end in itself had no meaning for her. Frequently she would ask Sunday School workers at training conferences, "What is the goal of your Sunday School?"

Almost invariably someone would answer, "To lead boys and girls to Christ."

"No!" she would reply emphatically to her startled audience. "That, of course, is part of it—and you know the emphasis I place on evangelism—but if your task stops there, you will never be successful. Our job is to train men and women, boys and girls, to serve the Master.

"They must feel that there is a task for them to do, that there is a place marked *X* for every person in God's Kingdom. Here is my *X*; no one can stand on this place but me. Now I must help others to find their places.

"God has a job for every Christian, and no one else can fulfill it."

Growth came quickly in new Christians when these ideas took hold. Christians discouraged and aimless for many years sought her for counseling. She would tell them that their Christian walk had lost its stride, because they had not realized Christ's plan for their lives.

When understanding of God's purpose in their lives began to catch fire in their hearts, everything took on a new glow. Many were the professional people—doctors, teachers, lawyers—who found out they were called to be witnesses and missionaries right where they were.

A highly successful car salesman in the church came to the realization that he had an obligation to be a laywitness for Christ. He began to study his Bible with increased enthusiasm and even spent a year in seminary. Eventually he took over some of the teaching responsibilities in the adult classes. Every weekday morning he would come to the church and study for three hours in preparation for his classes. He never felt called to give up his secular work, but in his capacity as a layteacher, he had great influence among the businessmen of the community.

She Was Involved

Ever since their first meeting in 1949, just before Billy Graham's now-famous tent crusade in Los Angeles, Henrietta had greatly admired her young evangelist friend and encouraged her collegians to support his various campaigns in the Los Angeles area. So when Billy came to the Hollywood Bowl in the 1950s, all were anticipating a repetition of that 1949 tent crusade. But the Bowl meetings did not measure up to expectations. Many of the young people, disappointed that the crowds were no larger, began to pray about what could be done.

Hollywood's First Presbyterian Church then had a membership of over 7,000, and some began to think how inspiring it would be if, for one night, the entire congregation would come out to one of Dr. Graham's meetings. The idea was presented to Henrietta and to Pastor Evans, who quickly approved. Headed by collegians, a committee set a target date.

The committee members cut up pages of the church phone directory and recruited volunteers from the college department and from other groups who would each phone every name on one side of a page. They then selected people to go around to the various Sunday School classes to announce the event. Posters were hung up all over the church, and the leaders were instructed to push the special night as hard as they could.

All the while, Teacher and her collegians were praying furiously. Large banners were made so the members would be able to find the section in the Bowl roped off for them. Monday was chosen for the strategic night, because this was ordinarily the least-attended session.

The students' hearts nearly leaped from their chests in pride, as Billy read off the names of the various churches attending the meeting that night. For when he called out, "The First Presbyterian

Church of Hollywood," 5,000 people stood to their feet. And at the invitation, scores of them went forward to profess Christ.

Teacher's students were flushed with success. They immediately got hold of telephone directories for the entire Los Angeles area, tearing out pages and cutting them in half. Then, with Billy's approval, they passed them out on various evenings to volunteers, along with instruction sheets, the idea being that each person was to phone and invite every person on his list to the services. Though some people responded, this invitation-by-phone effort did not work as well as the previous plan, probably because the students had not thought through this citywide approach in sufficient detail.

Nevertheless, Billy was so grateful for the enthusiasm of Teacher's collegians that he broke his own rule of not preaching in any one church during a crusade, lest he obligate himself to do the same for all the churches. He brought his entire team to the college department the next Sunday morning and took over Henrietta's class to the great delight of the students.

During the Billy Graham Crusade in the Hollywood Bowl, some remarkable conversions occurred among the youth of the church. Among them were those of two rascals in the college department who had been raised in the church, yet had never become Christians. They had been involved in enough mischief in and around the church that the ruling elders had seriously considered banning them from all church meetings.

One night the two mischief-makers went to a Hollywood Bowl service to sneer at the proceedings. But when Billy gave the invitation, the two young men looked at each other and both headed for the altar rail. In time, one was serving his Lord on the mission field, and the other became a Presbyterian minister. Whether in special campaigns or in the usual course of her ministry, Henrietta witnessed or was instrumental in thousands of such transformations.

When Billy Graham was in Manhattan's Madison Square Garden for his 1957 New York Crusade, Henrietta flew back to see the amazing things God was doing there. Upon entering the packed hall one evening, she was immediately recognized and ushered to a front seat where she sat back to take everything in. She reveled in the ministry of Cliff Barrows and the huge choir and thrilled to the singing of George Beverly Shea.

But as Billy began to preach, the realization that she had taken the attitude of a spectator jarred her. *No matter where I am*, she thought, *the Lord never intended me to be a spectator.* Immediately she lifted her heart in prayer: O Lord, don't let me sit here just as an observer. I want to be a participator. Use me here for your purpose."

As she prayed, Henrietta was unaware that a friend with her unconverted sister was in the Garden audience that night. For years this friend had wanted Henrietta to talk to her unbelieving sister about Christ. But because the sister lived in the East, the friend had become resigned to the fact that Henrietta and her sister would never meet.

As the invitation was given, the friend spotted Henrietta and quickly brought her sister over to meet her. Henrietta took the woman into the Inquiry Room and, in a few minutes, introduced her to Christ. As the days and nights rolled on, Henrietta led many others to the Savior as well.

She frequently shared this experience with others afterwards, pointing out that God does not call us to sit on the sidelines and watch. He wants each one of us to be on the field, playing the game.

Wherever she was—whether in New York, London, Athens, Galilee or Hollywood—Henrietta Mears played in the game, finding the lost, bringing them to Christ, training them for His service and encouraging them to others. Only eternity will reveal how many she loved into the Kingdom in her lifetime.

Notes

1. Barbara Hudson Powers, *The Henrietta Mears Story* (Old Tappan, NJ: Fleming H. Revell Co., 1957), pp. 72-73, adapted.
2. Ibid., p. 51, adapted.
3. Ibid.
4. Ibid.
5. Ibid., pp. 132-33.
6. Ibid., pp. 51-52, adapted.

ELEVEN

Leading Men to Leadership

T his is our supreme task as Christian educators; to gear youth into Christian service—regardless of what the specific occupation may be—and to encourage the utmost skill in the fulfillment of this service."

THE SUMMER DAY WAS HOT AND SUNNY—BEACH WEATHER TO SOUTHERN Californians. A rickety cattle truck, with brightly colored towels flapping against the wooden sides, clattered down Sunset Boulevard past the sumptuous homes of some of Hollywood's brightest stars. On board the truck, dressed in their beach togs, the collegians of the First Presbyterian Church of Hollywood were headed for the surf.

The students sang heartily, the clanks and squeaks of the old truck keeping time to their vigorous songs. And swaying back and forth in the middle of the happy gang, singing and laughing with them, sat Henrietta Mears. Next to her was a collegian with a contagious love for people. Everywhere Jimmy went, his warmth and joy for life glowed with a heavenly iridescence, made all the more captivating by a congenital abnormality in his physique.

As the rest of the passengers joked and sang, Henrietta said to the young man, "Jimmy, have you ever thought about going to seminary?"

Spiritual Horizons

Quite honestly, Jimmy had to admit that such an idea had never appeared on his spiritual horizons. But now she had raised the idea in his mind, and his horizons were, consciously or unconsciously, extended—something Teacher loved to do with her students.

Years later, while pastoring a church in California, Jimmy A. Arnold wrote to her: "One of my fondest memories of you was riding to Hollywood Beach near Oxnard in the late 1930s in one of Robinson Trucking Company's cattle trucks. I remember vividly...the happy trip back home singing with the gang, and you and Ethel May Baldwin right in the middle of it.

"I was so impressed that you gave so unstintingly of your time and of your Christian spirit. Here you were riding in the cattle truck with us, singing, sharing words of wisdom along the way and asking the question which opened my eyes to greater service, 'Have you ever thought about going to seminary?'"

Henrietta never told a student that God was calling him into the ministry. She reverently left that sacred responsibility within the province of the Holy Spirit. But she knew that one of her most important tasks in Hollywood was to create an atmosphere which God could use to speak to young people about church-related professions.[1]

Two-part Emphasis

Ever mindful that God had called her to train leaders, Henrietta continually sought out leaders among her young people and trained them, all her energies, ambitions and abilities dedicated to helping each one achieve his maximum development. Her God-given ability to spot leadership potential in an individual seemed almost instinctual at the time. Watching a purposeful-looking football player walk by one day, Henrietta commented, "What a wonderful leader John would make." And he did!

Leadership was her theme and she voiced it at conferences, meetings, Bible classes and in a thousand conversations. But in her leadership emphasis, Henrietta Mears was charged with being partial on two counts—a partiality toward men and a partiality toward the Church. She readily pled guilty to both charges and offered a ready defense of each one.

Strong males. Her insistence on having males in leadership positions she defended by saying, "I know that if I can get the best examples of young men to attend, I can always get the beautiful young women to follow!"[2] So she worked hard at finding and placing strong male leaders wherever possible in positions of authority in her Sunday School.

Male leaders, she felt, provided boys with needed examples; she knew the girls would keep pace with the boys. She saw a close relationship between the attendance of men and their involvement in a church program on one hand, and the success of that program and the virility of the Christian message on the other hand.

"If there are no strong men leaders in the church," she stated, "you will wind up with 22 girls and perhaps three fellows in the youth groups. In the Church of the living God, God has always called men to be leaders."[3]

> *So through the years, Teacher has always kept a close check on the rolls to see that there is an equal number of boys and girls in the Sunday School; camp lists have been checked to see that there are as many boys as girls going to the summer conferences. "Bring me men to match my mountains, bring me men to match my plains, men with empires in their purpose..."' Teacher has quoted.[4] "That's the way it is in building spiritual empires. We need to see the vision of the living Christ, need to find men who will dare to be true to the calling of Christ, need men who will build an empire for God. There will always be enough work for the women to do as we follow in their steps."[5]*

Church-related professions. And was Henrietta Mears primarily interested in supplying leadership for the church-related professions—the ministry and the mission field? Yes, leadership for the Church was her first concern. To challenge young men to enter the ministry was perhaps the greatest of Henrietta's gifts. Yet, though stressing the need for men as leaders in the church, Henrietta recognized and utilized women leaders as well. For she nurtured leadership potential in whomever she found it, bringing women leaders along with the men.

> *When she began to organize the Sunday School, she couldn't find the right man to be the leader in the junior high department. So she approached the best feminine leader and said, "Very frankly, I don't want a woman to take charge of this department. But would you be willing to take it over until I find the right man?"*
> *The young woman accepted. As the months passed,*

*the standing joke between the two of them became,
"Have you found the right man yet?"*

"No, not yet!" Teacher would reply.

*For 12 years the question was the same and the
woman built the department into a huge success before
the right man was found, when she moved to a northern city.*[6]

In the course of her career in Hollywood, over 400 collegians
heard God's call and turned their energies to pulpits in America or
to missionary stations scattered around the world. One of her
greatest delights was traveling the globe to visit missionaries who
had been her pupils.

So significant, in fact, had been her influence in providing
leadership for the Church of Jesus Christ that, in 1961, Dr. Harold
John Ockenga, then pastor of Boston's Park Street Church and first
president of Fuller Theological Seminary in Pasadena, California,
wrote to her:

*What a work you have done! There is no young peo-
ple's or Sunday School work in this nation equal to
yours. When I think of the tens of thousands of people
who have studied the Bible under your leadership, of
the thousands of young people who have faced the
claims of Christ and made a commitment to Him, of the
hundreds of young men who have gone into the ministry and other young people into Christian service, I
cannot but stand back in amazement.*

*Your vision, your faith and your courage have been
unequaled, and only heaven can measure the fruit of
your labors....*

*As you know, it was one of my fondest hopes to have
you as a professor of Christian education in Fuller Theological Seminary. Your contribution to ministers
would have been the acme of your educational career.*

Inspired Students

But it is one thing to be a seminary professor and to instruct young men and women who have already committed themselves to the ministry; it is quite another to inspire university students who are still trying to choose a life's calling. And Henrietta Mears definitely had this latter gift.

Yet, while developing leadership for the Church was her primary concern, Henrietta's vision encompassed every area of life. She was no less desirous of seeing her young collegians step into the business world, teaching, medicine, indeed, into all occupations, as Christian leaders. Her nephew was one of the developers of color TV, a brother was the president of several banks at an early age and other of her close relatives were outstanding in the professions, in industry and in commerce.

These examples served in her mind as norms for the ambitious Christian youth she challenged: "Young people, I want you to think about what you are going to do with your lives. What are you living for? When you come to the last days God allows you on this earth, will you be satisfied?

"Remember," Teacher would say, invoking the words of C. T. Studd, the great missionary to Africa, "'Only one life, 'twill soon be past; only what's done for Christ will last.'"

Henrietta always made it clear that she was talking to young people about a great deal more than simply making a living; she was talking about making a difference for Christ in whatever area of endeavor He led them. "Our duty is to understand youth, but more, to help them understand themselves that they may release their varied abilities in the service of Christ and His Kingdom. We must help them to discover a lifework, not work for life."

Sometimes Henrietta's goals for her students, like her standards, left them gasping. As one of them said, "We can't all be Luthers in religion, Faradays in science or Gladstones in politics. I feel left out of Miss Mears' vision."

Aware of the high expectations she had for her young people Henrietta herself confided in private:

I know that when I tell my young people the marvelous things God has done through the lives of others, it encourages them to strive to achieve higher goals. But it doesn't necessarily follow that He will do the same through them. But He has done it for some, and I know that the principles I lay down for them are valid. Besides, I want them to aspire to the very highest attainments possible for men and women whose lives are possessed by the Spirit of God.

Spirit-led Goals

Teacher always stressed that "leadership begins with Christ. No matter how brilliant a youth may be, he must experience the regenerating power of the resurrected Christ before his real potential can be liberated."

Absolute surrender to the influence of the Holy Spirit was a cardinal factor both in Henrietta's own life and in her training of others. Through submission to God's Spirit, vision began to grow in her own mind, and she passed on this key to successful leadership to thousands of young people:

"Allow God to tell you what you are to do. But you say, 'Miss Mears, I don't know what God wants me to do. I've been praying about it for months, and I just don't know.' Well, is there the faintest glimmer of light? It may be ever so small. What is it? Follow it! And as you do, God will reveal the rest."

This advice was the encouragement that many students needed. They had some glimmer of light, but it had seemed to them too faint, perhaps too ridiculous. Teacher knew that a youth will be listless, aimless and bored unless he has something for which to strive. Once he has a goal, all his energies will leap into the game.

So in her seeking to inspire leaders, two factors went hand in hand: the Christian's relationship to God, and his goal. The contact with Christ produced the goal which in turn produced a greater desire to know Christ. And it was amazing to see timid students,

202 Leading Men to Leadership

who had not really found much to do in life, join the college department and burst into activity and accomplishment once they came face-to-face with the Lord, found their goals in life and experienced the empowerment of the Holy Spirit to accomplish them.

Henrietta reminded her students that goals were never met by happenstance. She stressed—and practiced—the need to be specific with God's plans. She pointed out how—when she first came to Hollywood—she wrote down on a piece of paper all the things she wanted to accomplish as director of Christian education at the First Presbyterian Church. "I wrote them down, and through the years every one of them has been accomplished—and many more. I didn't trust my memory, nor did I merely have vague ideas. I wrote down specifics."

Specific Plans

So, time and again in the college department cabinet meetings, she would have her students take pieces of paper and write down what they wanted to accomplish in their departments. She encouraged them to be as specific as possible, to the most necessary detail.

After they set down the goals themselves, Teacher directed her leaders to write opposite them how they were going to reach these goals. Again these means and methods had to be specific. Her style for committing such specifics to paper was brief, practical and efficient:

> *Don't bother with elaborate plans. The simpler they are the better. Often we hide behind fancy ideas and plans because we secretly believe they are going to fail and thus relieve us of our responsibility.*
>
> *Be practical. Don't try something you know from the beginning is not going to work. Think a thing through and choose the best way of doing it. And don't underestimate what you yourself have to do.*

But theory and practice are seldom the same. So time and

again, she would have to call her students to their senses as they planned some big event—a party, a meeting, a camp—when they had not allowed themselves enough time to do it. Or they had not enlisted enough personnel for the job. "Always make sure you have sufficient troops to win the battle," she would caution them.

Hard Lessons

Even so, Henrietta was careful to see that no leader was allowed to fail or, at least, to remain a failure. Perhaps some planned activity fell through or a committee failed in its responsibility. Or, as sometimes happened, a deputation team would come back from its mission almost in tears.

Perhaps the team had gone out to some campus, and the program had fallen apart, the message had been awful, the whole team effort a flop. Teacher would then have her team—dejected by failure—sit down, and she would say to them, "All right now, fellows, why did you fail?" And she would proceed to review the event with them.

As she debriefed them, the reasons for their failure would come to light: the program had not been well thought through ahead of time, Bob had not been prepared to preach, Louie hadn't figured out what songs they were going to sing, and Sam hadn't had time to practice them on the piano. Gary's testimony was not to the mark—and so on.

As the causes for failure were recognized and ways for overcoming them understood, a metamorphosis would take place; the team could hardly be restrained from racing out on another deputation.

Individual Potential

As the Lord rescued Peter from his many failures, lifted him from his discouragement and helped him to see his way through, so Henrietta sought to help her students in their down times. She also sought to maintain a balance between expecting her leaders to excel and in asking something of any one of them that was doomed to failure from the outset:

> *You would never ask me to sing the soprano solo on Sunday morning. It would be criminal. That is not my talent. My job as a trainer of leaders is to spot the potential of a person: What are his talents? What is his potential?*
>
> *It doesn't matter if he is doing anything now or not. I must see where he is capable of going. Then I encourage him along that line.*

God's Call

Henrietta Mears believed that God called people according to their talents. Many a young musician told her that he felt called into the ministry. Without discouraging this possible leading, she gently pointed out that God had already given him a wonderful talent. Couldn't that be God's call?

In the college department, hundreds of young fellows felt called into the ministry, and they invariably talked it over with Teacher. Her response often was like a bucket of cold water on a flame: "How do you know God wants you in the ministry, Bill?"

"Well, I just feel He does."

"But is there anything specific?"

"Well, no, I just think He wants me to be a minister."

"But is there anything else you could do?"

"Sure, there are plenty of other things I could do. But I can't. I just have to be a minister!"

That was the note she was listening for: "Woe is unto me, if I preach not the gospel!" (1 Cor. 9:16). Henrietta would never encourage a fellow to make the pulpit his career if he felt there was something else he would be just as content in doing. It was necessary that, as a preacher, he experience ultimate abandon to God's call. Anything less was not enough.

Basic Training

The call might be to the pulpit, but the training began with straightening up chairs and passing out hymnbooks. If a student was willing to do the menial tasks, he could be entrusted with the bigger ones. Bob was that kind of fellow.

He had been employed in a large chain department store and had worked himself up to a high position there before he was converted. In the college department, Bob would walk through a room, pick up and examine any scrap of paper found on the floor. When asked about it, he said, "I learned in Penney's that no detail is too insignificant not to be bothered about. A very important piece of paper may have fallen that could cost the store hundreds of dollars."

That attitude caused Teacher to admire Bob. For although he held down high positions in her group and later on in several missionary organizations, he never felt above being concerned with the most insignificant detail.

Total Involvement

The college department cabinet—comprising all the officers of the class—was always a large bureaucracy. Sometimes cabinets had as many as 75 active members, plus others who helped as needed. Inevitably, several college department presidents entered office with reform in their blood, determined to cut the seemingly over-large cabinet down to manageable size.

Teacher always vetoed any such cutbacks. First, as each new president was soon to learn, a few people could not run a large department with so much to do. Second, and of greater importance, more students on the cabinet meant more people involved in the activities and, therefore, more leaders being trained.

She had a third reason for the large cabinets: college young people want to be in on everything that is happening in a group. If they feel they are being excluded or their talents are not needed, they will soon flag in interest and drop out. So "use them or lose them," she would say, even though it meant her having to create jobs—when none was open—for new people to keep everybody busy.

One day Henrietta received a letter from an anxious out-of-state parent saying her son Al would soon be visiting Teacher's college department. Al hadn't been involved at their home church, but now that he would be attending college in southern California, his mother hoped Henrietta could do something with him. Henrietta went on the alert.

When Al walked into the college department for the first time, Henrietta boldly grabbed him and asked him to usher—as they were shorthanded. She knew he might never come back if he weren't put to work immediately. Then, after the class hour, she told Al what a wonderful job he had done and asked him if he wouldn't usher again next Sunday morning.

Soon Teacher moved him up to the position of chief usher. Al now had to line up all the ushers for every meeting and, of course, be there himself. Next semester, Al was elected a director of the department and became one of the most outstanding program chairmen the department ever had. He spent all his college career in the department and later became an active elder in his church.

Many years later Al told Henrietta that she was the only one who had ever inspired him to think seriously about religion. One of the reasons for this was that she had made him feel important and needed. She had put him to work.

As the college department was spiritually strong, Teacher was confident of its ability to maintain a biblical emphasis. So, though she never entrusted a major responsibility to a student who had not made a profession of faith, she often would take a non-Christian and—as she had Al—get him active in a less essential job. She believed that working in a group meant involvement in its thinking. And placed at the very center of the activities, the fellow was thereby given full exposure to the gospel.

Once or twice this approach did lead to problems, but for the most part it had the desired effect. And one more individual took his first steps toward becoming a leader. It was one more of the many facets in her innovative leadership training program.

Deputation Teams

One of the most exciting areas of activity and training were the deputation teams. Under a director of deputations were assistants called captains, each one in charge of a specific responsibility. There was a captain for the jail work, another for the city missions, a third for the delinquent boys' camp, a fourth for hospitals, one for each campus in the area, and the like.

Under each one of the captains were the individual deputation teams. And all these teams met together on Friday nights for training. Not uncommonly, 50 or more students gathered together on the second floor of the church for three hours of study and preparation.

These training sessions were broken down into periods. First was Bible study, followed by lessons on how to do personal work. After that the teams met separately to talk over their specific responsibilities. Sometimes church leaders were brought into these small meetings to advise the deputy trainees.

Finally, all the teams were brought back together for prayer. By this time the students had been thoroughly instructed and inspired as to what had to be done the following week. One team was going to a little town to hold street meetings. Another would be speaking twice in the jails to hundreds of young people. A third was lined up to play two or three games of football in the boys' camps and then to hold services for them. Yet another team was to visit fraternity row at the University of Southern California for evangelistic meetings.

With such challenges before them, the students felt the need for prayer. They would get down on their knees and, for a half hour to an hour, seek the Lord's guidance, asking Him to direct their steps.

Many lives were transformed in these sessions. One girl had been invited to sit in for the evening activities even though she was not a team member. She was so thoroughly impressed with what was going on that when prayer time came, she burst into tears and, for the first time in her life, prayed. All the sins of her past came out. On and on she went, confessing, weeping and asking for the Lord's forgiveness. With hardly a dry eye in the room, she rose to her feet a new person and became one of the most active deputies.

The impact of these deputation engagements were little short of tremendous. Once 50 young people rented an old truck, loaded it and several cars with students and drove up to the little town of Fillmore. One of the gas station owners in the town was a Christian and let them park the truck on his property. They took the sides off the truck and transformed it into a stage, complete with a piano. As people walked by, the student chorus sang and gave testimonies, while the rest of them passed out tracts and witnessed.

That night, as prearranged, they gathered in the city's auditorium, now filled with people who had been personally invited that afternoon. The collegians again sang for them, gave testimonies, and one of the deputies preached an evangelistic sermon. Many present found Christ.

Many times the deputation teams went to college campuses, to fraternities and sororities. The team of collegians that went to the University of Southern California organized a whole week of meetings with the renowned Bible scholar, Dr. Wilbur Smith, speaking on the deity of Christ. The team secured the use of the campus philosophy building's main hall, seating about 200.

They plastered the campus with nearly 350 posters and put invitations in every mailbox. Announcements were made in all the fraternities. Someone got hold of two late model Buick convertibles and loaded them up with students, added loudspeakers and went up and down fraternity row at noontime, playing "Onward Christian Soldiers" and blaring the news about the meetings. Around-the-clock prayer meetings met on campus for several weeks in advance of the meetings.

When Dr. Smith finally began his lectures, the auditorium was filled. Some of the philosophy classes dismissed for the week so those students could attend. Dr. Smith covered the virgin birth, the miracles, the atonement, the Resurrection and the person of Christ. On the last day he wove his own testimony into his talk and gave an invitation to which several students responded.

For a number of years, the church's summer deputation program sent teams of students to over a score of foreign lands to help missionaries and to work in international camps with other Christians. Under Henrietta's direction, for several weeks before these teams left and for several weeks after they returned, the college department heard their reports and saw their slides on Sunday evenings.

Teacher felt these mission-centered Sunday evening programs given by teams were profitable for several reasons: They always made a deep impression on those young people who heard missionary challenges from speakers their own age and whom they knew. The programs also helped the participants to organize their thoughts on vital subjects, to improve their self-expression and to involve them dynamically in their group goals—all of which made their Christianity more practical.

But most importantly, as they spoke before their friends, they were also committing themselves before the Lord. For they soon learned they could not speak on missions publicly unless they were willing to do something about missions personally. Many of these same students said that when they were asked to talk on prayer, witnessing or Bible study, they had to come to a fresh realization of the importance of these matters in their own lives before they could share them convincingly with others.

Little wonder then that these deputation teams produced many young ministers and lay leaders. Three of the deputation directors were Richard C. Halverson, who went on to become minister of Fourth Presbyterian Church in Washington, D.C., an executive in several major organizations such as World Vision and International Christian Leadership, and who is currently chaplain of the United States Senate; Louis H. Evans, Jr. who organized and built, from the ground up, the Bel Air Presbyterian Church near the campus of the University of California at Los Angeles and who is now pastor of the National Presbyterian Church in Washington, D.C., and Bill Bright, founder and president of Campus Crusade for Christ, one of the most vigorously evangelistic student movements of our time.

Creative Club

Reflecting her own lifelong interest in the arts, a Creative Club met in Henrietta's home for many years. This artistic assemblage was composed of aspiring musicians, writers, artists, poets and the like in the college department who wanted an opportunity to express themselves, but whose accomplishments, by their nature, could not be fitted into the regular church program. So Teacher brought them out to her home for lovely evenings of sharing what each had to offer: poems, short stories, musical compositions, architectural models, paintings, animations and so on. Many club members went on to invest their talent and experience in the service of the Church as choir directors, writers of Sunday School materials and other Christian publications, radio ministers and others.

Because the First Presbyterian Church of Hollywood was blessed with two of the country's leading choir directors—Dr. Charles Hirt and his wife, Lucy—much of the Creative Club's emphasis was musical. The Hirts worked indefatigably with the young people, providing them with a broad appreciation for all kinds of church music.

Several times a year, Dr. Hirt gave training courses, especially for collegians, which covered everything from song-leading to church musicology. He stressed the importance of knowing exactly what they wanted a hymn to accomplish in a given situation. Those the Hirts trained learned the difference between a gospel chorus and a hymn, between the solo chosen for a worship service and one designed for a college department singspiration. They also learned how to analyze the thoughts of what they sang and to phrase the music with meaning. One of the many benefits of this training was that budding ministers gained a deep appreciation for good church music.

Timothean Club

Another important leadership training project was the Timothean Club, made up of those interested in church occupations—the ministry, missions, Christian education and even church administration. This large group met monthly, usually with one of the ministers and with a variety of speakers, including denominational leaders, who addressed the students. These guests would share their experiences with the students and freely answer their questions.

Every aspect of administration was covered, and for several years a few youth at a time were permitted to observe the session (a Presbyterian term for the body of ruling and teaching elders who govern a church) and other official meetings of the church. The preachers took the pre-seminarians to their libraries and explained step-by-step how they prepared sermons. At times on Sunday nights, the ministers would have young men help them out in the church service. And, on occasion, some would go with the ministers to call on the sick or bereaved. This early training meant more to many of the youth than did seminary later on, because of their direct involvement in live situations during their younger, more formative years.

Summer Seminarians

As five or six seminarians returned every year for the summer months, Henrietta worked out an extensive training program for them. They were integrated into the church staff and had definite responsibilities to fulfill. But they were also expected to put in a number of hours every day studying.

The younger men were required to attend training sessions led by some of the older seminarians, including those in theology and Bible study, along with Sunday School organization, evangelism and camping. And, of course, they all worked in the Sunday School—teaching, organizing summer activities, participating in special seminars, working at conferences and so on. The Christian

This 1937 photo was the first taken of young seminarians who grew up in Teacher's college department at Hollywood's First Presbyterian Church. *L. to r. (front row)* are Bob Ferguson, Homer Goddard, Kenneth Cook, Henrietta Mears, Pastor Stuart P. MacLennan, Cyrus Nelson, Bill Dunlap and Kenneth Nelson; *(back row)* Don Cole, Dick Halverson, Ed Rogers, Paul Fisk, Charles Miller, David Cowie and Jack Barnhart. Teacher described her seminarians as "a noble army of men who follow in His train."

education office was a madhouse during the summer as these fellows went about their work, but the summer seminarian position was an enviable one, and pastors from other churches frequently asked Henrietta if their seminarians could spend a summer under her guidance.

Most of Teacher's seminarians possessed little of this world's riches. Tuition, textbooks and transportation costs invariably exhausted any funds they earned during the school year. And working at the church during the summer paid them only a bare subsistence income.

When it was time for one young man to return home from seminary for the summer program, he found he was a quarter short of the price for his coach train ticket—at ministerial rates.

Then he remembered he still had his storage locker key which he turned in with great relief for his deposit of 25 cents. Teacher's theologues in those days learned vital lessons about complete dependence on God, and many a time they prayed, "Give us this day our daily bread" with more than a passing interest.

Henrietta always bought her budding ministers their "preacher's suit" and winter overcoat, if needed. And she always encouraged these young man to think of her gifts as loans they would, in turn, pass on to others. By helping the seminarians in this way, she knew they would be well-groomed in a dark suit, whether in the pulpit, at a reception or perhaps at a wedding. Ethel May Baldwin had all the seminarians' shirt measurements on file and never missed the semi-annual Dollar Days sales at the National Shirt Shops.

On one occasion, Henrietta and Ethel May decked out one of the fellows with special care, for in a few days he was to be ordained. On the day of the solemn event they inspected Homer carefully to ensure he was presentable. As he stood before the congregation to pledge his fidelity to God and His service, the two women beamed with pride over his fine appearance.

But then the young preacher knelt for the prayer of dedication and—to their horror and the amusement of the other worshipers—two large holes in the bottoms of Homer's shoes yawned at the congregation. Henrietta and Ethel May had forgotten to shod his feet with something more than the preparation of the gospel.

After the service, one of the men present handed Teacher $10 and said, "Buy Homer a pair of shoes."

She bought him the shoes and, as she did so, she thought back to a time shortly after Homer Goddard's conversion when he was attending UCLA. Homer had come and presented Teacher with $40. Knowing the penurious state of his income, she registered such surprise that he must have wondered if she thought he had robbed a bank.

"Homer, where did you get all this money?" she exclaimed.

"I saved it, Teacher," he replied shyly. "I want you to choose some boys to send to camp, because it meant so much to me when I was sent to Mount Hermon last summer. You just have to take this money, Teacher. It is my lunch money that I saved."

Dave Cowie was another young man who had similarly been aided by Henrietta's "loans." One day he phone her and jubilantly announced, "Teacher, I have just paid my debt! I have just bought Dick Halverson his first 'preacher's suit.'"

Henrietta was just as solicitous about the nutritional needs of her "boys." But when a fellow had few resources, his need to eat regularly could pose a problem. Then she learned that the Tick-Tock restaurant at Cahuenga and Hollywood Boulevards provided full dinners at noontime at luncheon rates. And the price included unlimited quantities of rolls. She advised one needy student to eat all his lunches at this famous restaurant, as she felt this one good meal a day would get him through the day, regardless of how skimpy his breakfast and supper might be. And she checked on him frequently to see that he was following her advice.

Great Leaders

Some great men and women have a tragic fear of other great people. Anyone whose abilities might overshadow their own or might threaten their positions is kept at a safe distance. But Henrietta Mears had no such qualms or reservations. She reveled in the gifts and talents of others, even when their abilities went beyond her own. And she was genuinely delighted when some young person would discover something she had not seen or could take one of her programs further than what she had envisioned herself.

Consequently, when outstanding preachers, teachers and leaders were in town, she encouraged her collegians to hear them. And she often invited visiting churchmen to take over her pulpit in the college department. Many times she welcomed them out to her home to spend a few days. Remembering that, as a girl, her family's table was always open to guest preachers and missionaries, she opened her own. She would then invite young people to her home to meet some Christian leader, perhaps to have dinner with him and then to sit in her beautiful living room and talk about spiritual things together.

In this way, Henrietta Mears was assisted in her task of training Christian leaders by some of the most able men and women of God in the land. During her early years at Hollywood Presbyterian Church, she frequently called upon her good friend, Dr. Harry Rimmer, to speak to the collegians about such concerns as evolution and the Bible, the miracles of Jesus, prophecy and Old Testament chronology.

Later, another famous preacher, Dr. J. Edwin Orr, helped greatly to establish her "preacher boys" in doctrine. His brilliant lectures on the existence of God, justification, sanctification and a host of other relevant topics helped many a confused collegian to crystalize his thoughts.

A man of astounding learning and practical insight was Dr. Wilbur M. Smith, who did much to ground students in the faith. His emphasis on the Resurrection and the deity of Christ was a major asset to the overall curriculum of the college department. Dr. Smith was then professor of English Bible at Fuller Theological Seminary. Teacher made full use of the school's professorial talents for the sake of her young theologues.

For many years, Dr. William Evans—the father of Dr. Louis H. Evans, then pastor of Hollywood's First Presbyterian Church —lived in semiretirement in Los Angeles. This noted Bible scholar contributed many hours a week to instructing Teacher's young people. And for several years the high school and college department deputation teams met in his home on Friday nights to listen to his discussions of the Bible and how to preach it.

Among the over 50 books on the Bible that Dr. William Evans wrote was *How to Prepare Sermons and Gospel Talks*. Many of Teacher's seminarians cut their first homiletical teeth on this work. So when the students met at his house for deputation training, they knew they were sitting at the feet of a homiletical expert. They listened earnestly as he told them how to preach at the jails and in the missions, how to use illustrations, how to give testi-

Dr. Louis H. Evans, Sr., who succeeded Dr. Stuart P. MacLennan as pastor of the First Presbyterian Church of Hollywood, is shown with his father, Dr. William Evans, a noted Bible scholar and teacher, and with Dr. Henrietta C. Mears at Forest Home.

monies and the like. His instruction even included how to put authority into one's voice.

"Dr. William"—who had written a book on how to memorize Scripture—had memorized the complete Bible in the *King James Version* and the whole New Testament in the *American Standard Version*. The young people would delight in giving him passages from either version to quote from memory. One week the college department scheduled a contest to see who would be first to memorize 1 Corinthians 15 in its entirety.

The following Sunday, Dr. William preached on this same passage and began his sermon by quoting from memory all 58 verses. His dedication to the Word of God inspired many of the youth to study his book and to begin their own memory programs. He shattered the myth that only younger students, not college people, are eager to memorize whole chapters of the Bible. For at Hollywood

Presbyterian Church, even the older folk were busy storing up the Word of God in their minds as well as in their hearts.

Dr. William Evans died on a Sunday morning at almost the very moment when the church service began. In the college department Teacher announced that their beloved mentor had stepped into eternity a few moments before. Then she said, "Fallen, fallen is one of the mighty men of Israel!"

Her lesson that day was on Elijah's ride to heaven in the fiery chariot. She spoke at length of the mantle the prophet threw to his assistant, Elisha, and she said, "I pray that Dr. Evans' mantle will fall upon some of you young men here today."

And the mantle did fall on many, for Henrietta Mears never allowed the pulpit to be viewed as the last resort of those who had failed in other professions. Just the opposite was true. She set the stage for God's call by making the Christian ministry exciting, adventurous, worthy, dignified, challenging and satisfying.

Her youth lived and worked in an atmosphere of spiritual giants whose powerful preaching greatly impacted their impressionable minds. Sunday after Sunday, at worship services of Hollywood Presbyterian Church, the oncoming generation of leaders —eager to hear, learn and grow—filled the front rows, for they had before them the very finest men of God as their examples. These future theologues looked at their leaders and saw virile, intelligent, purposeful men who were profoundly conscious of a great God. Through them, Teacher did all she could to make the pulpit attractive to the most active and ambitious young Christians.

Prayer Fellowship

Another aspect of the college department training program was the prayer fellowship for the leaders on Saturday mornings. To be a director in the department meant meeting certain obligations: be present at the Sunday morning Bible hour, attend a majority of the other meetings and be present at the Saturday morning prayer meetings at Teacher's home.

Henrietta scheduled these prayer times because she believed

the leaders of a group needed time apart from the other members to refuel and refresh themselves spiritually for the task of leadership. Sunday mornings she reserved for the college class as a whole; in the Sunday School hour, the average member would not find a speed beyond his own steady pace. But on Saturday mornings with the leaders isolated, she would let them run ahead at a fast spiritual clip. The driving momentum of the class as a whole was generated from the impetus of the Saturday prayer fellowships.

Neither executive planning sessions nor gab-fests, these Saturday morning meetings were intentional times of prayer. For years, right at 6 a.m., Teacher would already be on her knees as students trooped in to join her. Or she would have her well-marked copy of Oswald Chambers' devotional book, *My Utmost for His Highest*, turned to the page for the day. After reading the Word and with very little discussion, Teacher would ask for specific requests. She would then make a few brief remarks on the greatness of God and His willingness to answer believing prayers. Then down on their knees the group would go.

The praying had no formal pattern; each prayed as he felt led, some praying aloud several times in the course of the morning. And always they asked the Holy Spirit to be their leader.

Teacher encouraged the students to be specific. "Don't waste words on the Lord. Tell Him definitely what's on your mind."

As the group prayed on, latecomers would straggle in and quietly kneel with the others. And before they rose, there would be 20 or more students earnestly talking over the activities of the department of the Lord.

Teacher generally closed the prayer time. To hear her pray in this intimate fellowship was an unforgettable experience. She climbed right to the bastions of heaven and threw the doors open for a fuller view of God. Her prayers were filled with faith, as she claimed things from the Lord:

> *Now, Father, Thou hast promised that if we ask anything in Thy name and according to Thy will, we can expect it. First of all, we want to see Thy glory. We long*

to know the power of the resurrected Christ. We are tired of living humdrum, routine, empty Christian lives. Fill us with abundant life right now! We don't dare trust ourselves.

As the deputation team goes up to Fillmore this afternoon, go before them! Speak through them! Give them the abundance of the power of Thy Holy Spirit.

And we ask for the class tomorrow morning, for these 300 students who will be there to hear the Word. Give me wisdom to proclaim Thy truth as it ought to be proclaimed.

Now, Father, we believe Thy promises! We claim the victory which Thou has said Thou wilt give to us, that Christ may receive all the glory.

Teacher created a mood with her voice, her utter sincerity and her closeness with God. She was never formal with God. She just spoke to Him as a person speaks to a friend, without worrying about grammar or niceties.

The most prominent characteristic of her praying was her complete enthrallment with the person of Christ. She knew Him and He knew her; they were on speaking terms with each other and exercised this relationship freely.

Henrietta was never sentimental or weepy when she prayed, though at times she would be broken before the glory of God. But more often she was like Elijah commanding the fire down from heaven. So no one had any problem hearing her when she prayed, for she was not a timid person, even with God. Those present when she prayed sometimes got the distinct impression that she was ordering the Lord to do things.

One who experienced times of prayer with Henrietta commented later:

The wonderful thing about Henrietta, I think, was—above anything else, the way she prayed. Her relationship with God was so great and so believing.

> *Many's the time I would hear her pray, and we'd be*
> *faced with a problem, and she'd say, "Now God, I know*
> *you're busy, but we've got to have this fixed, and it's got*
> *to be done right away—not tomorrow, not next week,*
> *right away. Now get on to it and get it fixed!"*
> *You could almost hear God saying, "All right, Henri-*
> *etta, all right. I'll take care of it."*
> *And it would get fixed. Her faith was—almost like*
> *her hats—unbelievable.*

Henrietta would say, "My friends often wonder if I can hear the Lord speaking to me. Well, I suppose it must be the Lord, because I keep answering Him back."

When the Word of God was being read, Teacher was all concentration. She would lean back in her red leather armchair, her head resting on her hands, her eyes closed and her brow furrowed. Any phrase that especially moved her brought such responses as "Isn't that tremendous!" or "Now that's what we need to learn!" or she merely gave her own peculiar grunt which all present took to mean "Amen!"

These Saturday morning prayer meetings fed both spirits and bodies, but the spiritual food was usually more orthodox than the physical, for Henrietta loved outlandish combinations of food. The first time the young people attended one of these meetings, they rose to their feet at eight o'clock in the morning, hungry, to find a spread before them of grapefruit juice and strawberry shortcake. That was it, no more, no less. In later years, she switched to orange juice and rolls dripping with orange topping which she would sop up to the last delicious drop without any crumbs remaining on her plate.

To watch her eat was a study in abundant living. She was always proper, but never prissy, tempering her refinement and breeding with much gusto and speed. And the students loved it, as they sat around her beautiful glass-topped breakfast table, enjoying a fourth go-round of rolls and laughing and talking with abandon.

As with everything else she did in life, Henrietta Mears ate with genuine gusto. Here Teacher tackles a healthy hunk of watermelon at a feed put on by her collegians.

Personal Counseling

After breakfast, most of the students would have to leave. But some would continue to hang around, often until well into the afternoon, for personal discussions with Henrietta. She was always available to the individual members of her cabinet—her leaders in training—for counseling, and she accomplished much in their lives during these times with them.

Henrietta Mears believed in mass evangelism, but she also believed that leaders could be trained only one by one. She illustrated this point by saying, "If you want to fill a dozen milk bottles, you must not stand back and spray at them with a hose. You may get them wet, but you won't fill them. You must take them one by one."

Henrietta Mears at about midpoint in her career.

So Henrietta would sit for hours on Saturday afternoons, counseling first one student leader and then another. And it was understood that, when she was talking to a student, listening to his problems and dreams, they were not to be interrupted.

Teacher's skill as a trainer of leaders was most apparent during these times of counseling. She was both direct and restrained. She pulled no punches when encouraging a person to step out into new vistas of service. Her favorite story for a frustrated leader was that in Luke 5 of Jesus and His frustrated disciples who had fished all night and caught nothing. The Master exhorted them to "launch out into the deep" (v.4) for a more successful catch of fish.

Similarly, Henrietta loved to exhort youth to plunge into the deep and adventurous waters of faith to prove the promises of God. But she always refrained from defining options and possibilities for an individual or from confirming any choice as the absolute will of God. She left decisions and responsibilities for them to the individual.

In 1947, some university students in the San Francisco area organized themselves into a fellowship called Students Concerned. They were not Christians for the most part, but were seeking reality and an answer to the problems of the world. Students Concerned scheduled a conference and invited two of Henrietta Mears' young leaders to attend.

The two young men felt they should accept the invitation because it could prove an open door for them to share with these unconverted students what God was doing in their lives. But to go meant a disruption in their studies and in other personal commitments. So they came to Teacher's house one Saturday and, after the regular prayer meeting, asked her what they should do.

Her only reply was, "Well, fellows, let's pray about it."

So they prayed. Afterwards, they again asked her what they should do.

Teacher read a few verses from the Bible and again suggested they pray, which they did. But again the fellows asked her for a decision.

She said they should pray until they were absolutely convinced one way or another.

They continued to ask her to decide for them, and she continued to tell them to pray, never suggesting what she thought they should do. This procedure went on into the late afternoon, until finally the young men came to a resolute decision to go to the conference.

The choice was theirs. She had helped them make it only in so far as she encouraged them to seek the Lord's will for themselves. Despite being a person of decided opinions, Henrietta Mears was also a professional counselor and knew when and how to exercise restraint.

Reproducing Disciples

Legion are the individuals who found Christ under Henrietta Mears' ministry, who entered into the highly charged atmosphere of dedication and service that she created at Hollywood's First Presbyterian Church and who went on to serve in positions of Christian leadership all around the world. They preach from hundreds of pulpits, serve in schools, speak over radio and television, lead choirs, direct Sunday Schools and work on dozens of campuses. Their feet have trod on European streets, in African jungles, on South America's high mountain ranges, in the sweltering cities of India and in all parts of the globe.

Most important of all, they are reproducing their kind wherever they go, for they learned from their beloved Teacher that the true disciple trains other disciples to take his place. The combined ministries of her spiritual children extend far beyond what she did in Hollywood, continuing to the present.

And this was her greatest dream—that her work in Hollywood might be but a spark to ignite brightly burning fires in every nation of earth so that, in coming generations, multitudes might hear the Galilean's call and be saved.

Notes

1. David Benson was one of these young people. Even before he was aware of her interest in him, Henrietta Mears had recognized his potential while he was still in the fourth grade. She encouraged him spiritually over the years, and he accepted Christ as Savior and Lord before entering high school. Then, while still a freshman in college, David felt called to the ministry. He was graduated from UCLA with a Slavic major and did graduate work at Harvard University before transferring to Fuller Theological Seminary and graduating with a Bachelor of Divinity degree.

   A gifted musician and communicator, David went on to found Russia for Christ, a Christian mission for the purpose of evangelizing the USSR. He has written and published widely, and among the books he has authored is *Henrietta Mears and How She Did It,* a work which became the forerunner for this present biography of Dr. Mears.

2. Barbara Hudson Powers, *The Henrietta Mears Story* (Old Tappan, NJ: Fleming H. Revell Co., 1957), p. 135.

3. Ibid.

4. Quoted from *The Coming American* by Sam Walter Foss (1858-1911). Public domain.

5. Powers, *The Henrietta Mears Story,* p. 135.

6. Ibid., pp. 135-36.

TWELVE

"Give Me This Mountain"

I *f you place people in an atmosphere where they feel close to God and then challenge them with His Word, they will make decisions."*

"As soon as Teacher had hung up her hat and put her Bible down on her desk in her office in Hollywood Presbyterian Church, she started looking around for a place to which she could take the young people from her church for their summer conferences. Even as [her] Grandfather Everts was famed for his characteristic cry of 'Give me this mountain!' now his granddaughter started looking around for a mountain that she could possess."[1]

Many happenings among the youth of the First Presbyterian Church of Hollywood, as they grew up under the mentorship of Henrietta Mears, are associated in their minds with high points of decision. She wanted her young people to build up happy memories, so that their thoughts of God would be woven into the tapestries of their lives with threads of laughter, camaraderie, worship and fun. Many of those happenings, happy memories and high points of decision grew out of the camping experiences she provided the youth of her church. That was why she believed it was important that a young person's camping adventures should be filled with every wholesome pursuit, so that in future years, reminiscences of camp would excite recollections of fun and friends along with God and His high calling.

Switzer's Camp

The early years of camping were filled not just with adventure but with the unexpected. In 1929, Teacher took 125 collegians to Switzer's Camp in the San Bernardino Mountains east of Los Angeles. From the road up to the camp was a four-mile hike on foot, and Henrietta hiked right along with the rest of them the first year.

But after that, she found a four-footed animal—a pack mule—much more to her liking. The food supplies all had to be transported into camp by burro pack train. And to keep the butter from melting during the long, slow trip with the burros, one of the fellows always carried it in ahead on his back.

The moon would already be peeking over the top of the mountain as the first of the hikers arrived in camp and wound their way to the Stone Chapel on the point. The beams of flashlights

Switzer's Camp (nicknamed "Switzer-land" by some) in the San Bernardino Mountains, a forerunner to Forest Home, was accessible only by a four-mile hike over this trail. Henrietta Mears went in on foot the first year; after that she chose to ride in to camp on a donkey or a burro as she did here in September 1929.

revealed the remaining hikers still coming up the pathway across the canyon. Those gathered on the wall of Stone Chapel would sing out their favorite choruses and then listen for a reply from across the canyon.

The first part of camp to be seen and the last to be forgotten, this unique chapel stood out as clearly in memory as it did in actuality. Perched boldly on the lip of a ragged gorge, yet built into the solid rock of a mountainside, Stone Chapel was a parable of the Christian life, daring all, yet held fast and strong. The first roots of the great conference work undertaken by Henrietta Mears were planted in this place: here one young person accepted Christ as his Savior, another pledged her life to Christ, and a third heard the call to leave work and start training for the ministry.

Being the only adult at the Switzer's Camp conferences in 1929 and 1930, Henrietta did all the cooking, cleaning, counseling and challenging. Yet her spirit of gaiety and enthusiasm made the time together an unforgettable experience for everyone. But busy as she was conducting these conferences in the mountains, she also fulfilled her responsibility to her charges "down below," always returning to the church for the midweek college prayer meeting with the students gathered there.

Mount Hermon

Also in 1930, Teacher sent four delegates to check out a Mount Hermon Young People's Conference that she had heard about. This conference center was located in northern California, over 400 miles away, and the very distance lent enchantment. Teacher's Christian "spies" brought back such glowing reports of Mount Hermon that the next year 80 young collegians made the long trip, and after that no less than 150 found their way to that alluring spot.

A big parade was always held on one day during the Mount Hermon Young People's Conference. Parade participants drove eight miles to Santa Cruz and the ocean beaches. One year, not to

"Mount Hermon or Bust" was the slogan for Teacher and her fellow campers from the college department in the years before Forest Home was acquired. In this 1930 photo, Teacher is next to the girl sitting on the right fender of the car. The 800-mile round-trip to Mount Hermon and back was too great a distance for that camp to serve all the youth of the church, a concern that led to Henrietta Mears' search for a permanent campsite in southern California—the Forest Home Christian Conference Center.

be outdone by the young people, Henrietta, Ethel May and Dorothy Drew Choate—Dr. MacLennan's secretary—rode in the parade, outrageously made-up and costumed as comic characters in a ramshackle taxicab. With much blaring of horns, the parade wound its way down to the beach where the traffic-stopping trio had the nerve to enter a fabulous ice-cream parlor and order a round of wonderfully extravagant chocolate sundaes.

For many, Mount Hermon became a place of reflection and retrospection, repentance and renewal. Yet, though Mount Hermon had long been established and was well equipped, its great distance from Los Angeles precluded it from serving any but the church's college students.

Camp Bethel

Henrietta also tried other camp sites in an attempt to find a place that would be suitable for the increasing numbers of Sunday School youth. The obstacles she had to surmount were enormous, but her tenacity and determination readily overcame them.

Eventually she heard about Camp Bethel near San Dimas, close to Pomona. The site was accessible to Los Angeles, yet far enough away to discourage parents from dropping in to see their children at camp and leaving behind a bunch of homesick offspring. It was also far enough away to discourage her collegians from running up for a meeting instead of attending an entire conference. Yes, Camp Bethel held the possibility of being able to get the various age groups off by themselves for a period of time, enabling Teacher to do something spiritually constructive with them.

Camp Bethel also made possible the services of Bill Stahl. He was one of her boys who was studying to be a doctor, and during the summer months, he worked for a physician in nearby Pomona. "Why, of course, Bill can be our camp doctor," Henrietta decided. Bill's most serious case at camp, however, involved nothing more severe than that of a curious moth crawling into the ear of a little girl, making it necessary to awaken Bill about two o'clock one morning to still the insect's flapping wings and entice it from the frightened child's ear.

The reasonable proximity of Camp Bethel to Los Angeles, Henrietta felt, also made it possible for David and Clyde—who had to attend at least one summer session at the University of Southern California—to attend conferences at camp. "They can be at camp during the afternoon for the recreation time and at night for the evening meetings," she pointed out, "And then they can leave early in the morning for their classes. They can study on the way in—one can drive while the other one reads the material aloud for both. It is certainly fortunate that they will need to take the same courses."

Yes, the travel distance was fine. But the facilities were another matter entirely. The camp site itself was one large dust bowl. And the swimming pool was little bigger than a large size bathtub. The main auditorium—when not occupied by humans—did double duty as a chicken coop.

The facilities were hardly ideal for holding a young people's conference, but Teacher held them anyway. Sister Margaret, working with next to nothing, usually managed the kitchen for the conferences. All her supplies had to be hauled in by car, with new supplies being purchased as needed in nearby La Verne during the week. Removing the back car's seat increased the car's hauling capacity and protected the upholstery at the same time.

During the early years of camping, Henrietta would bear almost the full responsibility for the spiritual tone of the conferences. As the time for each conference approached, she besought the Lord to show her what He wanted it to accomplish, what emphasis He wanted it to have, what direction it should take. At such times, she claimed Philippians 2:13, "For it is God which worketh in you both to will and to do of his good pleasure."

She not only served the camps as organizer, but also as purchasing agent, speaker and disciplinarian. And no matter how intensively she prepared, each camp invariably demanded of her decisions for which no amount of forethought could suffice. Fortunately, her remarkable ability to encounter unexpected situations and to come up with solutions enabled her to cope with the many problems that inevitably arose. So, whatever the crisis of the day proved to be, she was always equal to the challenge.

The young scientist. Teacher's boys began telling her about Bud Moon, a young fellow with whom they had become acquainted, who demonstrated all kinds of scientific marvels—and all the while speaking from the Bible. They urged Henrietta to invite this young scientist to come and speak at Camp Bethel. She invited Bud and he accepted.

He delighted everyone in camp as he shone his "magic light" round the walls of the chicken-coop auditorium. Multicolored jewels of light would spring into sight and glisten, as the light's rays reached farther and farther into the corners of the large room.

Bud also demonstrated a new kind of machine called a wire recorder with which he could record his voice. Then he would play it back and let them hear what he had recorded. But after he erased the word, not a sound came forth from the wire. He reminded his listeners of Matthew 12:36-37 where we are told that we shall give account of every idle word spoken, and of Luke 19:40 where Jesus said that, if the people had held their peace and not shouted their hosannas, the very stones would have cried out.

The campers envisioned every stone holding idle words they had said and were greatly relieved when Bud explained that God would erase all the evil they had spoken—or done—when they accepted His Son, Jesus Christ, as their Savior (see Acts 3:19).

All of Bud's scientific displays were calculated to illustrate and reinforce some biblical theme. So Teacher delighted in his attempts to bring "sermons from science" to her youth, even though there were times she feared this imaginative young scientist would send the entire camp sky high in an explosion during his demonstrations.

Years later when Bud Moon became known as Dr. Irwin A. Moon, director of the Moody Institute of Science, Henrietta would phone him and say, "Now, Dr. Moon, for old times' sake and for the many moments I have sat on the edge of being blown to bits, I want you to do this for me."

He laughed heartily, knowing she had never been in safer hands, and he always accepted. When Henrietta was once at the Mayo Clinic in Rochester, she chose Dr. Moon to take her place at an important missionary luncheon to bring a word picture of the world as he had seen it in his many trips abroad since those early days at Camp Bethel.

The 1936 flood. Teacher often commented that the spiritual foundations of Camp Bethel had to be secure, for the flimsy portable structures on their stilts most certainly were not. During the winter conference of 1936, torrents of rain fell all one night and water rose rapidly in the camp. Campers in their canvas-sided cabins could hear the rush of water under and around the cabins.

Henrietta and Mother Atwater, sharing a cabin, were up all night, keeping their gas stove going to keep out the chill and praying that the camp would be spared from serious harm. They had no idea how serious the flood was, as they prayed, nor how close it came, but they could hear the roar of flood waters racing around them.

Daylight revealed devastation all around them, yet the camp itself had escaped. Still, high water covered all the campsite except for a small island of elevated ground on which the dining hall sat marooned. This one dry place was large enough to handle the entire group of campers, but how to get there?

Henrietta ingeniously proposed parking all the cars side by side to form a bridge, so the campers could walk from one to the other without having to wade through the foot-deep water. The only flaw in the plan was that the campers did not possess quite enough cars to span the newly formed sea between them and the dining hall.

Some of the fellows gallantly offered to wade the remaining distance through the muddy water, carrying the girls across on their backs. The arrangement moved along nicely, with the girls arriving safely in the dining hall, until one hapless fellow stepped into a submerged hole and went down. Both he and his luckless passenger went sprawling headlong into the muddy mix.

As both boy and girl, their clothes miserably soaked and covered with chocolate-brown mud, struggled to right themselves, he stutteringly hastened to explain, "Honest, Miss Mears, I didn't mean to do it." And the girl, so suddenly a brunet, was left with the problem of restoring her long locks to their former blond color again. Fortunately, neither one of them caught pneumonia.

The redemptive disciplinarian. Henrietta Mears had a redemptive attitude toward discipline. Only in the most extreme case would she ever ask a parent to come and take his son home from camp. Always she would try to rehabilitate a delinquent by keeping him in the group.

Her guiding principle was: "An incorrigible is not necessarily impossible." But this philosophy, positive as it was, did not mean that Teacher precluded punishment when it was warranted. Then she could be firm.

Henrietta met every situation with a fresh and creative spontaneity. Rather than rigidly relying on a set of changeless rules, she sought and found guidance in the moment-by-moment leading of the Holy Spirit. She recognized that laws are necessary in human relationships, but she also understood that, when dealing with youth, the dynamics of their growing personalities can be stifled by an indiscriminate application of an inflexible code. "The letter killeth, but the spirit giveth life," (2 Cor. 3:6) was the creative principle of Henrietta Mears discipline.

Less than a mile away from Camp Bethel was a beautiful little park used for picnics and ball games. But for individual use, this park lay outside the established bounds of the camp. At the beginning of each conference, Teacher would warn one and all, "If you decide that you just have to go to that little park down the road, just pack your suitcases and keep on going toward home."

Some boys went to the park—once! When they returned, Henrietta was waiting for them. Momentarily, she remembered an incident in her Minneapolis church when a church worker told two boys who had turned the church balcony into a racetrack to get out and stay out. And that is what they did. Did they ever again enter another church? Teacher doubted that they had.

So what was the appropriate step for her to take in this situation? She was aware that most Hollywood youth had a scanty spiritual heritage, if any, and that disciplined behavior was not their most natural attribute. She had no tradition here on which to build, for camping was previously almost unknown at the church.

She decided that she would have to set her own norms of discipline. And these she would have to bring into being as the moment called for them. And this was one of those moments!

The errant lads were brought into her cabin. She asked them if they had understood when she told them the park was out of bounds. They answered affirmatively. Then she carefully explained that it was not against her they had sinned, but against the Lord, and that it was not her they owed an apology, but to Him.

This spiritual application of a disciplinary problem had its effect. The boys knelt with her and weepingly sought God's forgiveness. Their hearts were filled with joy as they realized that He forgave them, and His love was so real to them that they became sparks igniting the faith of many others.

Another time some of her youth were involved in a misdemeanor. One of the fellows, as he was preparing to go to Teacher's cabin, was warned by his brother, "Watch out, Bill. Don't let Miss Mears pray with you, for if you do, you'll be a goner!"

Bill and his friend came to Teacher, and the door was closed behind them. "Boys, we are going to pray about what you did this afternoon," she said. Bill was filled with great satisfaction, for hadn't he been warned exactly what to look out for?

As they knelt, he literally held his fists up in front of his face, ready to defend himself against Teacher's prayer. He had resolved that when Henrietta began to pray, he was going to run out, leave the camp and never come back to the Sunday School.

A minute passed in silence. Five minutes passed. Then 10. And teacher remained absolutely silent. The anxiety in Bill's heart grew as he sought to understand what she was trying to do.

Then Don, the other culprit, broke the tension as he blurted out, "Lord, if there is anything in my life that is keeping the Holy Spirit from blessing this conference, show it to me." Bill was thunderstruck. His own friend, his companion in guilt, had been the first to pray!

Still Teacher remained silent. Bill was overcome with shame. For the first time in his life, he realized that he had the ability of free choice: He could say no to God if he wanted to, and no one, not even Teacher, would question his decision.

"What about my life?" he thought. "God wants me and I am holding back." His fists shook as he fought to control his tears. Finally, he cried out, "God, here is my life. If you want me to be a garbage collector for the honor and glory of Jesus Christ, I'll be one."

Years later, Bill Dunlap stood before his congregation and retold this incident. "My life was changed from that moment on. My father was the founder and president of 42 department stores. I was slated to be his heir.

"And if Miss Mears had prayed one word that afternoon, I would have left the camp and today would be in the business world. But she kept still and allowed God to speak to us, and I learned then that I was not responsible to her, but to Christ. And that is why I am in the ministry."[2]

A few years ago, a fad among teenagers was to see how many human bodies could be stuffed into a telephone booth. One night, some of Henrietta's first teenage campers tried a variation in their cabin of this unique human packaging concept. Late that night, a great deal of noise was coming from one cabin of boys who apparently had no great need for sleep. Except for them, the camp had long since settled down.

Realizing the noise would not stop unless she got up and spoke to the transgressors, Henrietta rolled out of bed, pulled her red leather jacket on over her pink nightgown and proceeded through the darkness to the boys' cabin. Suddenly, at the height of their hilarity, a penetrating, stentorian voice cut through the night: "Boys!"

Someone inside whispered, "It's Miss Mears, you guys!" as if all didn't know that already. "Everyone be quiet!"

"If I hear another sound out of this cabin, you will all go home first thing in the morning. You need your rest. We all need our rest. Now, I want absolute silence!"

And she waited. Not knowing whether she was actually still outside their door, they remained silent. She thought she heard a slight shuffling sound, but not a voice was raised. Satisfied that all would be well, Henrietta slowly walked back to her cabin.

One of the more courageous boys—who eventually became one of her seminaries and later a minister—revealed to Teacher what had been going on in the cabin the night she descended on them and ordered them to be quiet. They had been busy making a sandwich of boys and mattresses—a mattress and a boy, a mattress and a boy—right up to the ceiling. When she called out to them and told them she didn't want to hear another word out of any of them, they were almost suffocating. But they knew she meant every word she said, and no one wanted to go home in the morning.

So one by one, they came off the heap, from the top layer down, unstacking boys and mattresses from ceiling to floor. As each boy climbed off the pile, he dragged his mattress with him. That was the scuffling noise she had heard. Otherwise, the entire operation was completed in total silence.

Through the years afterward, Teacher always recalled this incident with great delight. "All I know," she would say, "is that there were a lot of good ministers smashed between mattresses that night, for every single one of them went on to seminary. I don't know why it is, but it seems the most incorrigible boys make the best ministers."[3]

The prayer wrestlers. One evening at camp, some of Teacher's more earnest college men told her they were determined to pray until God would reveal Himself to them and they would see His glory. Never discouraging them for a moment, Henrietta simply cautioned them, saying, "Suppose God answers you, as He did Moses: 'I will do this thing also that thou hast spoken: for thou hast found grace in my sight, and I know thee by name' (Exod. 33:17). Are you ready to face the consequences? Make yourselves ready to do whatever God may ask you to do."

The young men left her and, taking one of the paths away from camp, walked to a dry river bed. Dropping down on their knees there, they besought God to hear them and to reveal Himself to them. Into the morning hours they prayed, wrestling with God, until He did come to them. They knew God was in that place. The light of His presence was manifest in each face as they returned that next morning to rejoin the others.

The honest doubter. Total darkness surrounded Camp Bethel that night. The stars studding the heavens shone in all their majesty against an immense field of black. And the campfire blazed and blinked, casting great dancing shadows, as one camper after another stepped forward to give his testimony and to throw a stick into the flames.

At the end of the line stood Bob, a great hulking figure of a man. As his turn came and he stepped up to the fire, every eye focused on him. He began to speak, slowly and softly, yet powerfully, explaining that he was not convinced of those spiritual matters about which everyone else seemed so definite and certain. Unable to accept these things by faith, he still cast his stick into the fire, but turned and walked out into the night "to seek truth," he said.

Before the stunned campers could recover, Teacher was on her feet, praying for Bob and endeavoring to give the others some assurance of his state of mind. She had two facts where Bob was concerned that she clung to tenaciously. She knew him to be utterly and completely honest. And she had the Scripture she often repeated to his mother to give her the security she needed: "Train up a child in the way he should go: and when he is old, he will not depart from it" (Prov. 22:6).

Solidly placing her faith in the promise God had given through Solomon, she prayed—and waited—for Bob at least to get older. She knew he had a brilliant mind and, as a child, had memorized much Scripture. She asked the Lord to recall it to his mind and reveal the meaning to him.

Out of Henrietta's sight, but never out of her heart or prayers, Bob went on to study at the University of Oxford, England. He excelled in his courses and in athletics as Teacher knew he would. But it was the news of the bull sessions he engaged in that interested her most. Bob was a great one for debate and would take either side to spark a discussion. Yet the word that came back was that he always took the side of Scripture in any debate. God was working!

An avid mountain climber, Bob could not resist the pull of the Continent, so near at hand across the English Channel. If he saved and scrimped, bicycled through Europe and lodged inexpensively at youth hotels, he could just cover the cost of a climb before returning home for the summer.

At his destination, the Matterhorn in the Swiss Alps beckoned, its eternal snowy cap reaching 14,730 feet into the heavens. He arose early one morning to go out and watch a group as they got ready for a climb. Safely tied to each other, the hikers pushed forward, and the fascination of it all drew him on.

Lacking the finances to join the group—his honesty would not permit him to associate himself with them—he followed at a good distance. He had no thought of going on the climb, but, as though he were in a dream, he soon realized he had passed the point where one is still an onlooker. Now he was a participator, though the other hikers were nearly out of sight. He was scantily clad and inadequately shod in sneakers, but it was now impossible for him to turn around and go back alone.

Up into the lucent mists he climbed, exulting in the handiwork of nature, yet not daring to take a moment to enjoy it. Like an angry giant whose domain was being transgressed, the mountain began to fight back, closing in on the lone figure, now inching along with only fingers for spikes and nerves for ropes. Finally the jealous giant had Bob in his trap, for behind him lay an impossible descent; before him an impassible crevasse.

For a few icy moments, he looked into the giant's maw. There hung the rope on which he would have to swing out over that bottomless abyss to touch down on the other side. Surveying his chances, he knew his cold hands might not even hold the rope, even if his arch was sufficient to reach the opposite ledge.

As he watched the sun declining toward darkness, he began to realize he was not alone, and this chasm was there to test not his physical prowess, but his spiritual potential. "God, if you help me make this, I'll serve you until I die," he prayed, and with that he leaped out over the abyss. The giant growled with frustration as the young climber fell into the dirt on the other side, sobbing with relief, gratitude—and faith.

But to remain immobile for long would mean to freeze to the spot, so on he trudged. He caught up with the group of hikers just as they were taking time out to rest. Amazed to see this lone hiker arrive in their midst and to hear his story, they insisted that he join their group for the return hike.

God continued working in His mysterious ways His wandering son to teach. Bob returned to California the summer following his climbing experience, and a girl persuaded him to go up to camp for a day of the College Labor Day Weekend Conference (by that time already being held at Forest Home). Once again, it was the night to voice decisions made during the camp. As the meeting moved along, Bob was once more in the line.

Sitting on the edge of her chair, Henrietta, along with those who had witnessed the Camp Bethel walkout, wondered what Bob would do this time. Once again throwing a stick on the fire, Bob told how he had gone out from a similar campfire in search of truth and how he had found that the only way to discover truth is by faith, simply believing God—the very thing he could not understand before. Now he was back, to start experiencing faith as a little child and to learn that even "if we believe not, yet he abideth faithful" (2 Tim. 2:13).

Instead of returning to Oxford where he still had a scholarship, Bob chose to attend Princeton Theological Seminary. He had not decided that God had called him to the ministry; he just wanted to learn more about the faith that now was in him. He filled out his application so frankly and so honestly that then-president, Dr. John Mackay, was perplexed as to why this fellow was interested in attending seminary. Not until Teacher gave assurance that Bob would cause no dissension in the ranks was he admitted.

With the lost beliefs of his childhood reforming into a mature confidence in God, the young seeker took up his studies with transformed dedication. On the mountaintop, he had seen the glory of his Creator, not in a flash of over-powering brilliance, but in the Almighty's ability to control circumstances and to humble a doubting heart.

Completing seminary, he entered the Presbyterian ministry, becoming a chaplain in the navy during World War II. When Henrietta took a year's leave of absence from the Hollywood Presbyterian Church on account of her eyes, it was to this man's direction that she committed her Sunday School. Bob Ferguson led the work on, inspiring his co-workers, instructing the teachers and insuring continuity.

Forest Home

The conferences continued at Camp Bethel, at Mount Hermon and at a Camp Radford, but none of these sites was adequate for the active camping program that Henrietta envisioned for the church. In the summer of 1937, while holding a high school conference at Camp Radford, Henrietta said to Cyrus Nelson, the conference dean, "The other day Bill Irwin phoned to tell me that I should drive up to see a privately owned resort in the San Bernardino Mountains called Forest Home. He thinks this might be something we could use. When we drive in to the bank this afternoon, let's find out where it is and go up."

William Irwin was a good friend of Henrietta's; his children were in her Sunday School. He knew how long she had been looking for a campsite, but all had been either too rundown, had no buildings and would cost too much to get started or had an asking price that was exorbitant. Finishing their business at the bank, they started out to locate Forest Home Resort, as it was known.

An impossible dream. From the answers they received to their questions, Forest Home apparently had been *the* resort in that area for many years. As they approached the tree-shaded highway coming into Forest Home, they were impressed. The coffee shop, gas station and lovely cabins in the circle by the fishpond looked inviting. Then Cy turned right, up past the dining room, the soda fountain, the round house and the beautiful lodge.

They were overwhelmed by the grandeur of the setting, the magnificent stonework and expensive timbers. Excited, but ever practical, Henrietta said, "Don't even bother to stop, Cy. Just turn to the left of that round house and go on back down the highway. I know we can't afford all of this," and she gave a sweep of her arm. "This is just ridiculous. The buildings alone are far too elaborate for our pocketbooks, and certainly we can't begin to pay for the land."

And so, back they went to the responsibilities of the high school conference that awaited them at Camp Radford, dismissing Forest Home completely from their minds.

Back home once more and settling into the work at the church, Henrietta had not had time to telephone Bill Irwin before he called her again. "Did you go to look at Forest Home, Henrietta?" he inquired.

"Oh, Bill, that is the most elegant place I ever saw, but I just knew we couldn't afford it, so we didn't even get out of the car. We just drove up past all those stone buildings and turned back on the highway at the round house. What could we ever do to run such a big place, even if we could afford to buy it—and we can't afford it!"

A reasonable offer. But Bill Irwin had some interesting facts to reveal. The owner was very sick and quite old, and he was facing major surgery. It was not at all certain he could survive the operation. His son did not want to chance the possibility of having to meet the inheritance tax on a place valued by the bank at $350,000. The tax could wipe him out completely.

Bill thought that a reasonable offer would be considered. The "reasonable offer" was $50,000, so an option on the property was taken.

Surveying their situation after the initial excitement of the option had died down, Henrietta wondered how even this figure—low in comparison to the investment and value of the place, but high in those times of deep economic depression—could be met. *But this is the moment for action and not for speculation,* she thought. *The option will close before I know it. I must get people up to see Forest Home.*

And so the news of the option on the campsite was scattered abroad, and friends invited to come on a particular day "and see beautiful Forest Home in the San Bernardino Mountains which some day might be our Christian Conference Center." Interest was instant! Henrietta's enthusiasm was always catching. People responded to the invitation in great numbers and all rejoiced in this beauty spot, just a mile above sea level and within easy driving distance of Los Angeles. So impressed were some that they began to come to Henrietta and insist that she put their names down on certain cabins, just in case she decided to sell them to pay for the grounds.

The day ended, everyone else went home, and Henrietta was left alone to think. *If I do let those folks buy these cabins, what will I use for the children and young people? The money gained would not even pay the price being asked, let alone leave any over to use for building dormitories. I wouldn't be as well off as I would be if I were starting with only the ground. I'd have people occupying the places my young people should have, and a debt, and still no place to hold a conference. Besides, winter is almost here, and no one is interested in Forest Home now. I guess we had better let the option go.*

And so they did let the option go. Their other responsibilities rolled on and on and over them. The months came and went. And no one seemed to remember Forest Home at all.

A divine intervention. But God, as it were, was standing on the highest peak overlooking Forest Home Valley. He beheld below Him tens of thousands of children playing, singing and praying. He saw youth lifting their hands to Him in dedication, resolved to go from the conference grounds to preach His gospel to the world. He heard glad choruses from innumerable hearts, ringing across the glens and down the canyons. He saw here an auditorium filled with hundreds of His faithful and there a chapel where children were kneeling in prayer.

And on the mountaintop, God said, "I want this place for My glory to dwell in." So He reached out to the sky and called around Him the thunderclouds. All day and into the night they gathered, billowing like the smoke from an immense furnace. A moment of hushed suspense fell over the earth as nature waited for the command.

Then the God of glory thundered, His voice shaking giant boulders from their beds and causing towering pines to bend to the ground in worship. Bolts of lightning crashed like heavenly spears from cloud to cloud, unlocking the suspended floods that now swept earthward like steeds racing to war. Down the torrents fell, forming into a gigantic wall of water.

The welling tide, bolstered by enormous rocks hurling along in its waters, uprooted trees, crashed against buildings and cut into mountainsides. From wall-to-wall of the valley, the roaring current leaped onward, its unbridled fury leaving disaster in its wake. On the Forest Home Resort property, three cabins down by the stream were washed away and a fourth was left hanging over the bank. Yet, though the surrounding countryside lay in ruins, the rest of the campsite remained relatively unharmed.

In the silence after the storm, the shrill tones of the telephone bell could be heard. Bill Irwin was calling and asking to speak to Henrietta Mears. The son of the owner of the resort grounds had phoned and offered to sell Forest Home for $30,000!

A realized goal. What excitement followed! Seminarians Dave Cowie and Bob Munger encouraged Teacher to buy, pleading that they would help her through the coming years.

"Oh, I know you won't," she rejoined. "You fellows will go away to your pastorates, you'll get married, and I'll be left to run the camp. God always demands one person to be responsible, and I must know if this is His will."

The following days were spent in seeking divine confirmation. Henrietta finally received it when she read the Lord's promise to Joshua: "Now therefore arise, go over this Jordan, thou, and all this people, unto the land which I do give to them....Every place that the sole of your foot shall tread upon, that have I given unto you" (Josh. 1:2-3).

In these words, she found her answer and the assurance of the seal of God's approval. A nonprofit corporation was formed known as Forest Home, Incorporated. The founding members of the board were Henrietta C. Mears, John Hormel, Dr. Stewart P.

MacLennan, William Irwin and L. David Cowie. The papers were signed, and God had His conference center.

"That I may know Him, and the power of His resurrection, and the fellowship of His sufferings, being made conformable unto His death" (Phil. 3:10)—this was the first message to ring out from the pulpit of Forest Home Christian Conference Center, preached by Dr. Cortland Meyers of Boston.

That declaration by Paul was the platform on which Forest Home's ministry was to be built—the crucified and resurrected Christ living His life through the believer. "To know Christ" became the prayer of hundreds of thousands of people, who, beginning with the opening conference, traveled to Forest Home in search of the meaning of life. They found it there in Jesus Christ.

Notes

1. Barbara Hudson Powers, *The Henrietta Mears Story* (Old Tappan, NJ: Fleming H. Revell Co., 1957), p. 173.
2. Among the many opportunities that have come to him in the ministry, Rev. Bill Dunlap was privileged to preach the gospel from the pulpit to then President Dwight D. Eisenhower.
3. Powers, *The Henrietta Mears Story,* p. 174

THIRTEEN

Going Up the Mountain

*T*he other day a young business executive came to my cabin at Forest Home and said, 'I don't know what it is, Miss Mears, but since I have come here, I have felt a great need in my heart.'

"Within a few moments he found Christ as his personal Savior. That's why we established Forest Home—that men and women might have a place from the noise and tension of the city to meet God."

HENRIETTA MEARS ENDED EVERY CONFERENCE AT FOREST HOME WITH A great bonfire in Victory Circle, the camp's outdoor amphitheater. Campers came forward at this closing campfire and placed small sticks in the fire to represent Christian decisions they had made, committing themselves to the fire of the Holy Spirit. A Book of Remembrance was signed by each person after he had placed his bit of wood in the fire and publicly given his decision. As a result, thousands of campers ever after traced their spiritual histories back to the signatures they wrote in the Book of Remembrance and to the campfires preceding those signings.

Because he had been invited, a certain young man once attended an annual New Year's conference at Forest Home. He had been raised in a moral atmosphere but had no great consciousness of guilt, although he was looking for direction in his

Night after night in Forest Home's famed Victory Circle, a fire's glow reflected on the white stones of the cross and illuminated young men and women stepping one by one from the shadows into the firelight to cast small bits of wood into the flames, symbolizing in this way their decisions for Christ.

After making a public profession of Christ in Victory Circle, each young person moved to a small table nearby where Teacher presided over a *Book of Remembrance.* Believing that writing one's name down after making a public decision helped to crystallize it in the mind, Henrietta Mears would hand the individual a pen with an invitation to sign the book, quietly encouraging him or her with a gentle, "God bless you." This scene was repeated many, many times in Teacher's lifetime.

life. In the meantime, he, along with everyone else at camp, was having a good time.

On the last day of the weekend, Jack was in the coffee shop for a bite to eat just as the final service of the conference was beginning. With him were some other friends who also were not too interested in religion. Suddenly the coffee shop door flew open and Teacher boomed out, "All right, everyone up to the campfire service. Come on, Jack, you can always eat later on. Everyone come along now. We're all going to the service!"

As Jack sat in the testimony service listening to others relate what had happened in their lives, he felt a compulsion to say something. So, when his turn came, he said, "I don't know what this is all about, but I feel like all of you are on a boat leaving, and here I am on the shore, watching you wave good-bye. I would like to be on the boat with you. I want what I see and hear in this place."

Henrietta quoted to him Christ's invitation: "Behold, I stand at the door and knock; if any man hear my voice, and open the door, I will come in to him, and will sup with him, and he with me" (Rev. 3:20). As she explained to him what these words meant, the young man accepted the Savior right then and there.

As he returned to his seat, he closed his eyes and prayed for the first time in his life—not for himself but for his friend sitting next to him, that he might also open his heart to Christ. When Jack looked up, he saw his friend standing in the testimony line, and he wept as he heard him confess his faith too. Jack Franck went on to become one of Henrietta Mears' most faithful staff assistants at the Hollywood church, and later on he took over the leadership of Forest Home, being instrumental there in leading hundreds of other people to Christ.

A Camping Philosophy

Henrietta Mears had a definite philosophy of camping, the crux of which could be summed up in one word: decision. If the Sunday School was the place where people were built up in the faith, then the camp was where they made their decisions.

Because Henrietta expected people to make decisions at Forest Home, most of what she said and did there was for that purpose. The one word "decision" permeated every meeting of every conference. Consequently, not only did thousands make declarations for Christ under Teacher's ministry at Forest Home, but innumerable Christians decided on life careers while there. No college conference ever went by without several young men resolving to enter the ministry or to spend their days on the mission field.

One of the elders at Hollywood Presbyterian Church said to Henrietta, "I don't understand it. Doesn't anyone around here ever decide anything important except at Forest Home?"

Her answer was simple: "If you place people in an atmosphere where they feel close to God and then challenge them with the Word, they will make decisions."

And they did!

Whatever theme was selected for a camp week, three concerns were foundational: (1) the acceptance of Christ as Savior and Lord; (2) the growth of the Christian; and (3) a world vision. The first was the milk for babes, the second was meat for the mature, and the third was for the task ahead—the energy for which was supplied by the first two.

This same three-pronged approach was true for every age level, though the fundamentals were applied differently—and appropriately—for each age level.

Christian camping was first of all Christian. A conference for children was not just a week of baby-sitting in the mountains; it was a golden opportunity to teach them the wonders of God's plan for their lives.

The Bible hour, whether for children or for adults, was the pillar around which the rest of the edifice was built. This hour was usually given priority in the morning when minds were fresh. Sometimes not only were group discussions coordinated with it, but so were printed materials, notebooks, suggested readings, questions times and the like.

From the high school camps on down the children met by cabins and discussed what had just been brought out by the conference Bible teacher. Although the platform hours could be shifted to satisfy immediate needs, the Bible hour was rarely changed. It anchored the other hours at home port.

A Two-relationship Emphasis

Two relationship emphases—the individual with his God, and the individual to his church—pervaded every activity at Forest Home.

The individual with his God. Henrietta saw, first of all, the advantage of taking people aside into the marvels and mysteries of God's creation and there allowed the Creator to speak to them about Himself. Surrounded by grandeur of His handiwork, they realized there the majesty of God. "God must have time to talk to people," Henrietta insisted. "In the city a person may hear one or two sermons a week. But at camp he is face-to-face with God for seven days." Her starting point then was to take advantage of the restful, quiet, inspiring seclusion of nature in order to introduce boys and girls, men and women to Jesus Christ.

Wanting each person to have that personal encounter and believing that once a person came face-to-face with Christ, the Lord would convince him of his need for salvation, Henrietta stepped into each conference with expectancy and excitement, igniting those about her. "God is walking in this place," she would declare. "This is holy ground. Let us be still and listen to Him."

From this expectancy sprang her confidence that she should give God the opportunity to work in the lives of those present. She believed that God must have freedom to speak to individuals, and that every plan should be submitted to His leading.

This waiting upon God's direction related both to those who did not as yet know Christ as Savior and to those who were already Christians but who had no definite goals to live for. Each conference, in other words, was a Damascus Road experience, where people encountered Jesus as Savior and Lord, where they, as did Paul, asked the crucial question: "Lord, what wilt thou have me to do?" (Acts 9:6).

The individual to his church. Despite all her emphasis on the individual's relationship to a personal God, she never lost sight of the camp's relationship to the Church universal or that of the individual to his own church. Forest Home was never envisioned as a denominational conference center or as one belonging to a single church, for its purpose was to enhance the Christian's effectiveness in his home church—whichever one that might be. Because of this emphasis, a deep loyalty was built up among ministers who through the years visited Forest Home. They saw their members returning as vital witnesses and more eager to work in their churches.

Since the life of the church should be enhanced by a conference, the day on which a conference began was vitally important. Many Christian camps begin a week-long conference on Saturday or Wednesday. But Miss Mears did not want her camps to run competition with the Sunday School or the worship service. So she insisted that her camps begin on Sunday afternoon.

Her reasons were: First, the conferee had the benefit of attending his own Sunday School and church. Second, beginning a camp on Sunday afternoon and ending on Saturday left no opportunity for a person to get out of the habit of going to church. Third, starting a conference on Sunday afternoon allowed it to begin on a higher plane. The conferees had already been to Sunday School and to a worship service before the conference began.

At the First Presbyterian Church of Hollywood on Sundays when the large conferences were beginning, Dr. Evans would direct his pulpit remarks to those who that afternoon were going "up the mountain," thus setting the spiritual tone for the coming week even before the conferees left the city. And those remaining behind felt a part of what was going to happen.

Finally, the problem of Sunday recreation was avoided. If some congregations believed that sports should not be permitted on Sundays, while others saw no issue here, spending Sunday afternoon on the trip to Forest Home, with the opening meeting Sunday evening, circumvented any possible offense without raising the question.

A Broad-based Fellowship

This sensitivity to the needs and outlooks of varying churches led Henrietta to build conferences on the broadest possible base consistent with her loyalty to Christ. Any one church's peculiarities that might needlessly offend other participating groups were not allowed, and with none was she more consistent than her own people.

When her students were still attending Mount Hermon conferences, Henrietta constantly lectured them, "Here, you are not the

Henrietta Mears meets at Forest Home with James McMillan of Van Nuys, California who was then the newly appointed general manager of the conference grounds.

First Presbyterian Church of Hollywood; you are the Mount Hermon Young People's Conference." And at Forest Home—even though groups from her church often outnumbered all other churches combined—Henrietta integrated leaders from the other churches into the center of the programming and tried not to let her people monopolize the conference.

The camps thereby energized each church that took part in

them. And since most of the Forest Home camp weeks, especially the larger ones, were interchurch and, therefore, interdenominational, the Christian community in southern California was solidified more than would otherwise have been possible. Many had friends in other churches whom they first met at Forest Home.

This interchurch fellowship led to joint evangelistic efforts in the area, but it did not lead to proselytizing. If a person came to Forest Home a Methodist, he left a Methodist. Those who knew Henrietta's thinking never believed that Forest Home was the exclusive property of the First Presbyterian Church of Hollywood. It was her vision that it belonged in spirit to all churches which wanted to use it for the glory of Christ. Forest Home, consequently, had no denominational ties or leanings.

One of the prominent Baptist ministers in southern California said one year, "I have 22 of my young people studying in Baptist schools for the ministry. They all made their decisions at Forest Home."

Because the camps were interchurch and interdenominational, they were also interracial. All college groups were invited to the College Briefing Conferences, including those with students from Afro-American, Japanese, Chinese, Hispanic and other churches.

Present at one of the early College Briefing Conferences, soon after the end of World War II, were a young man who had flown in Hitler's *Luftwaffe,* another who had flown with the Japanese military and a third who had been in the United States Air Force and had bombed Germany. None knew of the presence of the others at the camp, and none was a Christian. At the final meeting around the campfire, the German stood to accept Christ. The other two were so moved that they stood by him and also received the Lord. Then the three of them, with their arms around each other and the tears streaming down their faces, sang with all those present:

> *Blest be the tie that binds*
> *Our hearts in Christian love.*
> *The fellowship of kindred minds*
> *Is like to that above.*[1]

A Renewed Spirit

The Forest Home conferences served as a catalyst for many a revival in local churches and on campuses, and the spirit of cooperation displayed in the conferences continued as people returned to their churches. Not the least who benefited were the pastors, Sunday School superintendents, teachers and youth directors.

Many churches experience an annual summer slump: enthusiasm sags as ministers and lay leaders go on their vacations, and programs, choirs and Sunday School classes are recessed. But for those congregations that took advantage of what Forest Home had to offer, just the opposite was true. Camps played such a dominant role at the First Presbyterian Church of Hollywood that summer was the high point of the year.

In fact, so much was happening from June onward that the ministers staggered their vacations through the winter months, so they could be with their people at the summer camps. To attend the conferences with the flock was the best way to find out what was happening in the hearts of parishioners, to follow the decisions of the youth and to get close to those who needed counseling.

Henrietta saw the value of the conferences also in the life of the Sunday School. She encouraged her adult classes to meet together for prayer and fellowship while at camp. At the College Briefing Conferences, church groups were urged to have their own prayer and testimony time at the end of the day, and it was Teacher's custom to gather her collegians in one of the lodges for this type of fellowship.

Here cabinet leaders and department members were welded together in a close bond with the Lord, a cementing which produced many ideas for future enterprises. The officers for the coming year were just entering into their new positions, and these camp prayer-planning sessions helped to map out the course these leaders would follow. Old leaders also, who had become discouraged or stale in their work, received fresh inspiration and vision.

Not only were churches and Sunday School classes revitalized by her conferences, but campus Bible clubs were energized and often initiated at them. Often, during a testimony time, students from the same school would announce their intentions to win their campus to Christ and, by the end of the week at a high school or college conference, it was not uncommon to see several new Bible study groups organized for the coming year. A suggestion that Forest Home itself should create Bible classes for the school was quickly discouraged in favor of the students themselves taking the initiative in conjunction with their own churches. Forest Home was there to serve them, not to usurp their responsibilities.

A Volunteer System

The participating churches had the responsibility of providing counselors for their particular conference. Some Christian camps hire counselors for the entire summer, the thought being that if a counselor is paid and remains in a given situation for the summer, he will be better trained and more efficient. Henrietta Mears did not agree: After all, who better understood those with potential —or with problems—than their friends and fellow church members?

A volunteer from a church also had a better opportunity to follow through with his people. A professional counselor would have interest in a person as long as he remained at the camp, but a counselor from the conferee's church would be able to carry on with him back home. Henrietta stressed that as the volunteer teacher is the heart of the Sunday School, so the volunteer counselor is the heart of the camp.

But these unpaid volunteers were not untrained, for indeed they were. Again, each participating church was expected to prepare its own counselors. At the Hollywood Presbyterian Church, Henrietta and her assistants met weeks in advance with the counselors for a given camp and covered a thorough program of training.

Esther Ellinghusen, for example, prepared the counselors for her junior camps a month before the opening date. Since Esther was a professional teacher for this age group, she knew exactly what lay ahead of her counselors. She also invited in volunteers from other churches, and as many as 40 people would meet in her home to review the conference program, the age characteristics of juniors, program responsibilities and subject content.

Esther made steady assignments and expected the counselors to bring back reports which were then discussed by all. She had her counselors examine their own relationship to Christ to make sure that they knew why they were going to the camp. No wonder that hundreds of juniors came to Christ during their stay in the mountains. Not the least blessed were the counselors, many of whose lives had been changed during the weeks of training.

The college conferences had no counselors, though some of the collegians were trained to lead the Bible study groups. As Teacher's students had group Bible studies for their weekly Wednesday evening meetings at the church, so the entire college camp had daily Bible studies conducted in much the same way. Usually after the morning platform Bible hour, the camp population would break down into small discussion units of about 15 students each, sometimes by cabin or by church.

The leaders of these units were students who had volunteered to get the other students talking about the Scripture passage that had been presented the preceding hour. These discussion times were for many the high point of the conference. Never before had they been able to ask questions about the Bible or to give their opinions.

As a result, dozens of collegians accepted Christ right in their group, often during the informal closing prayer time. "I had never prayed before," was a common admission, "but it seemed so natural in our small circle of friends." When a counselor heard this, he knew that he had done his job well.

Was it an extravagant expenditure of time and personnel to train a different set of counselors for every week of a busy summer camp program? No doubt hiring one group for the whole season would have been simpler. But at Forest Home, the system followed paid big dividends as scores of these volunteers grew into a profounder realization of their tasks as Christians.

Too, a person who is an excellent high school counselor might be very inferior working with juniors, so an advantage of the volunteer system was that counselors for each group could be chosen for maximum suitability for a given age. Not only then was Teacher's Sunday School graded, so were her camps and counselors. More work? Of course, but work that was necessary for successful camps.

A Flexible Approach

"Teacher never told me to stop doing something; her command was always, 'Go!'" said Jack Franck after a decade of serving as director of the Christian Conference Center at Forest Home.

Henrietta Mears' firm convictions and her own strong will gave her ability to take command of any situation—and she often did. This constant thrusting forward, impelled by her enormous energy, gave some who did not know her well the impression that Henrietta made most of her important decisions on the spot with little thought given to analysis or planning. But her associates knew that, for Henrietta, careful planning and much prayer preceded all that activity.

Yet Henrietta did not approach every camping problem with her mind already made up. Each situation was met with a fresh dependence on the Holy Spirit and the dictates of common sense. She had no need to take refuge in previously thought-out patterns. And never viewing any set pattern as sacred, she felt free to make up her mind as she went along.

The planned program was never the master of Henrietta Mears; the goal was. If the target was not being reached, she threw the bow and arrow away and used something else. In Forest Home faculty meetings, she frequently asked, "Why are we doing this? What are we trying to accomplish with our programs?" In this way she was fulfilling one of her teaching objectives—to get her assistants to think plans through for themselves.

As the younger camps were much more programmed, this dynamic approach was most evident at the college conferences, Teacher's special interest. At a college conference, she was an amazing mix of the careful program-planner and the spontaneous improviser. She could shatter the most well-thought-through plans without warning, but always with reason.

Just as frequently, she threw aside her own ideas for the sake of something better. Often she would say that she did not want something that had already been planned. When asked what should be substituted, she might say, "Well, I don't know right now, but let's think it through and see what the Lord would have us do."

Henrietta's adaptability and willingness to make sudden changes in the schedule made each conference a creative experience for those involved and not infrequently left conference speakers gasping in stunned surprise. A speaker's usual task is to find out weeks in advance what he will be talking about and how many hours he will be allotted. He then systematically plans out exactly what he is going to do. But Henrietta, always demanding flexibility from her speakers, not infrequently asked them to change what they had prepared.

She could say to a potential speaker: "I want you to bring the most outstanding message you have," or "I want you to present that series on prayer I heard you give three years ago."

One world-famous evangelist said, "When I am invited to speak at Forest Home, I immediately exclude from my mind any message that I have already given somewhere else, and I ask the Lord to reveal to me what He wants for this particular occasion."

At an afternoon faculty meeting, Henrietta might come out with this sort of an analysis of the way a conference had been proceeding:

"Here it is Wednesday. The conference is half over and what have we accomplished? Oh, the messages have been good, but we aren't getting down to business. We must have a presentation of salvation tonight."

At that point, having already planned his sermon for the evening, the scheduled speaker for that night would begin to slump in his chair!

Dr. J. B. Phillips, famous translator of *The New Testament in Modern English,* was among the many outstanding Christian leaders invited by Henrietta Mears to minister at Forest Home. A guest speaker at the 1954 College Briefing Conference, he appears here at Henrietta's immediate left. In this photo are *l. to r. (front row)* Cy Nelson and Bill Dunlap; *(back row)* Bill Bright, Dr. Bob Smith, Dr. Mears, Dr. Phillips and Dale Bruner.

"As I walk around these grounds and talk to the young people," Henrietta would continue on, "I find that many of them do not know anything about Christ. Now let's pray that the Lord will reveal to us who should speak this evening. This is the turning point of the conference."

The group would then pray, someone would have the unexpected responsibility of that evening's message, and dozens of young people would find Christ.

Henrietta put as much work into the selection of her conference speakers as she did into everything else and succeeded in getting the very best for her camps. She flew in outstanding Christian leaders from all over the nation and the world. They came

Among the many foreign missionaries whom Henrietta introduced to those gathered at Hollywood Presbyterian Church and at Forest Home Christian Conference Center was Gladys Aylward, the tiny British missionary who served in China and whose life was the subject of a major motion picture, *The Inn of Six Happinesses.* Miss Aylward stands here between Dr. Mears and Jack Franck, then director of Forest Home.

from Canada, England, Germany—it mattered not from where, as long as they had a Christ-centered message. In this respect, Henrietta was extravagant with quality.

Her conference speakers all had to have a firm relationship with Jesus Christ; evidence of that relationship was requisite. They had to be basically conservative in that they subscribed to the deity of Christ and to the authority and infallibility of the Bible. She felt that, if a speaker's relationship to Christ was solid, doctrinal divergences could be dealt with, a view that allowed her to invite people of somewhat differing theological hues. And by featuring a broad spectrum of thoughts and personalities, she exposed her young people to a variety of ideas.

Being confident of her own beliefs and in God's ability to weld together divergent points of view, she did not fear differing opinions on a faculty. However, she did not appreciate speakers who were contentious. By avoiding conflicts and not allowing herself to be drawn into disputes, she could prevent anything from sidetracking the central purpose of a conference—to win individuals to Christ and to train them for His service.

From the lessons learned through her years of trial and error, observation and experience, Henrietta evolved basic principles for a dynamic approach to camping that has influenced conferences and youth leaders around the world. Missionary Lillian Dickson, for example, after visiting Forest Home and seeing how Henrietta Mears did things, returned to Formosa with the determination to build a "Forest Home" in that land for her young people there.

An Individualized Emphasis

Each camp at Forest Home was person-centered, but this emphasis on the individual was not by chance. Never one to be impressed by crowds, Henrietta Mears always saw the individual at the heart of every group.

"To get a crowd is the easiest thing to do," she would say. "If you want a group of boys, throw a hamburger feed. Anyone can get an organ-grinder and a monkey and have a crowd.

"It's what you do with those in the crowd that tells the tale. It is the individual who counts. One man, Luther, started the Reformation in Germany. One man, Moses, led the children of Israel out of Egypt. One man, Paul, carried the gospel to the Roman Empire. God always works through the individual."

Teacher always asked, "Who is going?" and let the numbers take care of themselves. So at times, a college conference would have over a thousand students present, yet the individual was never overlooked. The small discussion groups and individual church prayer meetings maintain this emphasis.

For the large camps the faculty was deliberately expanded so enough counselors would be on hand to meet individual needs.

This might mean that a given faculty member would have only one opportunity to speak, although he usually had more. But every speaker was instructed that his first responsibility was to counsel and his second was to preach.

Another technique to individualize the conference was to hold special seminars. If there were three meeting periods in the morning, the camp would be broken down into seminars during the second one. If only two hours were set aside for meetings in the morning—a more relaxed pace—then the seminars met in the afternoon.

These seminars covered a wide range of subject: "How to Do Personal Work," "The Ministry of the Holy Spirit," "How to Lead a Bible Study," "The Doctrine of the Scriptures," "The Art of Prayer," "The Book of Hebrews," "Your Missionary Calling," and the like. Often, for those seminars with a missions objective, missionaries would be present to discuss their fields with any interested students.

Sometimes these seminars ran for a three-day course and then began again in midweek with a different audience. At times, not only were morning seminars held, but also duplicate afternoon ones, repeating the morning discussion for a new class. During a week then, one conferee could take in a complete course in four different subjects. Some of the most outstanding Christian leaders came to Forest Home conferences purposely to conduct these seminars and to counsel without ever appearing before a conference as a whole. All these elements combined to let individuals know they were important to Christ, because they were important to those who served Him.

How marvelous when nearly a thousand collegians gathered in the main hall and overflowed it to sing the songs of Zion and to hear the Word of God. But how much more wonderful when they gathered in small clusters with the leaders or by themselves to pray and to talk person-to-person. The main meetings were but the backdrop; the real drama was played out on center stage by individuals working with other individuals.

A Fun Schedule

Henrietta also appreciated the fact that people came to a conference to have fun. No matter the age group, they had to be given plenty of time to enjoy the outdoors and to work off their energies. And knowing that people love to be with their friends, she made sure that social times were built into the schedule. These times were not merely expedient, but a part of the spiritual program of the camp.

Recreation chairmen were carefully selected, and the play periods were guarded from being infringed upon by some extra meeting. Usually the entire afternoon was available for recreation with competitions encouraged at the younger camps and trophies presented to winning basketball, football or baseball teams. Teacher often took an enthusiastic part in planning and watching such events.

The evening platform hour was after dinner, the other platform hour being right before lunch. Since the evening meeting was usually the most important time for a public challenge for decisions, many of the conferees would afterwards go to the prayer chapel or to some other place for quiet thought. Or churches would gather together in their prayer groups.

But most of the campers would filter down to the Club House for a soda or a hamburger, and where "spontaneous" sings would break out. And right in the middle would be Henrietta Mears, downing a banana split with her usual gusto and singing at the top of her voice.

To the uninitiated, these Club House sings seemed to be spur-of-the-moment. But those close to Teacher knew they were preplanned and initiated by her. She made sure several good song leaders and at least one pianist "just happened" to be there to get things started. A couple of soloists or someone with a guitar was added.

With her eagle eye, Teacher would spot and point out to her leaders those students wandering around the campgrounds who were not coming to the sing, and she would hustle the leaders off to corral the strays and bring them to the Club House, especially if they had not made a decision for the Lord. In the informality of these sings, Teacher would call upon somebody she knew in this fashion, "Sam, I know what has happened in your life in these last 24 hours, and I wonder if you wouldn't like to share it with the others."

Sam had probably been at Teacher's cabin for counseling; now he began to tell how he had accepted Christ. A few more testimonies over the sodas, a prayer song or two, and Teacher would give an invitation. Somehow, for some, the smell of onions and root beer and the fellowship of one's friends all combined to make the gospel more palatable. This sort of intensive but informal planning helped break down the resistance of those who knew all about church but nothing about a personal walk with Christ.

Afterwards a string of students might follow Teacher to her cabin for a prayer meeting. And not infrequently, one of the speakers or counselors, feeling the need for a fresher, more vital walk with the Lord, would ask her to pray with him.

An Individual Aflame

Those who had the privilege of working with Henrietta Mears at Forest Home knew that a roster of top speakers and hundreds or thousands of conferees alone did not a conference make. It helped, of course, to have a well-planned program with much prayer and hard work to bring it all together. But at least one person must also be aflame with a vision of God's purpose. At Forest Home, this person was Henrietta Mears. Even though she at times made mistakes—as every believer has—she was the Lord's chosen vessel whom He used at conferences in many marvelous ways.

Often when a conference seemed to be going along well, and the rest of the faculty members were satisfied with developments, Henrietta would drop one of her anticomplacency bombs, discomfiting her colleagues by blowing their preconceptions and self-satisfaction sky high. The average faculty member initially might feel nothing is lacking, but after 15 minutes with Teacher during one of

Always available to the individual, Teacher personally counseled and led thousands to Christ. As one young man later wrote Henrietta Mears: "At Forest Home I walked up to you and asked if you would give me 15 minutes to tell me the secret of God's blessing [on] your life. We sat down and had a Coke and you said, 'I can give it to you in one sentence: "I can do all things through Christ which strengtheneth me."' You gave me the secret and the 15 minutes."

her status quo-shattering sessions, he would come to the conclusion that something indeed was very wrong. But what was needed?

Henrietta would proceed to ask and answer the questions. More emphasis on the power of the Holy Spirit was needed. What had been said about God's concern for the lost? The morning Bible studies weren't vital enough. The conference was drifting without a purpose. They had to pray more as a faculty. The testimony times were stale. They were rehashing worn-out ideas. The conference needed something fresh, alive. In short, Moses was on the mountaintop, but as yet had not seen the afterglow of God's glory.

A Powerful Influence

Henrietta Mears' efforts at Forest Home had a powerful influence on the lives of so many who, in turn, went on to impact the lives of others for Jesus Christ. One of these many was Jim Rayburn who went out from Forest Home to establish his own national youth ministry, Young Life. Jim readily expressed his indebtedness to what he learned at Forest Home:

As a young man just out of college and beginning to work among young people, I heard of Henrietta Mears' ministry at Hollywood Presbyterian Church and particularly at Forest Home. What I heard, chiefly her continual exaltation of the person and work of Christ, her emphasis of a personal conversion experience, and a vital and dedicated relationship to Him in the Christian walk, these things were so impressive that I tried to incorporate into my work everything I heard about her way of doing things....

I knew it was right, if she did it. Through this influence upon my life, she has had a great deal to do with shaping the progress and ministry of the Young Life campaign.

And others were affected, too. What armies of courageous missionaries have marched out from Forest Home, their banners flying, their voices hymning the glories of Zion, some to labor to old age, some to meet an early martyr's death. One such martyr was Dr. Paul Carlson who was gunned down in the Congo (now Zaire) in 1964 by anti-government rebels known as Simbas. In a book of testimonies about the heroic medical missionary, Paul's brother, Dwight, wrote:

I can vividly remember a Sunday morning when I visited Paul at Forest Home conference grounds in southern California. I was just 10 years old at the time, and it was there that I was challenged to dedicate my life to God for whatever purpose He might desire.

When the invitation was given to go forward and to seal whatever commitment we had made, I turned to Paul for support and asked if he would go with me. He readily agreed, and we went forward together.

Paul was 15 at the time, and he subsequently reiterated his desire and willingness to serve Christ on several occasions, always with strong leading toward the field of medical missions. In all the years that followed, with their many and varied pressures, Paul never forgot his commitment.[2]

An Infinite God

Henrietta Mears was always reaching toward the limitless, infinite possibilities of her God, the One who said, "Behold, I will do a new thing...shall ye not know it?" (Isa. 43:19). She wanted to see, to hear, to know "the things which God hath prepared for them that love him" (1 Cor. 2:9). She loved Him and wanted to know more of what this omnipotent God was capable of.

One afternoon a disastrous rainstorm hit Forest Home. Danger hung in the air, as water poured down in catastrophic torrents. Henrietta gathered several people in her cabin to pray, though not knowing exactly what for.

After the storm subsided, they discovered that a huge boulder, torn loose from the mountainside, had washed down straight toward the camp's main water tank, stopping only one foot short of destructive contact. God had given them a miracle, yet this incident was but a minor miracle in comparison to what God still had planned for the ministry of Henrietta Mears at Forest Home.

Notes
1. John Fawcett (1740-1817), "Blest Be the Tie That Binds." Public domain.
2. Carl Philip Anderson, comp., *There Was a Man* (Old Tappan, NJ: Fleming H. Revell Company, 1965), p. 31.

FOURTEEN

The Expendables

P erhaps you have come into the Kingdom for such a time as this.' I would not forget these words spoken to Queen Esther by her uncle. I was overcome with a sense of destiny, of crisis, of God's speaking to me.

"All of my ministry was now in a different light. 'If I perish, I perish!' But as I returned from Europe, I knew that God had called me into the Kingdom for the hour."

THE ASHES OF A SCORCHED ERA WERE STILL FALLING ON A FRIGHTENED humanity in 1946. Half-alive, mankind had barely staggered out of the night of Auschwitz and Dauchau, only to be greeted in the predawn darkness by the new threat of atomic annihilation. One year had scarcely given the world enough time to clear away the rubble of Berlin, London and Nagasaki and to recognize the face of peace; yet already the shadows of Armageddon were lengthening across the nations as rumors of World War III filtered across a still unsettled world.

Young men, returning from battlefields where they had given a final salute to fallen comrades, were filled with apprehension about the future. Many did not believe the fire of WWII was really out; its smoldering glow flickered along their path as they searched for a surer guarantee of peace than that which their fathers had known.

A Ruined World

Also in 1946, Henrietta and Margaret Mears were in South America, enjoying a year's leave away from their responsibilities in Hollywood. The war years had taken their toll on Henrietta too. Faced with diminishing male leadership for her Sunday School, she had also coped with the increased responsibilities of ministering to servicemen, comforting those bereft of sons and cheering anxious parents. Teacher was now experiencing exhaustion and, again, the possible loss of sight.

On the calm beaches of Brazil, she sought to recoup her energies. As her strength returned and Americans began receiving visas for Europe—closed to tourists until late 1946—Teacher began to think about visiting the fields of war where hundreds of her college boys had served. As always, thought led to action, and she applied for the necessary visas.

"Impossible!" responded the American ambassador in Rio de Janeiro. "Only official persons are receiving visas to Europe."

"But I am official," Henrietta remonstrated. "Over 700 young men from our church fought in Europe, and I want to see for myself what conditions prevail there, so I can better counsel them as they return home."

Her logic was not lost on the ambassador, who then spent an entire afternoon making long-distance calls on Henrietta's behalf. As the days passed while Henrietta and Margaret waited for a decision, they viewed films of the Nuremberg war crime trials. Finally, after wearily pursuing their visas and travel papers in all the necessary embassies, they obtained the decisive permits from the American ambassador and boarded their ship.

They were fatigued from all their last-minute preparations but satisfied that they were on their way to Europe at last. Margaret lay in bed with a severe cold. Henrietta spent most of the days on the ship resting, reading her Bible and praying, not realizing that God was preparing her for the most significant work of her life.

Henrietta's dining companion on board was a young French woman whose entire family had been killed during the war. As the Mears sisters reached France, they found this tragedy so often repeated that their minds staggered with disbelief. They wept as they saw the cities they had once known as majestic and proud—Rome, Brussels, Paris, Berlin—now broken and gray, seething with crime and confusion.

Children playing in the ruins of their cities and villages occasionally triggered an unexploded bomb; women lined up at relief food kitchens, seeking food for their families; their soldier-husbands limped back from war duty to fallen homes of scattered bricks and splintered beams; displaced persons searched for loved ones; and the aged sat silently, their eyes still glazed over with the horrors and terrors of days past.

As she traveled from one devastated country to another, Henrietta recorded her impressions. While in Germany, in early 1947, she wrote:

> *It's terrible to think of that which has come upon Europe! Nine people live in one room with no clothes but rags and with no money, no shoes, no food. Two*

*out of three have TB. Europe is prostrated, humbled
and ravaged.*

*There are over five million homeless orphans, bewildered and afraid. Their heads are often shaven as a
precaution against lice and other pests. One sees children who have not only lost a daddy and a mother, but
also a leg or an arm.*

*There are other millions of displaced persons, many
of them Christians. In helping Europe's suffering multitudes, our Christian agencies are having the opportunity to take the gospel message into many camps for the
homeless. The Christians have suffered indescribably
for their faith. Their convictions have brought them persecution and privation beyond those which men of lesser scruples endure.*

*Europe is on the brink of starvation. Last spring the
floods and then the drought of summer resulted in
scant harvests. Wheat and rye are 200 million bushels
under last year, when hunger was widespread. The
meager bread rations have been cut further in Britain,
France, Holland, Italy and Sweden.*

*Germany is fallen, but her fall was not cataclysmic;
it had been growing for years. Rationalism, secularism,
the cult of the scientific, the worship of man, relativistic
ethics—all these led to the godless society of Adolph
Hitler, who placed no authority above himself. He told
the women that the highest service they could render
was to sleep with German soldiers. Everything sacred
was violated.*

*But since this is a moral universe and God is at the
center, he would not let this continue without judgment.
God has brought a punishment on the nations that no
one can imagine. Peoples that divorce themselves from
God experience his judgment.*

*Out of 37 civilizations, only seven still exist. God
judges nations. When character fails, nations fall.*

But these same processes that brought Germany low are working in the United States today. Sixteen out of every 17 leading educators have repudiated Christian principles, and there is a growth of this repudiation in intellectual circles.

Among our GIs the medics and the chaplains here tell us that 60 to 80 percent are immoral. What has happened to these boys—lining up outside brothels?

But in America we see divorce and drunkenness increasing.

What is happening to our world?—crime, ruthlessness, killing, mass starvation, mass bombing, mass exportation of slaves! And there is no penitence among the nations today!

Germany is a vacuum; Nazism has left it with nothing. But communism is reaching into the vacuum....For the most part, however, disillusionment and undefined godlessness have taken over. Hardly anyone goes to church.

We are in an era of spiritual revolution. Men are hating culture and religion. They are rebelling against God.

The same is true of the other countries. Only 15 percent of the men in Britain go to church. Britain has forgotten God. In a city of 100,000, only 100 young people are in a church. Thirty million out of 45 million in France profess no religion.

A Renewed Vision

Henrietta Mears saw a renewed vision of the omnipotent God ascending from the ruins that lay about her, rising like the fabled phoenix bird from its own ashes to live again. As she and Margaret boarded the boat on their return to America, Henrietta felt a growing awareness of God's leading. She spent the days on the high seas in quiet meditation.

As she read the story of Queen Esther, she was impressed with the seemingly hopelessness of the situation when the decree went out for the Jews to be annihilated. Was not this as much of a threat as the crisis now facing the postwar world? She continued to read how Mordecai told Esther to intercede before the king on behalf of her people, and how Esther reminded her uncle that if one presented himself before the king without invitation, it might mean death.

Then Henrietta came to the words in Esther 4:13-16 that became her guiding inspiration through the demanding months that lay ahead:

> *Then Mordecai commanded to answer Esther, Think not with thyself that thou shalt escape in the king's house, more than all the Jews. For if thou altogether holdest thy peace at this time, then shall there enlargement and deliverance arise to the Jews from another place; but thou and thy father's house shall be destroyed; and who knoweth whether thou art come to the kingdom for such a time as this?*
>
> *Then Esther bade them return Mordecai this answer, Go, gather together all the Jews that are present in Shushan, and fast ye for me, and neither eat nor drink three days, night or day; I also and my maidens will fast likewise; and so will I go in unto the king, which is not according to the law; and if I perish, I perish.*

Although once again involved with her many tasks in Hollywood, Henrietta felt she was being moved forward by an unseen hand. She had known power in her life before, but this was something beyond any previous experience. Her messages were filled with urgency. She spoke of what she had witnessed in Europe and what she thought was God's solution to the chaos. Those about her saw a vitality and commitment in her that they had not known before. She was living on the tiptoe of expectancy, but what she was expecting was not yet clear.

At a reception held in honor of Henrietta Mears and her sister Margaret *(far right),* collegians of Hollywood's First Presbyterian Church welcome the two travelers home from their 1947 trip to South America and to war-ravaged Europe.

A Ringing Call

As the summer of 1947 approached, and as the international situation became more confused and threatening, Henrietta and those working with her began to pray with increased earnestness that God would reveal what they were to do. On Tuesday night, June 24, 1947, during the Gospel Light Teacher's Training Conference at Forest Home, God broke through and His power was released. Henrietta ascended the platform with a controlling sense of God's presence. As the hundreds of Sunday School workers, pastors and young seminarians listened, she spelled out all that she had seen abroad.

> *The seeds of destruction had been long in bringing*
> *forth their fruit. Atheism and moral expedience had*

> *been at work for centuries before Hitler's rise to power. There is no mystery as to what has happened to Germany. It can all be traced out step-by-step.*
>
> *And the same is taking place in America today. There must be a Christian answer to the growing menace of communism. Leaders are predicting that within another generation or sooner we will have entered World War III, which could bring an end to civilization.*
>
> *God has an answer. Jesus said that we must make disciples of all men. We are to take His gospel to the ends of the earth. We must become evangelists, even though evangelism is not recognized in our day as a valid program. And we must present the full doctrine of Christian truth.*
>
> *God is looking for men and women of total commitment. During the war, men of special courage were called upon for difficult assignments; often these volunteers did not return. They were called "expendables." We must be expendables for Christ.*

On and on she spoke, emphasizing the need for revival, for prayer and for renewed interest in the Word. "If we fail God's call to us tonight, we will be held responsible."

A Revived Youth

At this teacher's conference were four young men who had been powerfully moved by Teacher's ringing call. They were Rev. Richard C. Halverson, then assistant pastor of the Hollywood Presbyterian Church; Louis H. Evans, Jr., the pastor's son and president of the college department; Jack Franck, then one of Teacher's assistants in the Sunday School; and William R. Bright, who only a few months before had accepted Christ as Savior.

Following Teacher's Tuesday evening message, these four young men, along with several others, asked her if they could meet for prayer in her cabin. As they knelt together, they were overcome by a sense of helplessness and inadequacy. They prayed on into the late hours of the night with much weeping and crying out to the Lord, confessing sin, asking God for guidance and seeking the reality and power of the Holy Spirit. At times, no one prayed as God spoke to them.

Then, the fire from heaven fell, for God answered their prayer with a very real vision. Before them, they saw the college campuses of the world, teeming with unsaved students who held in their hands the power to change the world. Yes, the college campuses—they were the key to world leadership, to world revival.

Within two months, according to the camp schedule, the collegians of First Presbyterian Church of Hollywood were to come to Forest Home for their annual weekend summer conference. Yet a weekend was not long enough to share the vision fully. A week-long conference would be necessary, and one that long had never been tried before. And who would be the speakers?

Besides, one church group alone could not fulfill the vision. So, before the conference, all the campuses of America had to be contacted and their students invited to attend. Since all the advertising had yet to be done, could they reach enough in those two months to make it all worthwhile?

The sheer audacity of what they contemplated—a national collegiate conference with only two months to prepare—was breathtaking. Still, the immensity of the challenge swept over them and gripped them. What a great undertaking for God this would be!

As they began anticipating the many logistics involved in pulling together a conference of this magnitude in such a short time, their thoughts—whipped by winds of inspiration—rushed together like waves and then crested on rocks of yet unanswered questions. Yet the vision had come; God had spoken clearly, and they had heard. Teacher and the four young men went out into the early light of morning, transformed, commissioned, expendable. Theirs was a world to conquer for Christ, and the time for conquest was now!

Later that morning they met again in Teacher's cabin. Once more urgency prevailed as they prayed and talked throughout the morning and on into the afternoon. Already, less than 24 hours after the initial breakthrough of power, Teacher and these four young men began to organize their thoughts and to make plans, even as others in the camp became aware that something big was afoot.

As the young men were with Henrietta in prayer, God gave them a concern that something definite should be drawn up to express on paper what they considered to be their responsibilities. The thought was not to start another organization, nor to formulate a confession, but simply to state guidelines, so that standards might be before them as they sought to implement the enthusiasm God had given to them. The catalyst was the approaching college conference and the primary aim was the immediate evangelization of college campuses.

With this aim before them, Teacher and the four young leaders of this embryonic movement drew up a pledge which they incorporated under the title, The Fellowship of the Burning Heart. This name was based on John Calvin's seal which shows a hand offering a heart on fire, and around the whole is the inscription, "My heart I give Thee, Lord, eagerly and sincerely." They then drafted a statement of commitment followed by four specific disciplines:

> *The name adopted by those who wish to be expendable in this program of world evangelism is the Fellowship of the Burning Heart. It has taken as its emblem the famous Calvin seal. It is composed of those college-age youth who have offered up their hearts as a sacrifice to the Lord Jesus Christ in behalf of a needy world.*
>
> *Believing that the urgency of the hour in which we live demands the highest type of Christian Discipleship, I desire to unite in the Fellowship of the Burning Heart by the following commitments:*
>
> *I am committed to the principle that Christian Discipleship is sustained solely by God alone through His Spirit; that the abiding life of John 15 is His way of sustaining me. Therefore, I pledge myself to a disciplined*

devotional life in which I promise through prayer, Bible study, and devotional reading, to give God not less than one continuous hour per day. (Ps. 1.)

I am committed to the principle that Christian Discipleship begins with Christian character. Therefore, I pledge myself to holy living, that by a life of self-denial and self-discipline, I may emulate those Christlike qualities of chastity and virtue which will magnify the Lord. (Phil. 1:20,21.)

I am committed to the principle that Christian Discipleship exercises itself principally in the winning of the lost to Christ. Therefore, I pledge myself to seek every possible opportunity to witness and to witness at every opportunity to the end that I may be responsible for bringing at least one to Christ every 12 months. (Matt. 28:19; Acts 1:8.)

I am committed to the principle that Christian Discipleship demands nothing less than absolute consecration to Christ. Therefore, I present my body a living sacrifice, utterly abandoned to God. By this commitment, I will that God's perfect will shall find complete expression in my life; and I offer myself in all sobriety to be expendable for Christ. (Rom. 12:1,2; Phil. 3:7-14.)

The original leadership of this emergent revival movement immediately signed the pledge. Then as deputation teams subsequently went out to other youth groups with word of the impending conference, they also were invited to join the Fellowship. And so the names of the concerned grew as the time of the conference drew near.

As the day progressed, the five laid plans for the coming college conference; it was to last eight days, and as many collegians as possible would be invited. Special letters of invitation were to be written to hundreds of young people across the country. Churches had to be visited, pastors informed, youth leaders inspired. Other conferences, too, had to be brought into this vision, especially the approaching high school camp. Much work had to be done, and it had to be done quickly!

That evening, Henrietta and her four cohorts returned to Hollywood to speak at the college department's Wednesday evening prayer meeting. As Teacher entered the room, one of those present said to another, "I have never known before what the book of Exodus meant when it described Moses' face as shining with the glory of God, but now I see: Look at Teacher's face!"

Jack Franck, Lou Evans, Dick Halverson and Bill Bright gave their testimonies of what had happened the previous night at Forest Home, telling about their vision of having a conference for collegians from across the nation. And the word "briefing" would be added to the title of the conference, for, just as soldiers during the war had been briefed before their missions, so this College Briefing Conference was to prepare men and women to go out commissioned and trained to win the world to Christ.

The Teacher spoke, reiterating her remarks of the night before. She spoke with the authority of a person who had just stepped from the presence of God. Nothing was histrionic in her manner, nor was anything calculated or contrived; she was simply a prophetess declaring the mind of God to men. Yet she once again imparted her vision, this time to her college department, and they responded by pledging to work around the clock so other students might know what was happening and might come to the Briefing Conference.

Thrilling, hectic days followed as everyone involved in conference preparations worked at top speed on one assignment or another. Sometimes they felt like runners racing pell-mell through a forest at night without any light, nor quite sure where the path led or where the rocks were. Their course was unknown, none of them ever having traveled it before.

Even Teacher with all her spiritual insight and expertise was astonished at the various demands God was imposing on them. Yet an inner confidence illumined her. The way was new and unknown, but she knew who led them. And this conviction was for Teacher and her collegians their pillar of cloud by day and their pillar of fire by night.

One of the brochures they sent out at this time read:

A Call to Arms: In the nineteenth century, God chose, through Dwight L. Moody, 60 Oxford University students as missionaries to carry the gospel of Jesus Christ to the whole world. In this twentieth century, He is calling for greater numbers. Youth from all walks of life, from our colleges and universities, from our businesses and industries, must go forth to carry this same gospel to millions still in darkness.

As the opening of the Briefing Conference drew near, other churches were informed by deputation teams going out from the college department of Hollywood Presbyterian Church. One week after the initial prayer meeting at Forest Home, Teacher, along with the original four young men and one other, drove to the Mount Hermon Conference Center near Santa Cruz, California, where a high school camp was in progress. At this gathering were more young men who had been trained in Teacher's college class: Homer Goddard, Bob Ferguson, Bob Munger, Bill Dunlap and Cyrus N. Nelson, Mount Hermon's conference director at the time.

As the deputation from Hollywood told these leaders at the Mount Hermon camp what had happened at Forest Home, the Spirit of God fell again, bringing confession and dedication. They decided to have the deputation team speak to the entire conference that evening. Before an audience of nearly 1,000 teenagers and older guests, the four young men gave their testimonies and Henrietta spoke. Hundreds came forward to dedicate their lives as expendables for Christ.

But the team had no time to stay at Mount Hermon. The deputies left that night to return to Hollywood. Hours later, as they came over the Grapevine—a steep, winding, often fog-shrouded stretch of Highway 5—and began the long descent into the Los Angeles basin, they had their devotions, one prayed as another drove. The early morning rays were faintly breaking through the night mists, and a new era in Christian missions was beginning.

About the same time as the deputation teams were making contacts, this notice, promoting the approaching college conference, appeared in some of the literature then being circulated:

> *The Answer Has Come: "And it shall come to pass in the last days, saith God, I will pour out of my Spirit upon all flesh: and your sons and your daughters shall prophesy, and your young men shall see visions and your old men shall dream dreams!" (Acts 2:17). We believe that this day has come. Now, if ever, is the time for God again to speak and to revive His people.*
>
> *God has spoken. The revival has started. On Tuesday night, June 24, at the Forest Home Christian Conference Grounds in the beautiful San Bernardino Mountains of California, the Holy Spirit spoke to a small group as they knelt in prayer in Miss Henrietta Mears' cabin. He gave them a vision with a plan for worldwide evangelism, filling them with the power of the Spirit in a manner not unlike the experience of the disciples at Pentecost. The Holy Spirit has continued to lead. Great and mighty things have been done since that unforgettable night a few short weeks ago.*
>
> *There is continued evidence that this revival is the work of the Holy Spirit and not something conjured up in the minds of men. This has been demonstrated by the fact that this experience was followed by personal confession of sins by individuals in great numbers and complete consecration of life on the part of many heretofore lukewarm Christians. Such action must necessarily precede any great religious movement, thereby providing "cleansed vessels" through which the Holy Spirit may work.*
>
> *The tragedy of our times is that we live in a militant-*

> *ly pagan world. Social, economic, political, and spiritu-*
> *al chaos has overwhelmed world leaders, and the*
> *urgency of the hour has brought God's people to their*
> *knees in one last plea. God, in His tender mercy and*
> *loving kindness, has granted a revival to stave off what*
> *many of our leading statesmen have termed "the com-*
> *plete annihilation of civilization."*

This message was published across the nation while hundreds of telephone calls went out to pastors and their youth. Brochures were quickly written and printed by the thousands. Teacher, herself, wrote innumerable letters to young people, encouraging them to prepare themselves at the Briefing Conference for whatever God wanted. Typical of the many letters she wrote is the following:

> *Dear Don:*
> *I need you and God needs you! I have come back*
> *from Europe and South America with an overwhelming*
> *sense of the crisis hour in which we live. The needs of*
> *the world are appalling. I believe, Don, that you are a*
> *young man of destiny, for who knows but what "you*
> *have come into the kingdom for just such a time as*
> *this." I believe God has made no mistake and that He*
> *has a plan for you in this hour.*
> *As never before God is calling for expendables. He is*
> *watching for men to match the mountains of opportu-*
> *nity; He is looking for youth who will say, "I will face*
> *this hour and find my place in it, and if I perish, I per-*
> *ish." We need men who will put God first.*
> *Don, you are among those we are counting on. Gear*
> *yourself into the group, and help us achieve something*
> *for God in this hour. I would that we had young men*
> *driven along by a mighty vision of what God could do if*
> *only He possessed them. I believe young men of today*
> *are going to do things that will stagger this generation,*

> *but all this will pass. We must have young men to deal*
> *with things not of time, but of eternity.*
>
> *Don, come to the college department and help us! I*
> *say again, we need you desperately. The task before us*
> *is for the many, not the few.*
>
> *I do want you to come to our College Briefing Con-*
> *ference and sit around the table with us and discover*
> *how we can best serve in this day. We must have plans*
> *definite and workable. The conference is solely for*
> *briefing. Don, I am counting on you.*
>
> *Yours in His Service,*
> *Henrietta C. Mears*

Day after day the work continued. At times, Henrietta's colleagues feared for her health. She pushed herself as never before. From early morning to late at night, she and her staff wrote, traveled, phoned, interviewed, prayed, spoke to churches, talked with pastors, organized deputation teams, programmed meetings and worked on housing for the conference. In addition to all this, Henrietta kept up with the "normal" summer pace at the church and at Forest Home, with a new camp for several hundred people being planned each week.

Never a passive spectator, Henrietta Mears obviously believed in active participation, for, in her mind, revival meant organization, planning and work. However, through all this expenditure of energy and time, she never lost her perspective. Her own daily Bible reading and prayer time was never sacrificed.

Indeed, she carefully weighed each responsibility before the Lord in advance of undertaking it. She knew what to do because she believed God had told her to do it. During the busiest day, when dozens of major decisions were yet unresolved in her office, Teacher and her staff would take time to pray, perhaps for an hour or more.

This keen sense of balance between communion with God and activity was one of the most instructive lessons to be learned from the 1947 revival. Many Christians receive a vision of what God wants, but then they wait for God to do the work. When nothing happens they become discouraged, and soon what they thought was a vision leaves them.

On the other hand are those who work and plan, but to no avail because no vision guides them. Henrietta showed how to release unlimited energy and power by combining both of these fissionable elements.

All during these two hectic preparatory months, lives were being transformed by the Spirit of God. Even those who had been dedicated Christians, having actively engaged in the Lord's work for years, now felt a renewing concern for world-wide evangelism and for a more meaningful walk with Christ. The College Briefing Conference had not yet begun, and already the Spirit of God was at work reviving hearts and lives across the land. Even so, these manifestations of God's moving were only mercy drops. The showers of blessing had yet to fall.

FIFTEEN

Fallout from Victory Circle

*T*o know God is to have a reservoir of sustaining force that never fails. This fortitude pervades every nerve of the Christian as Christ lives within him and fulfills God's perfect will. It is not something we pump up. We can't work for it. We accept it as a gift."

FROM DOZENS OF CAMPUSES ALL OVER THE COUNTRY, THE CONFEREES CAME, expectant and skeptical, sincere and cynical, some waiting on God for blessing, others disbelieving His existence. Many came out of curiosity; most were convinced that God was already working in their hearts; few knew what to anticipate.

Forest Home in 1947 could comfortably accommodate 500 guests, but no one knew for certain just how many collegians would attend the Briefing Conference. Cars and buses rolled up the mountain all Sunday afternoon, bringing delegates, until near evening it was all too obvious there would not be enough places to house all the conferees. Already 600 had arrived, yet more students continued to pour in.

Greeters went out on the road to welcome the newest arrivals and to alert them to the fact that all accommodations were now filled to capacity. Undaunted, however, the latecomers responded to the housing shortage with the adventurous spirit of pioneers. Many slept in their cars or out under the trees. But they stayed for the conference and for what God had to give them.

That the leaders lacked a definite schedule for the week was no secret. Outstanding God-led Christian pastors had been invited to participate—Dr. Louis H. Evans, Sr., Dr. L. David Cowie, Dr. Robert B. Munger and others. But the one rule accepted by all was that the hour-by-hour program was to be led by the Spirit of God, and no leader was to speak who had not been singled out by the Spirit working through the entire faculty, chaired by Henrietta Mears. She and a few others met in prayer all the first afternoon and later marched around Victory Circle—the open-air meeting place where the early evening testimony times were held—claiming that the walls of stubbornness and disbelief would be felled by the Lord.

The Student Movement

The first meeting of the conference began in Victory Circle as the testimonies of how God had started the movement were again told. Then all the students were invited to share their thoughts and aspirations. Some stated frankly they could not accept such "emotional and illogical" beliefs. Others expressed their desire that God would reveal whatever He had for them. An overriding conviction of sin was in the hearts of many students, as one after another stood to ask God's forgiveness of past errors and faithlessness. Some professed Christ as Savior, often with tears.

As night fell, the testimonies went on. Only the stars and a fire illumined the scene. No one moved to stop the meeting which had no real leader other than the Holy Spirit.

Henrietta was overwhelmed with a realization that God was working and that the destinies of many lives were in the balance. As the testimonies continued, she slipped out—unnoticed except by a few—and returned to her cabin. There, with a handful of the faculty, she prayed for an hour that God would have complete sway over the situation.

She returned to Victory Circle and found the collegians still talking about their spiritual ambitions and problems. Stepping before them, she spoke about sin, confession, forgiveness, cleansing and the Holy Spirit. She laid before them the need to be absolutely honest with God and to submit completely to His will. She asked the 600-plus students to pray that God's purpose for their lives would be fulfilled. This first Victory Circle lasted over four hours, as did those on subsequent evenings.

Throughout the conference, confession of sin continued. One husky, young football player, well over six feet tall, began to weep uncontrollably. He confessed that he had been living a lie since he had returned from the war, having presented himself as a hero who had shot down many enemy planes. But in reality, he now admitted, he had washed out of flight school and had spent the war years on the ground repairing damaged aircraft.

His large frame shook as he fell on the ground, his face in the dust, sobbing and asking God to forgive him. Two nights later, this same lad dedicated his life to the ministry. Several years later, this dedication came to fruition before many of these same friends as he was ordained.

One fellow who was singing tenor in the conference quartet

gave his life and talent to the Lord. Through the years following the first Briefing Conference, God honored this musician's fidelity, opening up one door after another to him. He contracted with the Metropolitan Opera Company in the United States and with other companies abroad. But he still returned to Forest Home to sing and give his testimony.

The president of the USC Men's Council gave his life to the Lord, as did many others who were campus officers. Several of the young men decided that God was calling them into the ministry or onto the foreign mission field. Many ministers and missionaries, subsequently scattered across the nation and around the world, made their decisions during that week.

Placing a large map at the front of the main hall, Henrietta encouraged young people who felt led to certain countries to write their names on those places. The map remained up for the entire week, as students, prayerfully and individually, wrote where they thought God was calling them. A student from USC wrote his name on Japan and went on to serve Christ there. Dick Halverson signed China, and several years later he went to the Orient and ministered to thousands of Chinese until God led him into other avenues of service.

Another wrote his name on Russia. J. Christy Wilson, a recent seminary graduate, put his name on Afghanistan and subsequently took up teaching and pastoral duties in that inaccessible Muslim nation, even becoming a tutor in the royal house for a time before the country fell to Communist rule. And many students who had no clear indication of a specific country initialed campuses, considering their schools their first missionary responsibility.

Not all who came to that first Briefing Conference were converted. One brilliant and cynical lad stood at Victory Circle to defy everything that was being presented. He scoffed at the idea that he was a sinner and openly disclaimed the existence of God.

Naturally, everyone began to pray for him, and many tried to convince him of his error. He laughed at what he thought to be the ambition of the leaders "to get my scalp on your belt." As he left the conference unconverted, Henrietta continued to pray for him, affirming that God was not limited to Forest Home.

The week following the conference, during the echo service at the college department in Hollywood, he sat quietly as he listened to the testimonies of those who had found Christ the week before—among them was his own brother. Finally his skeptical heart was overcome by the reality of Christ's life, and he made a profession of faith.

That night he returned home and began work on a lengthy thesis in which he attempted to explain why he was becoming a Christian. Teacher was hesitant when informed that he wanted to read his thesis to the college department, but she eventually gave way to his request. Several collegians were converted after hearing his testimony. Both he and his brother later entered full-time Christian service.

Eighty-seven colleges and universities from nearly every part of the country had been represented at this first College Briefing Conference. As the delegates returned to their campuses, they were filled with a sense of mission to win their schools to the faith. Not unnaturally—since Teacher lived just across the street from UCLA, and many of her young people studied there—a large contingent from this school had attended the conference. So, after the school year opened, UCLA continued to be a focal point for witnessing and for deputation teams. On various occasions, Bible studies and prayer meetings composed of Bruins would meet in Teacher's home, and she encouraged every possible effort to win young men and women on this campus to Christ.

In those early years, Bill Bright was still in secular service. But during that 1947 student revival movement, he felt God's hand leading him into campus work. He was already a leader in the college department's deputation ministry and, as such, he often directed the work toward the campuses.

After completing seminary years at Princeton and Fuller, he continued his student-directed missionary efforts with Teacher's assistance. He and his wife, Vonette, lived for years with Henrietta, using her home as a center for their emerging crusade. God blessed Bill's efforts, and Campus Crusade for Christ evolved into the international work it is today.

The Continuing Blessings

Many were the continuing blessings begun by the 1947 College Briefing Conference. Among these, three stand out: the holding of subsequent yearly college conferences, for formation of the Hollywood Christian Group and the impact of the 1949 conference on Billy Graham.

The yearly college conferences. That first Briefing Conference set a precedent for what became an annual summer gathering of collegians seeking to find God's will for their lives. These week-long conferences soon ranked among the most important such events for the inspiration and training of university students in our time.

In the course of these conferences, certain lessons were learned:

> 1. Time was given for the Spirit of God to work. The evening hours were not filled with music before the message nor with other meetings afterwards.
> 2. Along with freedom in the schedule went an expectation that God was going to do something. Most everyone believed this, although people didn't know exactly what it would be.
> 3. The faculty meetings were devoted primarily to prayer. Levity was out of place, as the seriousness of the mission was allowed to settle on the faculty members' hearts. At these faculty meetings there was much weeping over the lost and crying out to the Lord for blessings.
> 4. Henrietta kept the purpose of the conference ever before the faculty, and conference techniques were bent or thrown out if they failed to comply with that purpose.

5. The faculty moved, thought and prayed as a unit. No matter who was speaking, the faculty was there en masse to support him. Their number included no prima donnas. God Himself was the soloist, and no one dared upstage Him.

6. The revival began in the hearts of the faculty before it spread to the conferees.

The Hollywood Christian Group. After the conference of 1947, the exuberant young people returned to tell their friends of what had taken place on the mountaintop. Louis Evans, Jr. shared his experiences with Colleen Townsend, a young starlet he was dating. A Mormon by choice, she had completed a year and a half at Brigham Young University in Utah when discovered by Hollywood scouts and catapulted into the dazzling heights of stardom.

Lou gave his testimony to the young actress who later said, "He talked about having been encountered by Christ. He was so alive and vital—I was impressed. I attended the next conference, and there I, too, encountered this living Christ. I didn't fall on my knees or weep; I just walked by myself and dedicated my life to Him."

Colleen had already been involved in the college department before her dedication to Christ, but now she gave herself to the kind of unselfish and gracious service of others that has characterized her life as a Christian.

Other Hollywood personalities were also being influenced by the effects of the revival. Among them were Roy Rogers, Dale Evans, Tim Spencer and Connie Haines. Henrietta had long sought how to reach the stars behind the celluloid curtain for Christ, and now the Spirit was bringing them to her. At one time, some of these Christian celebrities met in her cabin at Forest Home to pray for guidance as to how they could win their friends in the film industry to the Lord.

True, Hollywood actors and actresses attended churches. Dennis Morgan and Virginia Mayo, for example, were members of the

First Presbyterian Church in Hollywood. But even in the house of God, being famous presented difficulties; they still could not escape the lingering stares of the curious in the congregation. Miss Mayo frequently came on Sunday morning with a hat covering most of her face.

So a church-centered program was out of the question, if an effective evangelistic movement were to take hold among these people, especially if non-Christian personalities were to be reached. The only solution was to hold meetings in private homes without publicity, the guests being brought by invitation only. At all costs, the public had to be kept away.

Since Henrietta and Margaret had a home that compared favorable with those of the Hollywood great, and since it was located in the middle of the stars' estates, the decision was made to begin weekly meetings there. Henrietta knew that no tricks or gimmicks could be used on a crowd who made the mastery of gimmicks their livelihood. The secret of reaching the stars was Christ crucified and resurrected, the source of abundant life. And Henrietta believed that Dr. J. Edwin Orr represented this approach. Dr. Orr had been speaking at Forest Home conferences, and his logical and direct messages appealed to her. His uncluttered, unaffected style gave room for the Holy Spirit to work, so she asked him to help her reach the film capital.

The first meetings were immediately successful. The Mears' spacious living room was packed with the famous. Some of them rejected Christ, but scores of others found the Savior in these meetings as marvels of conversion resulted. Tim Spencer, leader of the famous cowboy singing group, The Sons of the Pioneers, had been enslaved to drink for years. But he found Christ, was transformed and eventually became president of the movement already being called the Hollywood Christian Group.

A beautiful young dancer listened eagerly to the testimony of Colleen Townsend as they spoke together on a set. Georgia Lee, with her husband, Ralph Hoopes, was known to millions through television, but now a new life was opening up to her:

A number of Hollywood personalities took part in *Decision,* a film made of Forest Home. At the premiere of *Decision,* were several members of the Hollywood Christian Group: *(l. to r., front row),* Connie Haines, Eva Pearson, Colleen Townsend, Lois Chartrand and Henrietta Mears; *(back row),* Bob Mitchell, Charles Turner, Bill Beal, Louis Evans, Jr., L. David Cowie and Murray Bernard.

Colleen invited me and my husband to one of the first meetings of the Hollywood Christian Group. The next week, Ralph and I were there and listened to Dick Halverson tell of his conversion, how he had sinned and then saw that not only he but everyone needed a Savior. There was a discussion after the message in which Dr. Orr and Miss Mears explained Jesus Christ the Savior to us, so that Christ became a reality in my life instead of just a fact in my mind.

That night, I knelt to pray as usual, but in a different way I prayed that the Lord Jesus would come into my life, forgive my sins and use me to His glory. Since that night, Ralph and I studied Scripture almost every day.

Georgia Lee and Ralph Hoopes gave themselves to the Lord with the total abandon that often characterizes the newly converted. And their enthrallment with Christ only grew greater as they sought to serve Him with increasing zeal. Ralph eventually entered the ministry, assisted by his vivacious wife—who also accepted roles in many Christian films, notably some produced by World Wide Pictures, the film division of the Billy Graham Evangelistic Association.

Not only did Billy Graham launch his film crusades by first employing the talents of the Hollywood Christian Group, many of the converted stars allowed their testimonies to be published in national magazines. And some appeared on TV and radio to tell what Christ meant to them. A few even left the industry and went into the ministry.

In the 1940s, and the early 1950s, motion pictures—and those who acted in them—were still widely regarded by evangelicals as "of the devil," making suspect anyone having anything to do with the industry and those in it. So Henrietta Mears, as an acknowledged evangelical leader, demonstrated no small amount of courage—and love—when she helped to launch the Hollywood Christian Group. And she seized every opportunity to help other church leaders realize that Christ was as much at home in the hearts of actors and actresses as in their own.

She once invited Ruth Bell Graham, wife of Dr. Billy Graham, to a meeting of the Hollywood Christian Group being held that day in the home of a top actress. As Henrietta and Ruth sat together on a small sofa, the actress was called upon to give her testimony. At first, Ruth thought to herself, *How can this woman, who plays such questionable roles on the screen, talk this way about Christ?*

Then, in the midst of her skeptical thoughts, Ruth became aware of Henrietta muttering under her breath, "Bless her heart! I just love that girl. She is the dearest person."

Some time later Ruth Graham wrote to friends:

> *It was a good thing that Miss Mears couldn't hear my thoughts when that actress was giving her testimony. I*

was raised in the Orient, where—if one was built like a woman—she overcame it the best she could. I sat there looking at this movie star like the chief of the Pharisees, but Miss Mears was encouraging her.

See what I mean? Some of us talk about love, but Miss Mears loves. No wonder God uses her!

Over the years the Hollywood Christian Group continued to grow as hundreds of Hollywood denizens were converted. From 1949 to 1951, Dr. Orr chaplained the group, as did Dick Halverson. And for a time, it had no single leader. Henrietta did what she could as adviser and confidante, urging the group on, but increasing illness in the 1950s kept her from fully sponsoring the group herself.

As the fellowship increased in size, it opened its doors to others in the film industry than just the top stars, such as cameramen and technicians. And instead of meeting in exclusive homes, the meetings moved to the banquet hall of the Knickerbocker Hotel. In this way, what had started as an exclusive movement for a few took on a broader appeal for the many. Other groups as well branched off from the central movement, so that today several evangelistic efforts operate among the movie and television people.

The impact on Billy Graham. At Forest Home, as the 1949 College Briefing Conference drew closer, the tempo of activity was increasing and the work load growing heavier. Teacher herself was searching for a more meaningful walk with Christ, and the earnestness of her quest kindled revival fire in the souls of many discouraged Christians. She had invited Billy Graham, then a little-known evangelist from the South, to speak to the conference.

"When she made known her selection, a would-be adviser strongly counseled her not to have him, for Billy was not from an established church and not considered by some as an orthodox voice of the church. But Billy Graham came to Forest Home. No one advises Miss Mears but God."[1]

At this time in 1949, Billy was going through the greatest spiritual and intellectual battle of his life. He was wrestling with a number of doubts that for months had cost him all peace of mind. He was facing a crusade in the downtown section of Los Angeles that was only weeks away. He felt inadequately prepared and had doubts concerning the crusade's outcome.

Most troubling of all for Billy were questions in his mind concerning the authority of the Bible as God's Word. Could he by faith accept all of the Bible as the inspired Word of God and preach it with authority and power if there were portions that presented intellectual difficulties he had not the wisdom to resolve?

Complicating the faith-reason battle for Billy and deepening his doubts were arguments posed to him by a friend of many years who was adamant in his insistence that a doctrine not intellectually tenable in its entirety must be rejected. Billy's friend, himself a prominent Canadian evangelist who had shared pulpits with Billy during their Youth for Christ days, was moving away from reliance on "thus saith the Lord." But Billy still wanted with undoubting faith to be able to say with Paul, "I declare unto you the gospel which I preached unto you...by which also ye are saved...how that Christ died for our sins according to the scriptures; and that he was buried, and that he rose again the third day according to the scriptures" (1 Cor. 15:1-4).

Nevertheless, despite his own concerns, Billy agreed to come to Forest Home for the conference. But because of his exhaustion, apprehension and extreme nervous tension, he asked to come merely as a conferee. But Henrietta retained him on the faculty along with herself and Dr. J. Edwin Orr.

Arriving early at Forest Home on the Sunday the conference began, Billy had several extra hours to confer with Henrietta and Dr. Orr and to plan for the coming week. He was candid with his colleagues and spoke with them at length about the struggle he was going through. They agreed that Billy would speak at the morning platform hours, and Dr. Orr in the evening when he would be stressing the ministry of the Holy Spirit.

Billy's doubting friend from Canada was also at the Briefing Conference.[2] He continued to be critical of Billy's simple faith and continued reliance upon Scripture as the Word of God. A particularly cutting remark he made about Billy—which he said later had been garbled in the retelling—deeply hurt and disturbed his old friend. By midweek, although his messages to the youth had been effective, Billy came to an impasse in his conflict. Seeking resolution, he and Dr. Orr spoke and prayed together about complete surrender to God and the infilling of the Holy Spirit.

That night Billy followed a trail into the woods and wandered up the mountain. He knew he had reached a personal crisis in his spiritual life and determined to end this battle that raged within him. This duel with doubts had to be resolved once and for all.

In desperation, he knelt by a stump, put his Bible upon it and prayed:

> *Lord, many things in this Book I do not understand. But Thou has said, "The just shall live by faith." All I have received from Thee I have taken by faith. Here and now, by faith, I accept the Bible as Thy word. I take it all. I take it without reservations. Where there are things I cannot understand, I will reserve judgment until I receive more light. If this pleases Thee, give me the authority as I proclaim Thy word and through that authority convict me of sin and turn sinner to the Savior.*[3]

The young evangelist arose from that place of prayer with faith strong in his soul. At his very next platform hour with the young people at the College Briefing Conference, he gave his challenge for them to dedicate their lives to Christ with such power and authority that 400 responded to the invitation.

"'I could feel an immediate difference,' said Miss Mears. 'I did not know then what had happened. But there was an authority, a sureness, a fire in his spirit, that hadn't been there when he first arrived.'"[4]

This experience at Forest Home transformed Billy Graham's entire ministry, according to his own testimony. He launched into his September Los Angeles crusade with a surging optimism that

Henrietta Mears, Donn Moomaw and Billy Graham enjoy a reunion and a time of fellowship together at a Forest Home banquet.

God was going to act. And act He did. Thousands attended and hundreds were converted—ordinary folk and notables alike. The newspapers picked up the story and overnight Billy Graham's name became a household word.

Billy Graham's Forest Home experience was, by his own admission, a turning point in his life. Throughout the following months and years, he frequently visited or phoned Henrietta, seeking advice, praying with her and informing her of new triumphs for Christ. Not surprisingly, Billy declared of Henrietta Mears:

> *Dr. Henrietta C. Mears...has had a remarkable influence both directly and indirectly, on my life. In fact, I doubt if any other woman outside of my wife and mother has had such a marked influence. Her gracious*

At a Forest Home banquet in Hollywood, Henrietta Mears is flanked on her right by her close friend, Dr. Charles E. Fuller of the "Old Fashioned Revival Hour" and on her left by the Honorable Arthur B. Langlie, then governor of the state of Washington.

spirit, her devotional life, her steadfastness for the simple gospel, and her knowledge of the Bible have been a continual inspiration and amazement to me. She is certainly one of the greatest Christians I have ever known!"[5]

The Conference Afterglow

At that 1949 College Briefing Conference, an afterglow of the revival fires of 1947 ignited not only Billy Graham, but scores of other young men and women. The evening messages, delivered by Dr. Orr with a depth of presentation rarely equalled, were central to the 1949 conference emphasis on the Holy Spirit. Dr. Orr outlined his talks with great care on blackboards, explaining point by point about such doctrines as justification and sanctification. Those meetings were not short—Dr. Orr's talks sometimes lasted as long as two hours—but the young people hardly seemed to notice.

After speaking each evening, Dr. Orr would usually call for a period of silent reflection and quiet prayer. The presence of the Holly Spirit was powerfully evident, as He convicted young people of their sins, filled them with grace and instructed them concerning their callings. Sophisticated collegians stood one after the other to repent of evil deeds and thoughts and to confess Christ as Lord. To see several college men, previously aimless dawdlers, rise to admit their frustrated existence and to surrender to the Spirit was unforgettable. Many have since gone into the ministry or to the foreign field.

At some of the meetings, various faculty members spontaneously rose to confess inadequacies. During one altar call, a young minister, prominent in the group, asked Dr. Orr to pray for him. Dr. Orr brought him to the stage and had other members of the faculty lay their hands on him as they asked God to take over his ministry and to glorify Himself in his life, a prayer God has since honored mightily.

The Shared Witness

One evening, Henrietta, in the sincerest and most straightforward way possible, shared her experiences from her own college days when she had been searching for more significance in her Christian life. Her face was radiant as she told of finding in the Bible the simple truths of commitment, trust and fellowship with God. Many lives were changed by her testimony.

In faculty meetings as well as in open conference, Henrietta lay bare her soul. She led by being led by God. Like Paul who used himself as an illustration and who made his most effective points as he revealed his most private thoughts, so Teacher gave herself to those about her in such a way that they felt close to her innermost struggles. This mood was picked up by the other faculty members with the result that they did little "preaching down" to the collegians. They were one family seeking together the heights and depths of the grace of God.

The years 1947 and 1949 were high-water marks of revival. In the ensuing years, Teacher tended to look back on those earlier years as examples of what God could do if men and women were willing to pay the price. At times she seemed to have fixed 1947 and 1949 in her mind as standards by which everything else had to be evaluated.

But in the mid-1950s, her attitude moderated, and lingering triumphs of the past gave way to the exciting realities of the present. Both in service—for what remained ahead of her still considerable—and in character, she was yet to climb higher, ever higher.

Notes

1. Barbara Hudson Powers, *The Henrietta Mears Story* (Old Tappan, NJ: Fleming H. Revell Co., 1957), p. 183.
2. Never able to reconcile his doubts with the witness of Scripture, Billy's friend and former fellow evangelist turned away from the faith he had once helped others find, left the ministry and now works in the secular media.
3. Powers, *The Henrietta Mears Story,* p. 184.
4. Ibid.
5. Ibid., "Introduction."

SIXTEEN

O for a Thousand Tongues to Sing

*A*s faith gives birth to achievement in the natural world, faith in God and in His Word gives birth to achievement in the spiritual world."

DURING THE MORE THAN QUARTER-CENTURY THAT MARGARET AND HENRIETTA Mears lived together, sister Margaret was always close at hand to remove the humdrum of daily living, giving Henrietta the opportunity to accomplish the full life of ministry the Lord had placed before her. Margaret's assistance to her sister was as varied as it was limitless; she organized the household, bought the clothes for both wardrobes, promoted Forest Home, assisted with teas and accompanied Henrietta to meetings.

Margaret's service was all the more endearing for its artlessness and spontaneity. And though she had a deep reverence for things sacred, she also had a delightful way of dispensing large doses of cold common sense when her sister's religious fervor—in Margaret's eyes—became impractical. Yet Margaret's down-to-earth manner never detracted from a genuinely regal bearing that prompted one admiring observer to describe her as a lady with "her beplumed head held as though she ruled five kingdoms.'"

At the age of 72, quick-witted and individualistic, Margaret could hold her own in discussions with Henrietta's collegians as she expounded her views on politics, the way the Korean War should be fought, the latest trends in women's styles, the UCLA football team or liberalism—flitting from one subject to another in a way that kept the young folk roaring with laughter. She especially enjoyed poking fun at the students when, in their youthful exuberance, they failed to see the larger view of life. She kept their feet on the ground as much as her sister kept their hearts on high.

Margaret was greatly loved by the collegians she had hosted so often, and they grieved when—five days before Christmas in 1951—this generous, kind-hearted lady was felled by a stroke as she decorated the home for the season. Less than two days later she quietly passed away. The following Wednesday at the college prayer meeting, before 200 college students who knew her so well, Henrietta Mears bore witness to her faith in perhaps one of her finest moments:

> *I had thought that I would not come tonight. Then I*
> *realized what an opportunity I would be passing up if I*

Furs, feathers, flowers—and hats —were hallmarks of the Mears sisters, Henrietta *(l.)* and Margaret. "Miss Margaret" was her sister's best friend, constant companion, gracious hostess, fellow traveler and lifelong partner in ministry. Margaret, who was several years Henrietta's senior, also selected most of the hats for which the two ladies were famous.

did not come. I have been teaching you collegians for the last 25 years that God is able and that He does sustain us in any situation. I am here tonight to tell you that my God is able, that He is my sufficiency at this very moment.

As life passes you by, you will be going through experiences that you think you absolutely cannot endure. But God is faithful. He will not permit you to suffer a temptation which you will be incapable of bearing. And this I know, that if we will commit our way to Him, and will trust in Him, He will bring all these things to pass.

A Royal Home

After her sister's Homegoing, Henrietta wondered if she should continue living in the large six-bedroom house they had shared together. It did seem foolish for one woman to remain in such a large house. Perhaps she should sell it and move to an apartment.

Yet the thought of a cramped apartment appalled her. And what of her work? True, a very small apartment would just suit her personal needs. But an even larger residence could be used and shared by so many. She could open it and use it for church groups, college student affairs and special group needs.

As Henrietta weighed the pros and cons of where she should live in the future, a good friend, knowing Teacher liked beautiful homes, phoned and invited her to go and see a home which she was putting on the market. Henrietta accepted the invitation, and the two drove to Bel Air where, directly across from the UCLA campus, they drove up the driveway to a house that was a miniature French castle.

They went inside. As Henrietta wandered from room to room, she again thought, *I have plenty of furniture to fill these rooms. I wouldn't have to buy a thing unless I wanted to. And that dining room, big as a football field—well, almost—my collegians would love it.*

As she verbalized these thoughts aloud, her friend said in amazement, "Why, Miss Mears, I didn't bring you here to sell you this house. I just thought you would enjoy seeing this beautiful place."

Henrietta set about discovering whether or not the Lord approved of her buying this house. She must be sure of His leading in this matter, for whatever would she do with a house that was even larger than the one she now possessed? And she would not allow herself to be stampeded into a decision by the suggestion that someone else might come along and buy the house first. If that happened, well, then the Lord didn't want her to have it anyway.

So she was unfazed when she learned that the dream house

was sold to another. After all, she had some speaking engagements coming up, and the conferences at Forest Home would occupy her full time, so she decided the Lord had not meant for her to have the house. And it was settled as far as she was concerned.

Then one day, a short time later, Bill Bright casually remarked, "Miss Mears, you know that property on Sunset that you were looking at? Well, there's another 'For Sale' sign on it."

The Lord then revealed to Henrietta that this house was His plan for her, and everything began to unfold in rapid succession. One of her "sons" offered to buy the old house in which he and all his friends, along with Miss Margaret, had enjoyed many, many happy times. Bill Bright indicated that he and his wife, Vonette, were willing to move into the new house with Teacher and help with the expenses, pointing out that he could carry on his campus work from the Castle.

That settled it—and 11 years of happy association followed. Vonette was the perfect hostess, taking over the household where Miss Margaret had left off. God had set his seal upon the entire venture—beyond the shadow of a doubt.

Henrietta and "family" moved into the Castle, unpacked and uncrated possessions and soon every piece of Henrietta's furniture and objets d'art was in place. The Venetian goblets, acquired when she and Margaret had been in Europe, glistened and sparkled in the lighted display cabinet. Hand-carved ivory from Hong Kong, India and Africa lay side by side with a Bible covered in mother-of-pearl and a carving of the *Last Supper,* along with other treasured objects in the beautiful curio cabinet. Hand-painted figures of Napoleon and the Battle of Waterloo ringed a table lamp that reflected the scene in a mirror on an exquisite marble-and-gold table.

Henrietta was never concerned that Napoleon would get knocked off the table by some awkward athlete. Her philosophy that "one would act like a lady or a gentleman, if so attired" held true. She felt the difference in people was in their power of appreciation, no matter whether it was a breathtaking sunset, a handsome set of Limoges china, a figured lamp, a hungry child or a person's need for Christ.

So, from the beginning, Henrietta's home served as a cultural training ground for her high-spirited students. Teacher's objets d'art remained in their places—and surprisingly—most remained in one piece. As she had known all along, her collegians did value and appreciate the beautiful.

Soon came the night when God's blessing was invoked upon this home and household, and the Castle was dedicated to the Lord for all the plans He had for its future service. After that, Henrietta and the Brights—and, in time, their son, Zachary—settled down to the business of just living, doing the day-by-day things before them, ministering to those who rang the doorbell, lifting voices in song and laughter with the groups that filled the rooms, knowing God was in their midst.

For more than a decade, this home served as a gathering place where hundreds met the Savior, going on their way with lighter and happier steps as they went down the stairs and out to share their witness of the greatness and goodness of God.

The work of Campus Crusade for Christ was growing rapidly, and with Bill and Vonette Bright and other members of the Crusade staff living with her, Teacher was always in close touch with the student movement on the various campuses. Among those converted through Bill Bright's influence was a broad-shouldered football star at UCLA named Donn Moomaw. A common spectacle on Saturday afternoons was to hear some 50,000 fans chanting "Moo-maw, Moo-maw, Mooooo-maw!" with the opposite side roaring back, "Moo-maw, hee-haw!"

Donn's new faith quickly caught fire and, seeing the change in him, many came to know his Christ. Teacher loved this explosive, open-hearted fellow, and many were the hours they talked and prayed together. When Donn finished his university studies and was headed toward seminary, he needed finances. So he was very happy when an American professional football team offered him a contract. But the contract had a hitch—he would have to play on

Sundays. He asked Teacher if she would come to see him play on Sunday.

"Donn," she said, "you already know my answer to that."

Donn searched the Bible, committed his future to the Lord and rejected the contract. A short time later, a Canadian team gave him a bid—with no Sunday games in the deal. Not only did this arrangement meet his financial needs for seminary, it introduced his name to British sports fans, a fact that enhanced his witness when two years later, he readily joined Billy Graham in Harringay Arena for the Greater London Crusade of 1954.

A Joyous Reunion

Many other conversions and spiritual transformations also took place in the Castle, as did meetings of rejoicing for what God was doing. Among the momentous happenings that took place in this home was one that grew out of an idea taking shape in Teacher's mind. She had been recalling the Christian organizations which had been brought into existence since she had answered the Lord's call to come to the Hollywood Presbyterian Church.

"Why some of my own young people have been instrumental before God in founding some of these organizations," she mused. "They have much in common. Wouldn't it be wonderful if somehow we could all get together and share what the Lord has been doing and pray together?"

As the thought took root and grew, over 50 closely knit organizations appeared on the list she was making. "We leaped to action when she told us her idea," recalled Ethel May Baldwin, "helping to get out invitations, preparing the day's speaking and prayer schedule and getting in supplies to feed the group.

"The day finally arrived. The doors of her home swung open wide, and she stood welcoming her guests and friends. One does not expect to have an experience like this again, this side of heaven.

"They came with such joy and exuberance that one felt they had been waiting a long time for just such an opportunity to share and pray together, as Teacher had now made available to them. She reveled in the successes of the Lord, and wept and smiled and prayed throughout the day and on into the evening hours, as she listened to one after another tell what the Lord had accomplished through him and his organization. Truly our hearts did burn within us, as the mighty workings of God our Father were brought to our attention."

A Redefined Role

During the 1950s, Henrietta Mears' influence was felt around the world. But especially in America did she have the opportunity to share her insights and successes with others engaged in Sunday School work. Time and again she traveled to cities across the nation to speak at Sunday School conventions, inspiring pastors, teachers, superintendents and directors of Christian education. After her tours, like a match igniting a forest, she left fires burning in thousands of hearts in hundreds of churches, as pastors and educators went back to their tasks with renewed vision.

In recognition of her leadership in Christian education, an independent Christian university granted her an honorary Doctor of Humanities degree.

Along with that of its founder, the influence of Gospel Light Publications[1] grew beyond expectations. Dr. Cyrus N. Nelson, one of Teacher's former collegians and seminarians who was associated with Gospel Light in the 1930s, left his post as director of Mount Hermon Conference Center to assume new responsibilities as president of Gospel Light.

"Little did I realize then," said Cy, recalling Gospel Light's beginnings, "when I saw Miss Mears writing away on lessons in those early morning hours at the church, that one day these lessons would be distributed by the millions around the world. Her dedication in giving out the Word has brought blessings and hope to multiplied thousands."

William T. Greig, Sr., Henrietta's cousin by marriage,[2] had for

A shipment of books for a new 1950 curriculum course has just arrived in the Gospel Light warehouse, and looking over one of the first copies are *(l. to r.)* William T. Greig, Jr.; William T. Greig, Sr.; and Cyrus N. Nelson.

many years been a partner and executive in a large Minneapolis printing firm. During the 1940s, he gave valuable counsel in the technical phases of Gospel Light's publishing program, and spent most of his time in 1949 and 1950 in California working with Dr. Nelson.[3] Then in 1950, as Gospel Light was entering its period of greatest growth, Bill Greig, Jr., became involved and launched the Minnesota offices at Mound, near Minneapolis. When he sold his interest in the Minneapolis printing business in 1951, William Greig, Sr. moved to California and joined the growing publishing concern full time as vice president.

With these men taking the reins of Gospel Light, Henrietta— freed of major management and administrative responsibilities—assumed the role of editor-in-chief. She also was able now to devote herself more fully to her many other involvements such as Forest Home and, of course, to her first love and responsibility, the Sunday School of the Hollywood Presbyterian Church. Henrietta's handing over of authority and responsibility reflected her conviction that her work must pass on into the hands of capable men who would, during her lifetime, expand her original vision beyond what she herself had seen as well as carry on the work after her death.

In 1950, as increased growth created a need for greater facilities, the company relocated four times, finally settling in Glendale, California. And by 1958, the Gospel Light staff, now numbering 50, had multiplied five times what it had been only a decade before. *Teach* magazine, a new publication for Sunday School workers, was soon to become the leader in its field, passing on information and inspiration to tens of thousands of Christian educators around the world.

By 1952, Gospel Light had published its first Vacation Bible School course, *Sailing with Christ,* and within a few years became a pacesetter in its field. Due to increasing demands, the original curriculum was enlarged and expanded, its full cradle-to-grave range prompting a continuing revision program with the addition of colorful visual aids and other teaching accessories. The product line was expanded to provide for teaching materials for every area of a church's Christian education program. New courses kept the teaching relevant to the times while holding to Gospel Light's six basic goals for its Living Word Curriculum:

- Teach the Bible, God's inspired Word
- Present Jesus Christ as personal Savior and Lord
- Relate the Bible to the students' lives
- Train and inspire teachers and leaders
- Strengthen the Christian home and build the church
- Build the Body of Christ.

Henrietta Mears speaks to guests at a celebration in 1958 in recognition of her sixty-eighth birthday and the twenty-fifth anniversary of Gospel Light Publications.

Cyrus Nelson, president of Gospel Light Publications, watches Henrietta Mears blow out the candles on the birthday cake honoring both these events.

As the 1950s moved into the 1960s, Gospel Light grew to the point where the company was publishing over 700 individual items with unit sales running into the millions. Demands from around the world saw overseas markets boom in the 1960s with major distribution outlets in Toronto, London, Johannesburg, Sydney, Auckland and Tokyo. Every month shipments were going to over 80 countries of the world, and reports flowed back of Sunday Schools being transformed and people being reached with the gospel all around the globe.

A Needed Rest

The wisdom of Henrietta's decision to commit her ministries gradually to others became manifest in the 1950s through a series of illnesses she suffered. In 1951, shortly after returning from a trip around the world, Henrietta collapsed while addressing the women of the church. The doctors could find no cause, so the diagnosis came back that everything was fine.

But those close to Henrietta felt they knew the cause. People who had decided that no one else could help them constantly phoned the office for counseling appointments with her. And when they learned that she would be back in less than two months, would say, "Oh, I'll just wait until she gets back."

Such incidents happened over and over again until the combined cares of many literally submerged her, and the physical body could take no more. As Henrietta recuperated in the hospital, she would smile when Ethel May would say to her, "This is the Lord's way of letting you get away from everyone's problems."

A New Ministry

In 1952, just after Margaret's death and after her own strength had returned, Henrietta and Esther Ellinghusen decided to take a trip around the world. Their excitement ran high as they visited schools, mission stations and hospitals. One evening in Hong Kong, some missionaries drove them through the red-light district of the city and invited the two Americans to help pass out tracts to the unfortunate streetwalkers. In the semidarkness, Henrietta and Esther enthusiastically handed out hundreds of brochures and leaflets to eager hands.

On university campuses in Japan, they saw well-printed Communist literature being read by hundreds of students while Christian materials were either scarce or nonexistent. Many missionaries they met—some of whom had gone overseas from Hollywood Presbyterian Church as a result of her teaching—begged them for Sunday School materials in the languages they worked in. Asian pastors bemoaned the absence of adequate Sunday School manuals, and everywhere the two women went church workers asked them for help in supplying their children and young people with Christian literature.

Their desperate pleas for help started a stirring in the women's hearts to see something done. For, in country after country that they visited, they saw people, particularly children, being taught without materials or curriculum—and nothing was available anywhere. The need was obvious—and growing—Henrietta vowed to help meet it. And when she got back home, she did!

On Formosa, Henrietta and Esther visited the compounds, schools and hospitals of Lillian Dickson, the indefatigable "angel" of thousands of homeless orphans and lepers on that island. In one of the homes for lepers, they saw helpless folk living—and dying—on bare boards. Lillian explained their desperate need for mats to serve as mattresses, whereupon the two visitors immediately wrote out a check to pay for the purchase of 100 mats.

Upon returning to the States, they began to interest others in the work of Lillian Dickson. In the next few years, they introduced her work to many churches and groups that provided her with much-needed assistance. Henrietta and her friends, particularly Eleanor Doan of the Gospel Light staff, did much to encourage the eventual formation of "The Mustard Seed, Inc." the organizational title by which Lillian Dickson's work became known to countless thousands of American friends.

Still, the enormous need for Christian materials in foreign languages continued to burden Henrietta's heart and mind, her thinking overshadowed by the lack of Sunday School literature for peoples of other countries. "When I see children in Hong Kong sitting on a curb, pouring over Red comic books, students in Tokyo University districts with their arms loaded with Communist literature, and similar scenes repeated throughout the world, by God's grace, I must do something," Henrietta told her friends.

Unbeknown at first to Henrietta, she had already influenced some initial efforts at producing gospel literature in other languages. One of her college "girls" who had gone to Guatemala as a missionary had started a translation program there. She had found the job an immense one, however and, after much work and prayer, found a man with printing knowledge who could read proof and lay out the pages of the material. It was some time before Henrietta and Gospel Light became aware of this endeavor, but Henrietta—when she learned of it—was glad to know it was in capable hands.

Some time later word came from a missionary in Japan who had quite a bit of experience in translating Gospel Light's Sunday School lessons. He and his wife previously had been missionaries in Peking (now Beijing), China and had translated and printed materials there. When Peking became troubled, he moved the work to Shanghai.

Eventually China was closed and the couple had to evacuate, leaving behind the Gospel Light materials they had translated and printed there. But undaunted by their experience, the couple went to Japan, learned that language and again began a translation program. When the first books in Japanese rolled off the press, Gospel Light was notified of the work started by this couple in China and more recently begun by them in Japan.

This information was an encouragement to Henrietta and to Gospel Light. Yet from the bush areas of other countries, from crowded cities in Third World nations, from remote border areas and little-known places in distant lands came increasing numbers of requests for Gospel Light materials translated into other languages. "Our answer will be 'Yes, we can help,'" Henrietta said with deep emotion.

The same burden was beginning to haunt Cyrus Nelson and William Greig, Sr. as they received letters and reports from various parts of the world asking for Sunday School literature in national tongues. More and more of Cy's time was taken in answering these letters from other countries, so Bill Greig, Sr. volunteered part of his secretary's time. Other staffers even offered to stay and help after work. But answering letters in itself was not going to meet this ever-growing need.

Finally in 1961, Henrietta Mears established the GLINT (originally Gospel Literature in National Tongues, now Gospel Literature International) foundation to facilitate the development of Bible-teaching curriculum for national churches. Gospel Light's Living Word Curriculum was given without charge or royalty to responsible and cooperating missions and church groups for adaptation, translation and publication in foreign languages.

From the beginning, Cy Nelson had a special love for the ministry of GLINT. So he volunteered to assist the newly established foundation in a dual capacity: He served as the first chairman of GLINT's board of directors. And, since the organization initially had no paid staff, he continued replying to requests, acknowledging gifts and handling the other paperwork necessary to the ministry's operations until GLINT's first executive director took over from him.

Needs of various projects were made known to interested friends by the GLINT board and the first funds began to come in for translation programs in India, Africa, South and Central America and Europe. The vision caught fire immediately as missionaries pledged their support and time as money was raised. Within a short period, over 100,000 children were reading Gospel Light Sunday School books in Greece. And translations of the same books were being introduced into major linguistic areas of India under the direction of missionary Anna Nixon.

Henrietta Mears was overjoyed to know that at last there was a beginning to the help needed by scores of missionaries and countless Christian nationals worldwide in making the Word of God known to those in other lands. Although begun by Gospel Light, GLINT is a separate missionary organization, guided by its own board selected at large and mandated to assist groups worldwide in providing Sunday School literature wherever needed.

Some of the board members made trips abroad at their own expense to assist various groups in organizing translation programs and to encourage them to persist. Esther Ellinghusen, Cyrus Nelson and William Greig, Sr. visited various mission fields to counsel the literature committees and to lend encouragement and help in the production of books. Eleanor Doan also made several trips abroad, visiting workers producing materials in varied places and meeting with the initial organizational groups in the Philippines and Brazil.

The stories growing out of GLINT's many endeavors soon confirmed that this new venture bore the seal of God's approval. One account concerned a converted Hindu who was skilled in languages, but who could not write because he had lost his fingers to leprosy. This new Indian Christian found a friend who could act as his scribe, and the two worked together, the leper dictating his translations to the scribe until they had several books available for printing.

Both men refused any pay for their work, saying, "It is our gift to Jesus who gave Himself for us."

Often at GLINT board meetings, as reports of such sacrificial ministry would come in, Henrietta would say, "Let's send $100 or $200 just to encourage their hearts that someone cares about their literature translation programs." And often a subsequent report would reveal that the GLINT check had arrived at the very moment a bill had to be paid.

Other reports soon abounded of churches in far-off countries doubling and tripling in a few months time as the new Sunday School manuals were introduced. As had happened in Hollywood, now in dozens of other places in Asia, Africa and other places, young people were being converted and trained for Christ's service. The new ministry GLINT rapidly grew to take its place in the front ranks of twentieth-century missionary advances.

A single purpose. Henrietta Mears established Gospel Literature International to fulfill one very vital purpose: to put the best possible Bible-teaching tools in the hands of teachers and learners all around the world. GLINT accomplishes this purpose in a number of ways:

GLINT makes possible the translation and publication of Bible-based, easy-to-use Sunday School materials by arranging the free use of Gospel Light Publications' curriculum. Gospel Light has given to GLINT the exclusive rights to overseas adaptation and translation of its copyrighted study materials. GLINT, in turn, grants those rights to carefully-selected missionaries and national Christian agencies for translations and publication overseas.

GLINT also has been granted the overseas publication rights to books published by Gospel Light's Regal Book division—the kind of quality Christian literature that is so sorely needed overseas. GLINT makes these copyrighted books available to selected foreign translators and publishers.

GLINT sometimes provides the "seed money" to help launch publishing programs. This money may be used to purchase equipment and supplies to underwrite certain printing and production costs or to set up distribution systems that ensure the widest possible use of the curriculum and books. Many of these programs would never begin without GLINT's financial aid.

GLINT has sponsored international training conferences to help national Christians and literature missionaries become better writers, editors, translators, artists, printers and distributors. These conferences enable specialists from the United States and Canada to share their skills with key overseas personal. GLINT has also provided scholarships for national young people preparing for publishing work.

Through printed training courses, special teacher-training conferences and a variety of teaching aids, GLINT is helping Sunday School teachers and pastors in many nations become more effective in their vital ministry of teaching God's Word and helping people grow in Christ.

A special organization. GLINT is a special kind of organization. It is a mission agency, yet it is not a sending agency. It distributes hundreds of thousands of dollars each year, yet it is not primarily a fund-raiser. It is the catalyst of a global publishing enterprise involving hundreds of people, yet it has only a handful of office staff.

GLINT was founded not just to begin a new ministry, but to respond to growing demands. It freely gives its resources to those in need. GLINT is solidly conservative in theology and works with a wide range of evangelical missions, national churches and denominations.

Instead of sending missionaries overseas, GLINT works with and through the missionaries and national Christians who are already there. They know the language, culture and local needs, and GLINT helps them meet those needs through culturally appropriate Christian literature and publishing services.

GLINT also believes that financial self-sufficiency is essential if national publishing ministries are to meet the changing needs of the people. It stimulates and aids such ministries in two ways: (1) by providing use of copyrighted curriculum and books, and (2) by providing "seed money" grants, not continuing subsidies, for specific translation and publishing projects.

GLINT carefully screens the many requests for its help, and works with reliable, dedicated mission agencies and national Christian organizations. After thorough field research and approval by the board of directors, it commits itself to work with only one organization in each language area. The foundation does not solicit individuals or organizations to use its aid; rather, it responds to requests that originate on the field.

To be effective, Bible study materials and books must be culturally relevant. GLINT does not expect translators to adopt the North American model of Christian education, but to adapt basic Bible-teaching tools for the special needs of their own cultures. It also encourages talented national Christians to develop their writing and artistic skills and to create original culturally unique Christian literature.

A great many tools are needed for the world's teachers of gospel literature, and these tools are continually changing to meet the needs of a changing world. A series of Vacation Bible School materials has been translated and printed, following the general themes of Gospel Light Publication's courses. Of course, many changes are necessary in the nine countries where they are printed to allow for cultural differences in expressions and art work. GLINT is excited to know that children worldwide are enjoying Vacation Bible School, learning the Bible, singing the songs, working in their books, learning to know God and praying to Him.

While much remains to be done in making Christ known around the world, GLINT rejoices in having had a part for nearly 30 years in translating and distributing materials that have won multiplied thousands of children, youth and adults to Jesus Christ as Lord and Savior and that have enlisted them in further spreading the good news of salvation.

Notes

1. After being launched as Gospel Light Press, the company formally changed its name in 1956 to Gospel Light Publications, the name by which it continues to be known today.
2. William T. Greig, Sr., married Margaret Buckbee, the same Margaret who stood with Henrietta Mears before the deacons and congregation of the First Baptist Church of Minneapolis, when both girls were five years old, to be examined on doctrinal matters before being admitted to baptism. Margaret Buckbee Greig was four days younger than Henrietta.
3. Dr. Cyrus N. Nelson, son-in-law of William T. Greig, Sr., was also married to a Margaret—Margaret Greig Nelson, better known as "Peggy" Nelson to her friends and associates.

SEVENTEEN

"I'll Not Be Here Next Year"

*I*f you ever happen to see in the obituary column that Henrietta Mears has died, don't you believe it! This old body may die, but I'll be glad of that. I wouldn't want to have to go through eternity with this deteriorating one. I'll have a new body.

"And what will I do when I get to heaven? Well, I am going to ask the Lord to show me around. I'll want to get in a rocket ship to inspect all the galaxies He has made. And maybe He will give me a planet of my own, so that I can start building something. Oh, it's going to be so wonderful!"

DURING HER LATTER YEARS, HENRIETTA MEARS PONDERED THE QUESTION OF her retirement and how she should go about it. But each time she took any steps in this direction, some new challenge would develop and she would arise to meet it. Soon it became evident that because of her own willingness to serve and remain active, retirement was out of the question.

When she finally realized that God did not want her to retire, she accepted His decision with renewed energy, comparing herself to Caleb of old (see Josh. 14:10-11), whose strength was not abated in old age. This acceptance now gave her determination to rise above any handicaps and to give herself in continued service to others.

As always, her home was open to guests seeking her spiritual guidance. She continued to attend the teachers and officers meetings for the Sunday School, and she was present at most of the functions of the college department, staying late to counsel students. When the Lord made it clear to Teacher that she was to remain at her post year after year—for over 30 years, she used to say,

> *Lord, as long as you see fit to keep me in that college department, you must make me attractive to those young people, and you must give me the message for this day and age that you want them to have.*

The executives of the class continued to meet with her on Saturday mornings, and the group more than ever expressed its love to their dear friend who, regardless of personal health, was giving herself to her beloved collegians—her family—as unstintingly as ever. Sometimes it seemed to them that Teacher actually relished the opportunity to test God's promise, "And as thy days, so shall thy strength be" (Deut. 33:25).

Receiving a Miracle

In 1957, while sailing with friends across the Pacific, Henrietta realized her eyesight was once again deteriorating. Even more

L. to r: Dr. Louis H. Evans, Sr., pastor of the Hollywood Presbyterian Church; Henrietta Mears; Dede Harvey, then a member of the college department; and Dr. Richard C. Halverson, then assistant pastor.

ominous, pains in her eyes were rapidly increasing. The sight in her good eye also became impaired.

Upon arrival in Australia, the new trouble was diagnosed as a ruptured blood vessel. Medical authorities there advised Henrietta to return to the United States and to her doctor there. They urged her not to prolong her trip beyond the time of the projected cruise.

In California her ophthalmologist, Dr. Paul Reed, a nationally honored specialist and an esteemed Christian leader, said to her, "There is nothing I as a doctor can do for you. But as a Christian, I suggest you pray and ask others to pray with you."

Henrietta knew that her sight lay in the hands of God who had

L. to r. are Dr. Richard C. Halverson, then assistant pastor; Dr. Henrietta C. Mears; Dr. and Mrs. Raymond I. Lindquist. Dr. Lindquist succeeded Dr. Louis H. Evans, Sr. as pastor of the First Presbyterian Church of Holllwood and was the pastor of the church at the time of Teacher's death in 1963.

created it and that God alone could intervene and stop the deterioration taking place in her vision. As prayer ascended on her behalf, God did hear and did answer. The next time Dr. Reed examined her eyes, he found no further deterioration in her good eye. God had stretched forth His healing hand once more on her behalf.

Even so, friends—who knew the determination of her courageous spirit and her willingness to accept infirmities as obstacles to be overcome—were amazed to find her reading again as avidly as ever. But she was motivated by a new dimension of thought beginning to open in her mind. She had long studied the doctrine of the Holy Spirit, and the ministry of the Third Person of the Trinity had been a lifetime reality in her experience. But now Henrietta began with growing eagerness to seek out a fuller understanding of His potential in her life.

Desiring the Gifts

What an unexpected thrill these times were for those close to her. Here was this dearly loved friend, this old warrior now approaching the end of her course, who had already accomplished more than enough to satisfy the most ambitious of individuals. Still she was searching, seeking, stretching for yet untapped reservoirs of divine power so that her life and ministry might attain to even more sublime heights of holy accomplishment.

"I have enjoyed spiritual gifts," she would say. "I have had the Spirit's presence. But now I want everything that He has for me. I want all the gifts."

And with a surprisingly youthful earnestness, she set out again to know God better. The observable outcome of this pilgrimage was seen not so much in her teaching or organizational ministries—more and more these responsibilities were being committed to her successors—but in that most important sphere of all: a holy, peaceful life.

Henrietta Mears mellowed after this experience, becoming even more sympathetic, gracious, kind and secure. Her eyes seeing with deeper penetration the opening doors of eternity.

Meeting Her Lord

Early in 1963, Henrietta was attending a garden party sponsored by some of the women of the church. Recognizing a musical friend in the crowd, Henrietta asked her to play something for them and began to lead the lady to the piano.

But the pianist begged off and apologized, saying, "Oh, Miss Mears, I am not really in practice. I'll play for you next year."

Henrietta registered a kindly disappointment, and only a friend standing next to her heard her whisper, "I'll not be here next year."

During the day of Monday, March 18, 1963, Ethel May Baldwin and Henrietta Mears drove past new construction sites in the San Fernando Valley. They talked excitedly together of the rapid expansion of southern California, of the influx of people to the area and of the opportunities they would have to reach these new residents with the gospel. The two women returned to Henrietta's Bel Air home still animated over what the future held for their work.

Tuesday evening, Henrietta talked at length on the telephone with Jack Franck about the coming prospects of Forest Home—so many new ideas were in the offing that thrilled and excited her. When she finally turned her light out, her heart was singing with the adventures of what still lay before her.

The next morning, her housekeeper, Mrs. Shearer, found that, during the night, Henrietta had died peacefully in her sleep. She had finally slipped through that veil between the present and the hereafter which she had described over the years as being so very, very thin.

Someone remarked, "It was nothing new for her to meet her Lord alone, for she had often done so. This time she just went with Him."

On her desk were found her preparations of several Bible messages which she was hoping to give in the near future, among them the lesson she had planned for her collegians at their Easter breakfast.[1]

Rejoicing in Heaven

Nearly 2,000 people filed silently into the sanctuary of the First Presbyterian Church of Hollywood to witness the most triumphant memorial service that most of them would ever see. Scattered throughout the audience that day acutely aware of God's presence at that moment were hundreds whom Henrietta Mears had personally led to Christ, some of them ordained ministers, many of them young people.

The opening words of the service were: "I am the resurrection, and the life: he that believeth in me, though he were dead, yet shall he live: and whosoever liveth and believeth in me shall never die" (John 11:25-26).

The soloist, one of Teacher's own boys, with profound and heartfelt feeling, sang, "How Great Thou Art!" And the choir, under Dr. Hirt's majestic leadership, sounded forth with Martin Luther's magnificent call-to-arms, "A Might Fortress Is Our God," as prayers of thanksgiving and rejoicing rose from hearts overwhelmed with the glory of God.

Many tributes to Henrietta were spoken, including one sent by telegram from Billy Graham: "I am certain that Henrietta Mears had a great reception in heaven. She made a tremendous impact upon my life and ministry."

Dr. Raymond Lindquist spoke of her energy, her enthusiasm and her ability to bring a person to his own fulfillment.

Dr. David Cowie mentioned her talent for showing a person his unlimited capacity to be filled with God's ability.

Dr. Richard Halverson recalled her many wise counsels, especially concerning her advice to stay in one place in order to establish a lasting work and not to move about from church to church. Her work at Hollywood was possible, he emphasized, because she stayed there for 35 years, turning down many invitations to minister elsewhere.

The Rev. Louis Evans, Jr. unfolded in his prayer a scene all were thinking about:

> *O Lord! We look upon heaven now and can see nothing but rejoicing, for she is meeting all those whom she has known on this earth who have gone before and all those whom she has not known on this earth who have waited for her all these years. Indeed, O Lord, heaven throbs with rejoicing on this day for thy saint, who walked in simple victory, because she walked in simple trust.*

In his tribute, Dr. Cyrus Nelson summarized the many accomplishments of Henrietta Mears:

Because of Dr. Mears' deep love of her Savior and her church, she had a great love for the world. She believed, that for the needs of all people in all places, Christ was the answer. Consequently, when she envisaged the work of the local church, she saw the Church universal.

"People must be called by God," she said, and she prayed the Lord of the harvest to send forth His laborers. It is a remarkable fact that over 400 young people went into Christian service under her influence. In 1962, there were more than 40,000 delegates at Forest Home, coming from 40 different denominations and hundreds of churches and groups.

Billy Graham, in 1949, found a renewed dedication at Forest Home, which enabled him to begin his now-famous Los Angeles Crusade. Writing in Christianity Today, he says, "I remember walking down a trail, trampling alone in the world, almost wrestling with God. I dueled with my doubts, and my soul seemed to be centered in the cross fire. Finally, in desperation, I surrendered my will to the living God as revealed in Scripture. Within six weeks we started our Los Angeles Crusade, and the rest is now history."

Dr. Mears also played an important part in the worldwide ministry of Campus Crusade for Christ. Bill Bright, the founder, listened to her one evening with intensity and conviction and, after her challenge, he knelt before God. This was his spiritual pivot from self to the Savior.

Then she opened up the doors of her home and, for almost 10 years, thousands of students crossed Sunset Boulevard from UCLA to hear the gospel there. The Hollywood Christian Group was born in her home. She was a founder of the National Sunday School Association, and a member of many boards of international Christian significance.

> *Her global vision also saw the potential of the print-ing press and in 1933 she founded Gospel Light Publi-cations, together with Miss Esther A. Ellinghusen, Miss Ethel May Baldwin and D. Stanley Engle. Today this ministry touches more than 20,000 churches and mis-sion stations across our country and the seven seas.*
>
> *Her last and perhaps destined to be her greatest worldwide ministry is GLINT, a missionary foundation formed to translate and distribute Christian materials around the world. And so GLINT was born in 1961.*
>
> *You will notice that facts stirred Dr. Mears to action.*

Her open casket, banked with numerous floral tributes, seemed to be but another platform from which she was speaking. Many young hearts asked themselves, "I wonder upon whom her mantle will fall?" But her mantle already lay on the shoulders of thou-sands upon thousands who had been directed to Christ by her life.

Concluding the memorial service, the choir began pealing out the heroic themes of George Frederic Handel's exalted "Hallelujah Chorus." The congregation rose to honor the King of kings and their minds turned reverently from the passing of a friend to the glory of the risen Lord. As the last chords faded into silence, a man whispered to his neighbor, "Dear Teacher! Even in her death she pointed us to Christ."[2]

Notes

1. Ever committed to the ministry of Forest Home, Henrietta Mears left her estate to the Christian camp and conference center she had founded 35 years before.
2. Officials at the Forest Lawn Memorial Park said that the crowd attending the grave-side service for Dr. Henrietta C. Mears was the largest gathered there in 20 years—an astounding fact, considering that many of Hollywood's greats are also buried there.

EIGHTEEN

So Many Enduring Monuments

I n our generation more has been learned about the universe than in all the previous history of mankind. This is the age of discovery. Those who think that there are no more frontiers to conquer are out of contact with their times."

IN 1983, ON THE TWENTIETH ANNIVERSARY OF THE DEATH OF HENRIETTA Mears, Dr. Cyrus N. Nelson, then chairman of the board for Gospel Light Publications, declared, "Few people have forged such strong ties of influence and impact and produced so many enduring monuments—monuments of fruitful lives and influential Christian institutions—as has Dr. Henrietta C. Mears....Dr. Mears is now with the Lord, but her vision and vitality remain."

Gospel Light Publications

Premier among the three major institutions established by Henrietta Mears is Gospel Light Publications which she founded in 1933. Of Gospel Light and its founder, Cy stated,

> *The sun never sets on the work Christ called Dr. Mears to do through the lives she taught and trained and the materials she wrote and edited. We at Gospel Light Publications are—and always will be—committed to the continuation and expansion of teaching the total Bible. We recognize and proclaim its absolute authority and transforming power of Christ....*
>
> *We at Gospel Light have dedicated ourselves to the teaching of God's Word in its completeness and without compromise. We are determined under God that the message so rich and meaningful to Dr. Mears shall continue to flow from our company to increasing millions of people around the world.*

The Gospel Light product line, already growing rapidly at the time of Henrietta Mears' death, continued to expand in the following years to meet the many needs in the field of Christian education. To build and strengthen the Christian home, the company launched *Family Life Today,* a magazine designed to help build strong marriages and family relationships and to support family ministry in the church. This successful magazine was acquired in its ninth year by Full Potential, a group of concerned Christians whose primary purpose is to expand the magazine's circulation and outreach potential while continuing a close relationship with Gospel Light.

To serve the world further through the printed page, Gospel Light, in 1965, launched its Regal Book division with two titles and a declared mission: to publish books and tapes that stimulate thinking, meet needs and influence Christian attitudes, values and relationships. As of late 1989, Regal Books had published several hundred with 283 currently in print and some 30 other titles awaiting publication.

Gospel Light was one of the first publishers in the Christian education field to introduce paperbacks into the Sunday School curriculum line. Two of Regal's first books are still best-sellers: Fritz Ridenour's *How to Be a Christian Without Being Religious* has over 4 million copies in print and Henrietta Mears' classic *What the Bible Is All About* in several editions and in more than 50 printings also has nearly 2 million copies in print.

In 1971, on February 9, a 45-second earthquake in the early morning rocked southern California, including Glendale, and damaged the Gospel Light building beyond repair. Dr. John Calvin Reid, a noted Presbyterian minister and Regal author, arrived later that day to speak to the Gospel Light staff in chapel. He surveyed the wrecked building with its collapsed roof and, with a chuckle, expressed his wonderment "at the lengths some people will go to to avoid hearing me preach. All you had to do," he added with a smile, "was just ask me not to come."

Employees meanwhile rescued projects and materials and set up shop in any habitable space available, in rented buildings, in nearby houses, in whatever could be found. Many worked at home temporarily until a six-story former bank building was located and obtained in downtown Glendale.

In 1970, just before the earthquake, Gospel Light's International Center for Learning (ICL) was established to train and motivate both lay and professional church staff persons for effective Bible teaching—primarily through the Sunday School—by providing churches with training seminars and resources. Holding more than

50 annual seminars in its first 12 years, ICL introduced a complete line of related products while training teachers and leaders to improve their instructional methods and organizational skills. In doing so, it helped them to increase the impact of their total Christian education ministries.

Different types of programs were offered by ICL as needs and conditions changed. Serving churches in six regions in the United States and Canada, ICL continued to equip Christian educators through seminars featuring age-level workshops, conducted in various cities by specialists in Christian education, presenting a totally coordinated Sunday School plan. In the past decade and a half, the International Center for Learning has trained educators to improve the teaching of God's Word.

The city of Glendale, in 1980, absorbed Gospel Light's downtown location into its emerging Galleria, one of southern California's then newest and largest shopping centers. In its selection of a new headquarters site, Gospel Light moved its center of operation to its present location at 2300 Knoll Drive in Ventura, California, where on a clear day the staff can glimpse the Pacific Ocean. The company's West Coast warehouse is also at this location, though the main Gospel Light warehouse is still located in Cincinnati, Ohio.

In 1982, Gospel Light acquired Vision House, a publishing company that offered a wide variety of books and audio tapes by a broad range of personalities. Among the notables joining Gospel Light through this acquisition were cults expert, Dr. Walter Martin, psychologists Dr. Gary Collins and Dr. James Dobson, and Bible expositor, Dr. Ray Stedman, pastor of Peninsula Bible Church in Palo Alto, California.

Gospel Light celebrated its fiftieth birthday in 1983—a few of the staff recalling those beginning years with Henrietta Mears—by renewing its commitment to making the written Word of God and Jesus Christ, the Living Word of God, known to all the world. The company's commitment is expressed in this statement of purpose: "The mission of Gospel Light is to know Christ and to make Him known; to provide His Church with effective Bible teaching and learning resources for use in making disciples, empowering them for godly living, equipping them for ministry and the evangelization of the world."

To accomplish this mission and to extend the vision of Henrietta Mears, Gospel Light continues to broaden its product line with new resources for individuals, families and churches in the areas of inspiration, evangelism, Bible teaching, motivation, personal growth, church growth and Christian living. Through these products, Gospel Light affirms its belief in God's Word as the total answer to man's total need; the good news of forgiveness, faith, peace, power, purpose and heaven.

The intervening years since 1983 have been full of progress and change, yet years that say the Sunday School has become an increasingly effective tool in the nurture and education of several generations of Christians. This fact is reflected in the company's continued growth and development during these years. Gospel Light's English Language products are now distributed overseas through seven centers: Toronto, Canada; London, England; Auckland, New Zealand; Sydney, Melbourne and West Ryde, Australia; and Johannesburg, South Africa. In addition to these distributors, scores of Christian bookstores on every continent make Gospel Light's English language products available to missionaries and other English-speaking customers. Regular shipments now go out to more than 85 countries across the world.

Growth is also evident in the establishment of two warehouses, sales representatives and Christian education workers strategically located throughout the United States, a growing staff and increasingly automated facilities in Ventura. Typesetting, word processing, bookkeeping, inventory control, order processing, editing, product design and other procedures are now computerized. Records are kept on microfilm, and Telecopies (fax machines) permit the instant exchange of hard copy between various in-house departments and field staff, customers, authors, printers and the like. Printing and book manufacturing is done in Pennsylvania, Ohio, Tennessee, Texas and California as needed.

Now facing the twenty-first century, Gospel Light remains first in its resolve to meet people's needs in an ever-changing world with the changeless gospel. No one can predict the future world in which today's children will be tomorrow's leaders, for times change and society moves on. But the importance of Christian education, the Sunday School and the Sunday School teacher remains the same. Something else also remains constant—Gospel Light's commitment to Jesus Christ and to the continuing development of the best in Christian literature and resources.

While the coming decades are creating many uncertainties, the late 1980s have already produced one certainty: a new baby boom means more children will be reaching Sunday School age in the near future than at any time in the last two generations. At the same time, the fastest-growing segment of population in the United States and Canada is the over-55 age group.

With these statistics comes (1) an exciting opportunity for churches to reach and teach more children and adults with the love of Christ, and (2) a certainty that the quality of today's Christian education will have a dramatic effect on the churches of the next generation. The fact that the Sunday School has the potential to impact the lives of increasing numbers of individuals adds urgency to the challenge of the future.

Gospel Light has responded to this challenge with the introduction of a totally new curriculum of Bible study materials designed to meet the critical needs of the coming decade in a way that will effectively minister to students, teachers and church leaders. The all-new Living Word curriculum has been developed by skilled staff members with much practical experience in Christian education. It is designed to contribute greatly toward building life-changing, growing Sunday Schools and churches.

So Gospel Light moves into the future fully aware of the importance of life-changing Bible study for boys and girls, men and women. Meeting the spiritual needs of lives being formed in a new age—in a world increasingly opposed to Christian values—remains our hope, our purpose, our prayer for today and for all the tomorrows yet to come.

Forest Home

"Forest Home is operated for one purpose—to conduct conferences for all ages where Christ will be held up and magnified," Henrietta Mears asserted during her 25 years of administering Forest Home. "We desire that each person attending will be introduced to Christ as Savior and will commit his life to Him as Lord."

"To know Christ," that initial message and prayer of Forest Home has echoed through the years in the thousands of conferences held there, attended by millions of children and adults. And it still echoes. And the multiplied thousands—now more than 2 million, hear the Bible messages, make eternal decisions, enjoy the fun and relax in the beauty of mountains, streams and whispering pines.

Forest Home Christian Conference Center is in its sixth decade of ministry on the mountain. And its leadership and board are looking to the future for as many more years of service as God ordains for the center.

Years before the Forest Home Christian Conference Center grounds were obtained, a group of 14 leading citizens, led by Truman Reeves, then State Treasurer of California, walked to the top of Mount San Bernardino facing Forest Home. There they stood and prayed, dedicating the mountain and valley "to the service of the Lord." This fact was not known until 1958 when some of the Forest Home conference members hiked to the top of the mountain and found the plaque. A new plaque was then made and installed by the King's Men Boys' Club with this inscription:

> *On May 30, 1876, this great mountain and valley were dedicated to the service of the Lord Jesus Christ in prayer by fourteen eminent citizens led by Truman Reeves, State Treasurer of California.*
>
> *Seventy-eight years later Forest Home Christian Conference Grounds stands as a monument to answered prayer. Erected August 14, 1954 by the King's Men.*

To Henrietta Mears, Mount San Bernardino—"this great mountain"—was her "Miracle Mountain." She deeply loved the old mountain and the conference center sheltered in its shadow.

> *I stood on the slopes of Miracle Mountain. Every view spoke of His greatness and majesty. I shall never forget Forest Home. It has meant so much to me and countless thousands of others like me that I vowed to give of my time...my talents that youth from all over the world might know the reality of Christ.*

From her commitment came committed people with great vision, and Forest Home played a significant part in capturing and perpetuating her vision. For not only was she able to stimulate men and women to work with her during the 25 years she administered Forest Home, but she also trained them to carry on without her. Since Henrietta entered heaven on March 20, 1963, another 27 years have passed, and the Forest Home staff today are no less dedicated to the vision she established. They are determined that it will be implanted and nurtured in the lives of all who attend Forest Home today, tomorrow and in years to come.

The year before Henrietta died, 350 women met on the mountaintop for the first Women's Auxiliary meeting. Henrietta was the guest speaker and she gave her listeners three challenges:

> *I want you to be women of prayer. Everything at Forest Home has been accomplished because of prayer. I want you to be women of planning...see so much work to be done at Forest Home that you'll have to cry for women. I want you to be women of vision—to start men and women, boys and girls out to the utter most parts of the earth. The seemingly trivial things are making it possible to do this.*
>
> *Ask the Lord to lift your vision to see what you can do to make Forest Home what He wants it to be for His*

*honor and glory. Everything we do for the Lord should
have beauty and loveliness and do honor to Him.*

The goal of the auxiliary was to have a membership of 2,000, as well as thrift shops and projects for area chapters, a Forest Home women's retreat in the fall and membership teas in the spring. Through the years to the present, the auxiliary membership has continued to increase, both in numbers and in undertakings for the benefit of the conference center.

Progress at Forest Home has continued, with enrollment increasing every year, necessitating construction of new dormitories to replace the aged ones; erecting new meeting halls; organizing new camps, such as the New Indian Village for juniors and Lost Creek Ranch for junior highs; building new duplexes and developing plans for much, much more.

Forest Home was growing and room was needed for the campers. Some of those who are conference leaders now were among those students and guests at the 1947 and 1949 College Briefing Conferences, among them: Rev. Donn Moomaw of the First Presbyterian Church in Bel Air; Dr. Richard C. Halverson, chaplain of the United States Senate; and Dr. Billy Graham.

As the '60s merged into the '70s, a dormitory that housed girls on the staff during the summer and women conference guests the rest of the year was completed and paid for by the Forest Home Women's Auxiliary. New Ponderosa cabins were built for high schoolers, and an Olympic-size swimming pool was put in. Plans included other buildings to be used year-round to accommodate increasing enrollments. And with the building of new facilities, many more conferences were scheduled for winter.

Henrietta Mears envisioned Forest Home as a place where she could lead young people to know Christ and to serve Him.

*I have learned through the years of dealing with
hundreds of thousands of youth throughout the world
that there is a nostalgia today "for reality." They will
spurn religion, but they want reality. It seems that here*

in this mounting sanctuary of templed hills with its craggy altars, we meet God as He is revealed in His Son. Christ is present as the answer to the individual life and to the world's problems. He says, "I am the way, the truth, and the life: no man cometh unto the Father, but by me" (John 14:6).

Henrietta was convinced that, in ministering to young people, more could be accomplished in hours of camping than in days of Sunday School. She had organized Indian Village for junior-age children, the Ranch for junior high and Main Camp for families. But what was still needed was a special place for the high school youth. Such a place would take time to develop, but already she envisaged it.

Finally fifteen years after her death, a large large camp was built on the Lakeview side of Forest Home. The new Henrietta C. Maers Memorial Lodge is the nerve center of the area with its lounge, game and counseling rooms and a comfortable meeting room. Crowning the lodge is a carpeted stair-step amphitheater, capable of seating 200 people comfortably.

At the Ranch in the late '70s on Western Street, at the entrance of the camp, two staff rooms, the Museum and a meeting room, were built and again paid for by the Forest Home Women's Auxiliary. Another improvement at the Ranch was the building of bleachers.

Next, at the junior high camp, came the building of the Barn which accommodates 250 students for bed, board and meetings, summer and winter. This facility doubles the prior capacity of the camp. Camp officials and churches alike thrill to see the number of youngsters attending the camps, coming to know Jesus Christ as Lord and Savior, and going forth year after year enriched in spiritual experience.

Many other improvements are made annually to keep the camp upgraded. A new Ponderosa duplex cabin, especially designed and built for handicapped guests and located opposite the entrance to Hormel Hall is already in use. Plans for future years

The Henrietta C. Mears Memorial Lodge, Forest Home Christian Conference Center, erected in 1978, five years after her death.

are on the drawing boards, designed to accommodate further expected increases in enrollments and to improve the overall quality of the conference grounds for year-round usage.

Forest Home is not merely a collection of cabins and meeting halls and dining rooms on 600 acres of mountain; it is people meeting God. Whatever has been constructed grew out of Henrietta Mears driving desire to reach people and to train them for the service of Jesus Christ:

> *Forest Home is a place a mile nearer heaven, with its God-given charm and beauty as everlasting as the rugged mountains that surround it. But this is not all: Forest Home not only answers the call of your being for beauty and challenge; it also speaks to the heart and says, "God is in this place!"*

> *How many have gazed into the starry heavens at night and said with David, "The heavens declare the glory of God; and the firmament sheweth his handy-work" (Ps. 19:1) or in the morning have looked upon the mountains rising another mile above them and said, "I will lift up mine eyes unto the hills, from whence cometh my help. My help cometh from the Lord, which made heaven and earth" (Ps. 121:1-2)? A peace that passes understanding fills our souls.*

Henrietta's gift to Forest Home of a rich spiritual heritage is found in the thousands of names in the *Book of Remembrance*. These are names of people of all ages and denominations who signed the book after they had cast their bits of wood into the fire, symbolizing their decisions. Of them, she said:

> *Wherever you go on the face of the earth, there are men and women living to the glory of God because their lives were touched and transformed at Forest Home. There are many in industry, in professions, in the mar-ketplaces of the world, as well as in the ministry. They have gone with a message. What a wonderful place For-est Home has been for us to see what faith in Christ can really accomplish.*
>
> *There we feel translated out of an environment filled with science and the technique of living, stuffed full with every gadget to make life more interesting but leav-ing life so empty. One glimpse of those hills, a mile nearer heaven, reminds us of the God of Power. And the river speaks of God's eternal mercy ever rolling down to an eternal sea; one glimpse—and we may not even know how it happened, but we feel whole again! Life has gotten its bearings.*
>
> *It's different because once more we are living in a land where eternal values count. We set our flushed faces toward the cool breezes of eternity and breathe deeply. We are made for this!*

This rustic signpost once welcomed guest to Forest Home and reminded them where they were in relation both to the Christian Conference center and to heaven.

GLINT

The work of GLINT was already well under way in 1963 when Henrietta Mears was called home to heaven—just two years after she founded GLINT. But in the years that immediately followed, GLINT's program was in evident need of hands-on leadership; leadership with a knowledge of the work being done overseas by people who wanted to provide Christian teaching materials but who lacked training in the writing, editing, producing and manufacturing of books. To meet this need, Rev. Paul Fretz, the missionary who had spearheaded GLINT's work in Brazil, was appointed GLINT's executive director. Paul moved to southern California to direct the work and, under his leadership, the work grew and prospered, particularly in India, the Philippines, Brazil, Japan, Greece and Korea.

The literature committees—when translating Bible materials from English into other languages—gave careful attention to cultural traditions in the different countries. The art work, puzzles and the like were also carefully adapted as each translation progressed. In some countries, several language groups had to be accommodated so that many people were involved in the translation effort, necessitating organized leadership to direct the work. In India, for example, 28 languages have been translated, each requiring detailed attention and much work to meet the needs of their people with the finished product.

Kenya has curriculum in eight language groups, the Philippines has five and Zaire has four. The Sunday School curricula has been published in its entirety or in part in 46 countries, involving upwards of 105 language groups, including materials for mainland China, three Arabic countries and three other countries behind the Iron Curtain.

In 1965, when Gospel Light's Regal Book division was established, a number of mission enterprises began requesting permission to translate Regal books that would be helpful to their people. Henrietta Mears' book, *What the Bible Is All About,* was the high school Sunday School course in four quarterly books. Then it appeared later in a modern book format, convenient to read and use as a basic Bible commentary. Through the years it has been one of the more widely translated Regal books, vying with Don Richardson's *Peace Child,* which has appeared in 17 translations.

In 1987, a children's edition—*What the Bible Is All About, Young Explorer's Edition,* prepared by Frances Blankenbaker— was published and received the coveted Gold Medallion Award as best book in its category. This edition went into three printings in less than a year and was immediately translated into Greek. Other translation permissions are pending.

Through GLINT the work of Henrietta Mears continues around the world as the printed page in many languages continues to proclaim the same message she did: Jesus Christ is Savior and Lord.

To date, GLINT has helped organizations in 41 countries to publish 474 books in 34 languages and translated from 194 Regal Books titles. These works are now being distributed in more than 50 nations, including six behind the Iron Curtain.

Currently, 86 books are being worked on in 30 languages. GLINT will be publishing for the first time in 14 of these languages. Altogether, when projects pending or in progress are completed, GLINT will have published in a total of 48 languages.

Many GLINT books are exhibited at International Books Fairs in such places as Frankfurt, Germany and Moscow, Russia's capital city, where they become known to even wider audiences. *What the Bible Is All About*, with recent translations in Arabic, Farsi (one of the languages of Iran) and Polish, has been exhibited at these fairs in both its original and *Young Explorers* editions.

After serving GLINT in Canada and the United States for 14 years, Paul Fretz returned to his denomination to serve the Missionary Church as associate missions director. He is still close to the work of GLINT, meeting missionaries and Christian nationals around the world who have translated Gospel Light's Sunday School materials and books. Succeeding Paul briefly as interim executive directors were Richard Reilly and Peter Angier.

Presently heading up the work of GLINT is Georgalyn Wilkinson who previously served eight years in Japan as field director of her mission board and six additional years in the United States as the mission's director of outreach. She faces the future with great expectations as she describes GLINT's past successes and future challenges with these words: "Our message is the Word of God. Our field is the minds of people. Our missionaries are the teachers of the world. Our tools are paper and ink."

In all that she ever said or did, Henrietta Mears had but one goal in life, to "make Christ magnificent in the eyes of man." In fulfilling that purpose, she succeeded magnificently.

In summing up the life of this woman of God, Dr. Raymond I. Lindquist, one of the several pastors whom Henrietta served as Christian education director of Hollywood Presbyterian Church, said this of her: "Henrietta Mears moved on wheels of wonder, worship and work. She radiated magnetism for the Master, communicated cheer and strength and the sense that life in Christ is the supreme adventure. She was a woman of vision, imagination and influence of God's good for all."

NINETEEN

Making the Impossible Possible

*R*emember, lightning that strikes is accompanied by thunder. So faith that strikes is accompanied by life and testimony."

WHAT HENRIETTA MEARS ACCOMPLISHED IN HOLLYWOOD WAS REMARKABLE in itself, but all the more so in the context in which she wrought it. Hollywood is no theological spawning ground; it was and is a superficial town, based on illusion. On the screen, cars fly, animals talk, flowers dance, aliens intrude, underdogs triumph, money beguiles, beauty tempts and brawn conquers. And stories then always ended happily, white hats always won and cowboys always rode off into the sunset—sometimes with the girl, but always with the horse.

Legion are the young men and women, many in their teens, who flock yearly to this land of make-believe, hoping to be discovered and catapulted into celebrity heaven, there to sparkle and glow for an admiring public and myriads of adoring fans. For the first weeks and months of their pilgrimage to the bright lights, they pay their obeisance to the agents and scouts to whom they commit their early destinies, body and soul. Eventually, rejection, failure and faltering funds cast deepening shadows of despair over once-bright dreams until the last hope flickers out to be replaced by oblivion, desolation and ruin.

Henrietta Mears came to the movie capital just when it was entering its golden years of film-making. Sound movies were coming into their own, and their heroes and stars were setting dangerous moral standards and patterns of conduct for youth everywhere in the world that films were shown. Stars were created, who rose overnight, becoming larger than life and glorifying glittering, glamorous, carefree, immoral life-styles that suggested life was little more than one long, never-ending party.

This celluloid city was to become Henrietta's place of ministry. But "can there any good thing come out of Nazareth?" (John 1:46). Could anything good, anything spiritual possibly come out of Hollywood? Henrietta Mears thought so. And she made it happen. But how did she make the impossible possible?

In reflecting on her long and successful career in Hollywood, Henrietta Mears frequently told Christian workers from other cities:

If God can do it in Hollywood, He can do it in your city. You may think that this has been easy for us out here and that you have an impossible situation. But I tell you honestly that I would have chosen any place on the face of this earth to go than Hollywood, if it had not been for God's definite leading.

What you see accomplished here is only a fraction of what can be done in your city, if you will just believe in a God who can do the impossible.

Henrietta Mears' Own Ten Commandments as a Sunday School Teacher

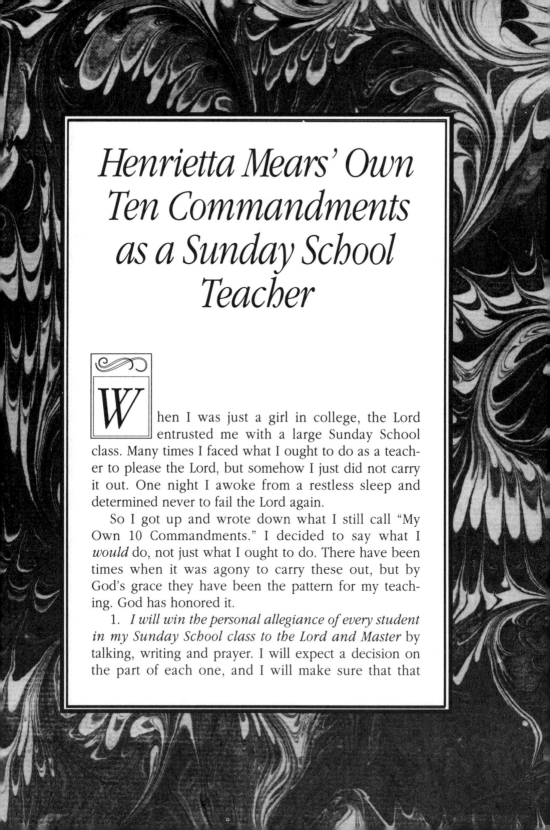

When I was just a girl in college, the Lord entrusted me with a large Sunday School class. Many times I faced what I ought to do as a teacher to please the Lord, but somehow I just did not carry it out. One night I awoke from a restless sleep and determined never to fail the Lord again.

So I got up and wrote down what I still call "My Own 10 Commandments." I decided to say what I *would* do, not just what I ought to do. There have been times when it was agony to carry these out, but by God's grace they have been the pattern for my teaching. God has honored it.

1. *I will win the personal allegiance of every student in my Sunday School class to the Lord and Master* by talking, writing and prayer. I will expect a decision on the part of each one, and I will make sure that that

decision is based on facts. No boy or girl will I ever give up on as unreachable.

2. *I will not think my work over when my pupil has made his decision for Christ.* I will help him to realize how necessary daily Bible reading and prayer are. I will also put helpful books in his hands and will encourage him to unite with God's people. I will show him the importance of church work. In all this, I will stay close until he is established, remaining at all times accessible to him.

3. *I will see that he finds a definite place in some specified task.* I will not rest until every student is an out-and-out aggressive Christian, for God has a place for each one to serve.

4. *I will bring Christianity out of the unreal into everyday life.* I will show my students the practical things they should be doing as Christians. The ministrations that the world needs so much today—meat for the hungry, drink for the thirsty—are judgment-day tests of genuine Christianity (Matt. 25).

5. *I will seek to help each one discover the will of God, because the Master can use every talent.* I will try to see in them what God sees. Michelangelo saw the face of an angel in a discarded stone. Christ saw a writer in a tax gatherer, a preacher in a fisherman, a world evangelist in a murderer. He takes the foolish things and the weak and despised to work His purposes.

6. *I will instill a divine discontent into the mind of everyone who can do more than he is doing,* not by telling him the pettiness of his life, but by giving him a vision of great things to be done enthusiastically, passionately.

7. *I will make it easy for anyone to come to me with the deepest experiences of his inner life,* not by urging, but by sympathy and understanding. I will never let anyone think I am disappointed in him.

8. *I will keep the cross of Christ central in the Christian life.* It is great to be out where the fight is strong, to be where the heaviest troops belong and to fight there for God and man.

9. *I will pray as I have never prayed before for wisdom and power,* believing God's promise that "if any of you lack wisdom, let him ask...and it shall be given him" (Jas. 1:5).

10. *I will spend and be spent in this battle.* I will not seek rest and ease. I will not think that freshness of face holds beauty in comparison with the glory of heaven. I will seek fellowship with the "man of sorrows...acquainted with grief" (Isa. 53:3), as He walks through this stricken world. I will not fail Him.

Henrietta Mears' Objectives for the Sunday School

1. *Canvass your neighborhood.* What is the potential of your city? Let us believe that any church in the United States can grow.

How many unchurched boys and girls are there in your community? Start where you are with the youth nearest you. Are they being reached?

Don't be afraid to count numbers. Gather figures and discover how many unchurched youth there are in your community. Many of these you could have in your Sunday School.

2. *Teach the Word.* The Bible is the living seed that brings life. We are born, fed, enlightened, equipped for service and kept by the Word of God.

Youth must know how to use this chart and compass. Other things may be good, but this is the best. Always specialize in the best.

3. *Win people to Christ.* Are children introduced to a living Savior in your Sunday School? This concern is paramount. Eighty-five percent of the boys and girls attending the Sunday Schools of America do so without ever taking Christ as their Savior.

If they are not won for Christ and built into the life

of the church, they will leave God's house and be lost forever. Carry out every means of winning them to Christ. All programs that deepen the spiritual life and strengthen the faith of youth enrich the church.

When a young person has been allowed to go through the Sunday School and reach college without taking a stand for Christ, it is difficult to win him back to the church. He has learned to live without Christ. Childhood is the time when God has made the heart tender.

Fill the child then with the knowledge of a personal Savior who has a plan for his life. The high-water mark of conversion comes between 11 and 13. After 20, one in 100 becomes a Christian, and after 30, one in 1,000.

4. *Enlist for service.* Let each child know he is accountable to the Lord for his life and that God has a job for him. What is more exciting than discovering God's plan in one's life? Find a place for every student to work.

5. *Look over your building.* Are the rooms attractive to the youth in your community?

Sometimes a can of paint will work wonders. Curtains will divide a large room into individual classrooms. Basements can be converted into department rooms with a bit of carpenter work. Look over what you have and be daring in your thinking.

When our Sunday School grew from about 450 to 4,200 in the space of two and a half years, we had to build screens; use curtains for partitions; discover every available space under steps, in closets, in offices; and buy adjoining apartments and houses, making a Sunday School out of what was at hand.

Nothing is as thrilling as to have to knock down partitions to build an annex or to change a porch into a room or to pitch a tent. Anything that indicates growth thrills people.

6. *Study your program.* As you study the program of your Sunday School, ask yourself if it is merely an assortment of ideas, or do you have a comprehensive, long-range plan? Every successful leader must plan his work and work his plan.

Plans must be sound. Christ left His disciples with a definite plan. A leader who moves by guesswork without practical, clear-cut plans is like a ship without a rudder. Sooner or later he will crash on the rocks.

Master the art of program-making. Visit a radio broadcast and note how each minute counts.

And balance your program. Don't run to extremes. See if you are putting due emphasis on attendance, worship, teaching, stewardship, missions, social life and evangelism.

Strive always for a successful program, remembering that nothing succeeds like success. Everyone likes to belong to a growing concern.

Henrietta Mears' Qualifications of Leadership

1. *Definiteness of purpose.* The apostle Paul said, "This one thing I do" (Phil. 3:13). What is the primary objective of your life as a teacher?

2. *Definiteness of decision.* "Choose you this day whom ye will serve" (Joshua 24:15). God is constantly asking men to decide. One who wavers in his decisions shows he is not sure of himself. He therefore cannot lead others.

Be definite. Many people are afraid to decide something because they may be wrong. Don't let this fear slow you down. It is better to decide and to be wrong, than to make no decision at all.

3. *Burning desire.* "He shall give thee the desires of thine heart" (Ps. 37:4). Set your desire on God. A leader must be consumed with a desire to achieve his purpose, and purpose and decision must be motivated by spiritual ambition. There is energy in such desire. What do you really long for as a Christian leader?

4. *Unwavering courage.* "Be strong and of good courage" (Josh. 1:6). No follower wishes to be dominated by a leader who lacks self-confidence and courage. "Be ye followers of me, even as I also am of Christ" (1

Cor. 11:1) was Paul's plan of leadership. His conviction and courage sparked the enthusiasm of others. This Christ-centered courage must conquer fears of failure.

Many people believe themselves doomed to failure or mediocrity. But there is no such word as "failure" in the Christian's vocabulary. This courage must help the leader to cultivate qualities of decision, promptness, action and the habit of finishing what he begins.

5. *A keen sense of justice.* No leader can command and retain the respect of others without impartiality and a feeling for equality. Christ gave His life that He might demand our lives from us. The leader must be willing to do what he expects others to do.

6. *Definiteness of plans.* Plans must be sound. Think, do not guess. Write out your plans. Do you cut your program into workable units so others can carry out your plans? Your achievement can be no greater than the soundness of your plans.

As a Sunday School teacher you are engaged in an undertaking of major importance both for time and eternity. To be sure of success, you must have plans that are faultless. If your first plan does not succeed, find another that will.

7. *Plan with others.* Don't try to go it alone. Christ chose 12 men to be with Him. Every plan you originate should be checked and approved by members of your department. No individual has sufficient experience, training or native ability to insure great success in spiritual things without helpers.